AFTER REAGAN

American Presidential Elections

MICHAEL NELSON

JOHN M. MCCARDELL, JR.

AFTER REAGAN

BUSH, DUKAKIS, AND
THE 1988 ELECTION

JOHN J. PITNEY, JR.

UNIVERSITY PRESS OF KANSAS

Published
by the
University
Press of Kansas
(Lawrence,
Kansas 66045),
which was
organized by the
Kansas Board of
Regents and is
operated and
funded by
Emporia State
University,
Fort Hays State
University,
Kansas State
University,
Pittsburg State
University,
the University
of Kansas, and
Wichita State
University

© 2019 by the University Press of Kansas

Library of Congress Cataloging-in-Publication Data

Names: Pitney, John J., Jr., 1955– author.
Title: After Reagan : Bush, Dukakis, and the 1988 election / John
Pitney, Jr.
Description: Lawrence : University Press of Kansas, [2019] | Series:
American presidential elections | Includes bibliographical references
and index.
Identifiers: LCCN 2019019342
    ISBN 9780700628759 (cloth)
    ISBN 9780700628766 (ebook)
Subjects: LCSH: Presidents—United States—Election—1988. | United
States—Politics and government—1981–1989.
Classification: LCC E880 .P57 2019 | DDC 324.973/0904—dc23
LC record available at https://lccn.loc.gov/2019019342.

British Library Cataloguing-in-Publication Data is available.

Printed in the United States of America

10 9 8 7 6 5 4 3 2 1

The paper used in this publication is recycled and contains 30
percent postconsumer waste. It is acid free and meets the minimum
requirements of the American National Standard for Permanence of
Paper for Printed Library Materials Z39.48-1992.

To J.P. and Hannah

I returned, and saw under the sun, that the race is not to the swift, nor the battle to the strong, neither yet bread to the wise, nor yet riches to men of understanding, nor yet favour to men of skill; but time and chance happeneth to them all.

—*Ecclesiastes 9:11*

CONTENTS

Vice President George Bush, the Republican nominee for president, said: "Read my lips: no new taxes." His Democratic rival, Governor Michael Dukakis of Massachusetts, dispassionately answered a debate question about capital punishment for someone who raped his wife (and looked silly riding in a tank). An independent group launched a racially charged attack on a Massachusetts prison furlough program for convicted murderers that Dukakis supported.

As John J. Pitney Jr. reports in this book, there is no shortage of specific explanations for the outcome of the 1988 election. In the conventional wisdom that formed then and has persisted ever since, nearly all of them turn on masterstrokes by the Bush campaign and its supporters, or blunders by the Dukakis campaign. But as Pitney shows, nearly all of them are overstated.

Campaigns do matter, Pitney argues. But they do so at the margins. Bush did not win at the margins. He won by 53.4 percent to 45.6 percent in the national popular vote—and more to the point by 426 to 111 in the Electoral College. Much more important in deciding the outcome of presidential elections, Pitney argues, are fundamentals—that is, the historical, economic, and political conditions that mark the country in an election year.

Not all of these conditions worked in Bush's favor. No incumbent vice president had been elected president since Martin Van Buren in 1836, although Richard Nixon came close in 1960 and Hubert H. Humphrey ran well in 1968. No political party since the Democrats in the Franklin D. Roosevelt and Harry Truman era had won three presidential elections in a row, as the GOP was bidding to do in 1988.

What Bush had going for him in the way of fundamentals turned out to be more important. The president in whose administration he served, Ronald Reagan, had earned the approval of most Americans. The economy was growing rapidly. Internationally, the nation was at peace; Cold War tensions with the Soviet Union had ebbed. In short, Bush benefited from both peace and prosperity—a fundamentally strong position from which the nominee of the incumbent president's party can run a campaign.

The scholarship on how fundamentals affect voting in general elections is less applicable when it comes to contests for the two major party nominations, in which party labels do not differentiate the candidates from each other. To be sure, a vice president in a popular administration who seeks the party's presidential nomination benefits from having been a member of that administration, as Bush was during both of Reagan's two terms. As popular as Reagan was in the electorate as a whole, he was even more regarded by the Republican voters who chose their party's nominee in 1988.

In addition, Pitney points out that Bush's rivals for the nomination were ill-suited by virtue of their own positions to mount an effective challenge. Robert J. Dole was the Republican leader in the Senate, a post from which no president ever had been elected. Jack Kemp was a member of the House of Representatives, which had not launched a president in more than a century. Al Haig was a high-ranking general, but unlike other generals who were elected president, he had not served in a popular war. Reverend Pat Robertson had never held office, which at the time was seen by most voters as disqualifying in a candidate for president.

The particulars of a presidential campaign, although less important in deciding the outcome of most elections than the fundamentals, are nonetheless significant in a different way. Once in the presidency, Bush felt compelled to break his "no new taxes" pledge. The voters did not forget. Despite his remarkable success in foreign policy—and arguably his wise decision to change his mind about the need for more taxes—he was a one-term president, defeated in his bid for reelection in 1992.

For the sake of transparency, let me start with some disclosures. My interest in the 1988 campaign stems not only from my academic research on presidential campaigns but also from my past political activities. I was a low-level volunteer in the Bush presidential campaigns of 1980 and 1988. From 1989 to 1991, during a leave of absence from my academic duties, I served in the research department of the Republican National Committee, where my daily work consisted mostly of cranking out talking points in support of the forty-first president and his policies. In the early 1990s, however, I stopped taking part in partisan campaign activities, and in 2016, I changed my party registration from Republican to independent. I do hope that the passage of time and my change of political affiliation has enabled me to write about this subject with the necessary detachment. The reader, of course, must be the judge of that.

As Booth Tarkington wrote in *The Magnificent Ambersons,* "at twenty-one or twenty-two so many things appear solid and permanent and terrible which forty sees are nothing but disappearing miasma. Forty can't tell twenty about this; that's the pity of it! Twenty can find out only by getting to be forty." While writing about the 1988 campaign, I often thought to myself, "Wow, things really don't work that way anymore. People back then could not see how different politics would be in decades to come." Just around their bend lay momentous changes, ranging from the collapse of the Soviet Union to the end of the Democrats' forty-year reign in the US House of Representatives. It would shock the 1988 political community to learn that, in the second decade of the twenty-first century, Democratic leaders held up Ronald Reagan and George H. W. Bush as examples of statesmanship and bipartisan cooperation. Republicans of the early 1960s would be equally shocked the GOP of the mid-1980s fondly remembered John F. Kennedy for tax cuts and anticommunism. More than thirty years after the campaign of 1988, I hope that I have been able to see some things that were not evident at the time.

I first discussed this book with Chuck Myers at the University Press of Kansas, and he graciously gave me a green light. His successor, David Congdon, has been most patient and helpful. I thank them both. Series editor Michael Nelson provided not only guidance and encouragement but also a detailed set of line-by-line suggestions that greatly improved the book. I am also grateful for the bracing, perceptive, and helpful comments of Jeffrey Crouch and John Robert Greene.

My old political foxhole buddies John Gardner, Lloyd Green, Jim Pinkerton, and Jeremy Shane read portions of the book and offered useful advice. The names of my frequent writing partners Joe Bessette, Andy Busch, Jim Ceaser, Bill Connelly, and Steve Schier do not appear on the cover of this book, but the text benefits enormously from what I learned in my years of collaboration with them.

Of course, my greatest debt is to my wife, Lisa Pitney. Like me, she did volunteer work for Bush, and in the years since, she has put up with my rambling monologues about all matters political. During the writing of this book, she was a model of loving forbearance as my mind darted through the decades. I could not have accomplished this work—or much of anything else, for that matter—without her support.

Our son J.P. and our daughter Hannah were born in this century, so they have no firsthand memory of the events that this book recounts. I do hope that they will read it someday, and that they might find it useful. With love, I dedicate it to them.

AFTER REAGAN

INTRODUCTION

On November 30, 2018, George H. W. Bush died at the age of ninety-four. For days afterward, Democrats and Republicans briefly joined to honor the former president. A common theme of the tributes was that his life belonged to another time. At his funeral, biographer Jon Meacham called him "America's last great soldier-statesman, a 20th-century founding father."[1] Reverend Russell Levenson, the Bush family's pastor, observed in his homily: "Some have said in the last few days, 'this is an end of an era.' But it does not have to be. Perhaps it's an invitation to fill the hole that has been left behind."[2] Funeral orations are for praise, not dispassionate analysis. Nevertheless, the eulogies had a valid historical point: in important ways, Bush had come in at the end.

The 1988 campaign, which had brought Bush to the White House thirty years earlier, provides a measure mark for judging how our politics had changed in the intervening decades. Hence, this book. Of course, it is hardly the first analysis of the topic; the 1988 race drew plenty of coverage, both at the time and in the several years that followed. The internet, at the time a little-known medium for scientists and academics, had not yet ravaged the print media's circulation and revenue. Newspapers could afford to put their top talent on the campaign trail for long stretches. Even midsize regional papers could get into the game. The big three news magazines—*Time, Newsweek,* and *U.S. News & World Report*—sold millions of copies and had the money to do serious reporting.[3] Cable news was starting to matter. CNN's daily broadcast, "Inside Politics '88" was must-see TV for campaign operatives, and C-SPAN was airing unedited coverage of major speeches and events. After the election, publishers produced a shelf of volumes about the race. The most famous was Richard Ben Cramer's *What It Takes: The Way to the White House* (1992), which journalist Jonathan Martin later called "the best book ever written about a campaign."[4] But in the late 1980s and early 1990s, even the most perceptive writers were too close to the election to see its full context. In the early twenty-first century, we can better understand what led up to the campaign and what came from it.

Bush defeated Michael S. Dukakis with 426 electoral votes and 53.4 percent of the popular vote. At the time there was little talk of a landslide. Some preelection polls had shown Bush getting a bigger margin, so the result was a letdown. Moreover, his totals looked modest next to Reagan's forty-nine-state sweep in 1984. In hindsight, the Bush victory seems more impressive. He secured a third term for a party that had been in the White House for eight years—a feat that would elude Al Gore, John McCain, and Hillary Clinton. Bush won a larger share of either the popular or electoral vote than any candidate in the next seven presidential elections. A *Time* report on the 2008 election began with the words, "When historians look back at the 2008 presidential landslide . . ." Obama's margins were smaller than Bush's.[5]

The America that chose Bush was different from the one that elected Barack Obama and gave a popular-vote plurality to Hillary Clinton. Among other things, it was whiter and less educated. In 1988, non-Hispanic whites made up 85 percent of the electorate.[6] In 2012, that figure was 72 percent, and in 2016, it ticked down to 71 percent.[7] Between 1988 and 2016, the share of voters with no more than a high school diploma dropped from 53 percent to 30 percent.[8] The nation also became more partisan. In 1988, 34 percent of congressional districts voted for a presidential candidate of one party and a House candidate of the other.[9] In 2016, only 8 percent of districts split their tickets.[10]

These changes would help scramble political alignments that looked durable in 1988. The GOP won five of the six elections between 1968 and 1988, so it was commonplace to talk of a Republican lock on the Electoral College. On Capitol Hill, Democrats had enjoyed majorities in the House of Representatives since the 1954 election. Senate Republicans did have a span of control starting in 1980, but after their big losses in the 1986 midterm, those six years looked like a fluke stemming from the Reagan landslides and a streak of GOP good luck in small states.[11] The 1988 election seemed to confirm that Americans liked divided government. Despite Bush's victory, the

GOP made no headway in either the House or Senate. One explanation was that voters preferred Republicans on "presidential issues" such as national defense while leaning toward congressional Democrats on distributional issues such as Medicare.[12] The notion sounded sensible, but the GOP presidential lock and the Democratic congressional lock were both more fragile than anybody knew in 1988. After the 1994 midterm, we had a Democratic president and a Republican Congress. Democrats would win the popular vote in six of the seven presidential elections between 1992 and 2016, and Republicans would dominate Capitol Hill during most of this time.

These shifts in party politics occurred amid dramatic changes in the issue agenda. Crime was the most memorable topic of the 1988 campaign. The controversy over the Massachusetts prison furlough program put the name "Willie Horton" into the political lexicon. CNN journalist Bernard Shaw made debate history when he hurled this question at the Democratic nominee: "If Kitty Dukakis were raped and murdered, would you favor an irrevocable death penalty for the killer?"[13] Crime had been a presidential campaign issue since the late 1960s, and it is easy to see why. Between 1960 and 1969, the rate of violent crime doubled, from 160.9 offenses per 100,000 people to 328.7. By 1988, it had nearly doubled again, to 640.6.[14] Americans expected their federal officials to do something about crime, even though it is mainly a state and local responsibility. The GOP had owned the crime issue since Nixon's election in 1968, and there was every reason to think that it would keep paying political dividends. Then an odd thing happened: after peaking in the early 1990s, the crime rate started plunging—as did its political value to Republicans.

Another break with the past involved international politics. During the late 1980s, Mikhail Gorbachev's policies of glasnost (openness) and perestroika (restructuring) had already led some American leaders to say that the Cold War was over. But for decades, there had been such talk during warm spells in US-Soviet relations.[15] In 1973, for instance, Nixon spoke of meeting some Russian children fourteen years earlier, "when the Cold War was still going on."[16] Cold War talk shifted back to the present tense whenever freezes followed thaws, and no one in 1988 could be sure that this period would be any different. Many Americans suspected that Gorbachev's reforms might just be camouflage for a regime that remained repressive and dangerous.[17] Even the most optimistic Americans had no idea that the Berlin Wall would fall in 1989, or that the USSR would crumble two years after that. Neither Bush nor Dukakis knew that their contest would be the last in which the Soviet Union was an issue.

Since the late 1940s, relations with that country had always been at the center of American foreign policy, never far from view in electoral politics. Americans judged presidential candidates for their ability as Cold War leaders and stewards of the nuclear arsenal. Aside from the 1964 campaign, when Democrats convinced millions that Barry Goldwater was a trigger-happy extremist, national security issues tended to favor Republicans. The 1972 Nixon reelection campaign charged that George McGovern would leave America practically defenseless, and the 1984 Reagan campaign symbolically pictured the Soviet threat through its famous "bear in the woods" television spot. The 1988 Bush campaign exploited Michael Dukakis's unlucky photo op in a tank to make him look weak on defense. Four years later, when the Cold War was undeniably over, Bush struggled to find national security attack points against Clinton. As late as 2012, Mitt Romney would try to make an issue of Russian expansionism, only to face a smirking dismissal from President Obama. And in 2016, the GOP was the more pro-Russia of the two parties.

In 1988, a generational shift was underway. In his 1961 inaugural address, John F. Kennedy proclaimed that "the torch has been passed to a new generation of Americans."[18] Every president from Kennedy to Bush was born between 1908 and 1924 and wore a uniform during World War II.[19] Five of them—Kennedy, Johnson, Nixon, Ford, and Bush—served as commissioned naval officers in the Pacific. Events of the 1930s and 1940s shaped their outlook. Many leaders from this generation were peculiarly wary of appeasement, seeing any act of international aggression as an echo of Hitler. "You know, if you look into history, America never went looking for a war," Bush said shortly after Iraq invaded Kuwait in 1990. "But in World War II, the world paid dearly for appeasing an aggressor who could have been stopped. Appeasement leads only to further aggression and, ultimately, to war. And we are not going to make the mistake of appeasement again."[20]

After 1988, the Greatest Generation would never get another president. Bob Dole ran in 1996, but he lost a campaign in which his he came under attack for his "old ways" and his "tired, old, worn-out rhetoric"—an obvious way of saying that his generation's time had passed.[21] Bill Clinton and his successors were all born after V-J Day. By the time that Bush took his last breath, World War II assumptions had weakened, and we again were hearing the slogan of the prewar isolationists: "America First."

Bush might also have been the last president of his social niche: upper-class, old-stock Eastern white Protestants.[22] From the nation's founding to the late twentieth century, this caste played an outsize role in the nation's economic, social, and political life. At a time when fewer than one in twenty Americans could go to college at all, people in this class enjoyed easy admission to Ivy League universities. They ran big law firms and financial institutions, and out of a sense of noblesse oblige, they often lent their services to the foreign policy and intelligence communities. In politics, they were the cornerstone of the Republican establishment. Bush's father was a Yale-educated Wall Street investment banker who went on to two terms as a US senator from Connecticut. After serving in the navy and attending Yale, Bush made his career in Texas, but it was old-line money and family connections that enabled him to do so.

By the time he ran for the presidency, he was a social antique. Changes in laws, mores, and educational practices had opened the doors of American institutions to people from more diverse backgrounds. Many Republicans looked with suspicion on the kinds of people who had made up their party's establishment a generation earlier. In response, Bush undertook sometimes comical efforts to transcend his background, proclaiming his love of pork rinds and country music. George W. Bush, who grew up in Texas and had the twang to prove it, was more successful at avoiding an elitist identity. Ironically, the GOP's most emphatic rejection of the old Eastern establishment came years later with the nomination of a New York billionaire.

George H. W. Bush and Michael S. Dukakis were born eight miles and nine years apart. Neither experienced poverty in youth, and both went on to earn Phi Beta Kappa keys and Ivy League degrees. Both first won office in the 1960s, later having both victory and defeat at the polls. But their lives were different. If Bush personified the GOP's yesteryear, Dukakis was a transitional figure, linking the Democratic Party's past and future. His parents came from Greece and were the first in their families to attend college. His father was the first Greek immigrant to graduate from Harvard Medical School.[23] As a doctor's son, Dukakis grew up in comfort, but as the son of immigrants, he could claim membership in the Ellis Island wing of Franklin Roosevelt's New Deal coalition. He could also identify with his fellow Massachusetts Democrat, John F. Kennedy. "Although the Dukakises certainly weren't financially and socially where the Kennedys were," Dukakis said in an oral history interview, "there was an immigrant tradition; there was the fact that this guy was a real pioneer in his own way."[24]

The party that nominated Dukakis was not the same as the one that chose John F. Kennedy. Southern whites, who had always been part of its base, were moving to the GOP. Franklin Delano Roosevelt had welded the party to organized labor in the 1930s, but union membership was now waning. The ranks of white-collar suburbanites were on the rise, and they were starting to make up an increasing share of the Democratic vote. Dukakis was part of that movement. His hometown of Brookline was once solidly Republican, but by the 1960s, it was trending Democratic. Dukakis started his electoral career in Brookline's local government, and in 1962, he won a seat in the state legislature. For the rest of his career, his approach to issues embodied what historian Lily Geismer calls "individualist, meritocratic, suburban-centered priorities of liberal, knowledge-oriented professionals."[25] At the national level, professionals were becoming more numerous and liberal. In 1988, people with postgraduate degrees made up 15 percent of the electorate, and split narrowly for Dukakis, 50–49 percent.[26] The trend would continue: in 2016, they cast 18 percent of the vote, and favored Hillary Clinton by a twenty-one-point margin.

By the time Dukakis ran for president, African Americans and Hispanics were also a growing force in the party. His lifelong advocacy of civil rights would give him credibility with these emerging segments of the Democratic coalition, though there were complications. He could give campaign speeches in fluent Spanish, which he had acquired from his undergraduate studies at Swarthmore and a college summer in Peru. If the Hispanic vote had been as big as it would be decades later, he probably would have fared better. As it was, his approach did not always play well in the still-Anglo America of 1988. "You know," lamented the Democratic governor of Kentucky, "back home, Bubba still thinks we ought to just speak English in this country."[27]

Some issues that would loom large in the twenty-first century were present in 1988, but in embryonic form. The reliability of financial institutions came to public attention with the savings-and-loan crisis of the 1980s. The failure of hundreds of thrifts cost the federal government billions of dollars and caused economic trouble in many communities. It briefly came up during the 1988 campaign, but neither side could use it to advantage because blame for the crisis was thoroughly bipartisan. By the early 1990s, the problem seemed to be under control. No one could foresee that it was a distant foreshock of the next century's Great Recession. Deindustrialization was another economic issue that had not yet reached full force. Manufacturing employment was already slipping, and Rust Belt economic distress had made its way into popular culture through songs such as "Allentown" and "Born in the USA." But the real turning point would not come until the early years of the twenty-first century, when automation would displace millions of factory jobs.[28] Many Americans would come to blame immigrants for their plight, but immigration was a secondary concern in the 1988 campaign. President Reagan had signed an immigration reform bill two years earlier, and most politicians thought that the new law would keep the issue at bay. Unexpectedly high rates of immigration would bring it back into public debate.

A careful consideration of 1988 helps us understand how much election politics had changed by the early decades of the next century. Both Bush and Dukakis financed their general election campaign from the federal treasury. Although there was some outside spending, federal financing put the parties on a more or less even footing. By the second decade of the next century, major presidential candidates bypassed public funds, instead relying on their own fundraising as well as the support of super PACs and dark-money organizations.

Forgetting nasty elections of the past, pundits in 1988 lamented the campaign's negative and divisive tone. From the perspective of some later races, the 1988 contest between Bush and Dukakis seems downright gentlemanly. In fact, as author Virginia Postrel has pointed out, it would be the last time for at least the next twenty-eight years in which the losing side generally regarded the president as legitimate.[29] Democrats severely criticized Bush's campaign tactics and presidential policies but did not deny that he rightfully held office. By comparison, consider the next four presidents. The Republican-controlled House impeached Clinton, and the party seethed when he escaped conviction in the Senate. George W. Bush lost the popular vote to Al Gore, and the murky results in Florida led many Democrats to question whether he fairly won the electoral vote. Although Obama twice won popular and electoral majorities, he had to contend with the myth that he was born in Kenya and was therefore constitutionally ineligible to be president. Although the idea was preposterous, a 2016 poll showed that only 27 percent of Republicans agreed that he was born in the United States, with the rest either disagreeing or saying that they were unsure.[30] Donald J. Trump was the most prominent figure to spread the birther myth. He won the 2016 presidential election despite losing the popular tally by 2.8 million votes. By the year after his inauguration, some progressive political activists were calling for his impeachment.

Retrospective analysis can help sweep away myths that gather around an election. As soon as the result is clear, pundits start showering credit on the winner and drizzling blame on the loser. The journalistic accounts that emerge in the months afterward tend to focus on the "inside baseball" of campaign decisions. The victor's strategic decisions appear to be wise or diabolically effective, depending on the pundit's opinion of the outcome. The other candidate retroactively becomes a stumblebum who either blew a winnable election or was so obviously doomed from the beginning that the party was foolish even to think about nominating such an incompetent. Sources in the loser's camp use press leaks to shift blame to internal rivals. After Bush lost his 1992 reelection bid, one GOP strategist reportedly said of another: "I'm gonna do somethin' that I've never done before. I'm gonna burn his ass where he'll really feel it—in the *Newsweek* book!"[31]

Some candidates really are better than others, and smart moves or mistakes can have an impact on the outcome. Much of what happens in an election, however, is beyond the power of the campaigns to control. First are the fundamentals of peace and prosperity. If international threats are at a low ebb and the economy is doing well, the party holding the White House is probably going to win, no matter how clever the opponent. Conversely, bloodshed and a limp economy will also certainly hand the White House to the other side. Think of the 2008 election, which took place in the wake of the Iraq insurgency and the Great Recession. Of course, this point raises another question: To what extent is the administration responsible for the fundamentals? Surely some credit or blame is due, but even here, luck plays a bigger role than we like to think.[32] The president, after all, has only limited power over fiscal and monetary policies, which in turn are just two of many influences on a complex global economy. Issues of war and peace similarly reflect decisions taking place in a hundred foreign capitals and the policies of past administrations. It is no disrespect to President Clinton to note that he had the good fortune of taking office just a year and a month after the Soviet Union went out of business.

The benefit of hindsight helps us see the extent to which the outcome of the 1988 election was a matter of time and chance. For much of 1987, many smart people thought Bush was politically dead. A summit with the Soviet Union had collapsed in the fall of 1986, and a few months later, Reagan appeared eager to take the Cold War out of cold storage with his now-famous "tear down this wall" speech. On October 19, 1987, the stock market sustained its worst crash since 1929. And for a while, the Iran–Contra arms-for-hostages scandal prompted whispers of impeachment. A year later, the economy was chugging along nicely, the United States had signed an historic arms deal with the USSR, Reagan was visiting Red Square, and Iran–Contra was in remission. No one can seriously contend that Vice President Bush had primary responsibility, but he still reaped the political benefits. At a postelection conference, Dukakis campaign manager Susan Estrich said that for all the talk of campaign strategy, "It was probably less important than Ronald Reagan, the economy, and world peace."[33]

None of this means that campaigns are irrelevant. Even if they only move a point or two in the popular total, they can make a big difference in the Electoral College. And according to political scientists John Sides and Lynn Vavreck, "Campaigns are often most effective when the polls are out of line with the fundamentals—when one candidate is doing much better or worse than he 'should' be, which means that some voters have not lined up behind the candidate that prevailing national conditions, or these vot ers' own beliefs, would predict."[34] Such was the case in 1988, when some midyear surveys gave Dukakis a lead that did not square with the national conditions that favored Bush. Moreover, the fundamentals that drive general elections are less decisive in nomination campaigns. In primaries and caucuses, voters choose among candidates who belong to the same party and often have similar issue positions. Campaigns matter even more at this stage of the process. Bush was not the inevitable nominee in 1988, and if he and his opponents had made different strategic choices, the party might have picked someone else.

The cliché is that elections have consequences. What is less obvious is that campaigns have consequences too. Whatever the role of the fundamentals in a general election, the political community tends to assume that the nominees' campaigns determined the outcome. Future campaigns will copy what the winner did and try to avoid the purported mistakes of the loser. The conventional wisdom about the 1988 campaign was that Dukakis's status as a Northeastern liberal was a huge liability. Four years later, Bill Clinton (who had placed Dukakis's name into nomination) sold the party on picking a Southern moderate. Another lesson was that negativity works. Many campaign professionals thought that the furlough issue enabled Bush to turn a double-digit poll deficit into a victory. As we shall see, this notion is questionable. Even so, Bush's victory encouraged ad makers to seek "game-changing" attack points, and subsequent elections had much harsher edges.[35]

The furlough issue had unanticipated consequences for the GOP. African Americans saw it as an appeal to racism, and they did not forget. Bush campaign manager Lee Atwater became chair of the Republican National Committee, and in a symbolic effort to make peace, he joined the board of historically black Howard University. In the face of student protests, he had to resign as trustee. A costly outreach effort at the Republican National

Committee proved to be a failure. In spite of GOP hopes that Bush could increase his share of the African American vote to a modest 20 percent in 1992, he got only half that much.[36] Decades later, African American political leaders would still cite the furlough issue as proof of Republican bad faith.

Candidates make promises and incur political debts that have a lasting impact. Perhaps the most famous campaign pledge of modern times came when Bush said at the Republican Convention, "Read my lips: no new taxes." Two years later, he broke his promise by acceding to tax increases. "I think a lot of us didn't have a sense of just how serious a pledge George Bush had broken," said pollster Peter D. Hart during the 1992 campaign. "Now I'm finding that it's cost him more than anything else and hurt politicians in general. The promise was as close as a politician can come to putting his imprint in Grauman's Chinese Theater. The voters took it as a blood oath."[37] In light of the queasy 1992 economy, Bush probably would have lost anyway, and polls ranked Bush's reversal behind other issues on the minds of those who voted against him.[38] Nevertheless, Republicans came to believe that the broken promise cost him the election, and their opposition to tax increases became more adamant.

Campaigns also leave scar tissue in the form of attacks and controversies that live on in memory. So this book will not end with election night 1988. It will also analyze how memories of the campaign influenced policies for the decades to follow.

1

RETROSPECT

1950–1980

George H. W. Bush was the last of the World War II junior officers to serve as president. In 1960, John F. Kennedy and Richard Nixon were the first of that group to seek the job. In *The Making of the President 1960*, Theodore H. White tells the story of that election, and he devotes a good deal of attention to the political and demographic changes that had swept America since 1950. Those changes influenced the careers of Kennedy and Nixon, just as they would for Bush and his rivals.

Television was a big part of the picture. In 1950, only 9 percent of American households had television sets. By 1960, that figure was up to 87 percent, and eventually nearly every home would have one.[1] Presidential candidates had run television ads before, but spots played a much larger role in 1960, with celebrities such as Harry Belafonte and Eleanor Roosevelt making appearances for Kennedy. The Kennedy–Nixon debates set an historic precedent: never before had the major-party nominees for president taken part in such events. Because of the perception that debates had worked to Kennedy's advantage, Nixon would avoid them in 1968 and 1972. After that point, however, they became a standard feature of presidential campaigns.

In part because of defense spending, and in no small measure because of the spread of air-conditioning, more Americans were moving to the warmer states in the South and West. Between 1950 and 1960, California gained eight seats in the House, and Florida gained four. (Growth was uneven, as rural states such as Mississippi and Alabama lost ground in the House.) Changes were also occurring within the Southern states, where small towns and farms lost population as metropolitan areas grew. Harris County, Texas, encompassing the city of Houston, saw more than a 50 percent increase, from 807,000 to 1.2 million. NASA spending would contribute to further growth in the 1960s, just as George H. W. Bush was launching his political career there. Bush later wrote: "Something was stirring at the political grass roots in Texas, especially in Houston and Harris County. Nixon carried Houston over Kennedy—the largest metropolitan area in the country to go Republican in 1960."[2] In 1961, an obscure college professor named John Tower won a multicandidate special election for the Senate seat of Lyndon Johnson, who had become vice president. Tower was the state's first Republican senator since Reconstruction—indeed, the first from any Confederate state in nearly half a century.

Multiple forces were changing politics in Texas and throughout the South. First, many of the people who moved to the South from other regions had been Republicans, and they carried their partisanship with them. Second, the sheer passage of time had worn away the South's Civil War hatred for the GOP. The last Confederate veterans died during this decade, and when Southerners thought the of the burning of Atlanta, the image in their mind's eye came from *Gone with the Wind*, not any firsthand memory. Third, newly affluent Southerners liked GOP positions on economic issues, including Eisenhower's support for state control over offshore oil drilling. Finally, Eisenhower's unique status as a war hero gave him strong appeal in this promilitary region. The 1960 results, however, made it clear that the Southern movement to the GOP was not just a personal phenomenon. Nixon carried Virginia, Florida, and Tennessee, and he ran close to Kennedy in Texas and the Carolinas.

Elsewhere in the country, population movements would have political consequences. Since 1940, African Americans had been pouring out of the South as mechanization diminished their job prospects on the farm. World War II and the early Cold War created millions of new factory jobs, as did the broader economic growth of the 1940s and 1950s. The departure of African Americans did not immediately transform Southern politics because racial discrimination had largely blocked them from voting booths. They did vote in their new communities, and mostly for Democrats, helping push big cities out of reach for the GOP.

In a chapter titled "Retrospect on Yesterday's Future," White marveled at the population growth that we would later know as the baby boom: twenty-eight million people in a single decade. "What was more exciting was the changing pattern of growth," he wrote. "Two thirds of the stupendous

28,000,000 growth of the nation had taken place in suburbia."[3] The new suburbs were filling up with people who made their living differently from the past. "Some time between the year 1950 and the year 1960 (census scholars fix the date uncertainly at the year 1955) for the first time in American history," said White, "the number of white collar Americans (professional, managerial, clerical, and sales people) had become greater than the number who held blue collar jobs (productive or operative)."[4] Many of these white-collar workers were clerks or secretaries who—like more 90 percent of adults overall—did not have college educations.[5] In fact, most American adults had not even finished high school. Thanks to policy decisions in the previous two decades, educational attainment would shoot upward during the next two.

Again, these developments had a great deal to do with the Cold War. The key federal education law of the 1950s was the National Defense Education Act, which began with these words: "The Congress hereby finds and declares that the security of the Nation requires the fullest development of the mental resources and technical skills of its young men and women."[6] The military–industrial complex hired large cadres of professionals, who tended to cluster in areas where defense contractors set up shop or where research universities were spending Pentagon dollars. One of these places was the Route 128 corridor around Boston, whose educated workers would be a core constituency for programmatic liberals such as Michael Dukakis. Connecticut was another New England state that would change because of rapid suburban growth. But vestiges of its old order were still in place.

PRESCOTT BUSH AND THE REPUBLICAN ESTABLISHMENT

In *The Deadlock of Democracy*, his classic work on party politics, James MacGregor Burns describes the establishment that dominated Republican presidential politics in the middle of the twentieth century: "Internationalist-minded men out of the universities, law schools, and metropolitan law and banking firms of the East: men like Elihu Root, Henry Stimson, John Foster Dulles, Douglas Dillon."[7] With their money and influence with important media outlets such as the *New York Herald-Tribune*, the establishment was able to secure the nomination for New York businessman Wendell Willkie, New York governor Thomas Dewey, and General Dwight Eisenhower. Richard Nixon, who started off as an outsider from the West, became the 1952 vice presidential nominee because he had made a favorable impression on Dewey and other establishment figures.[8]

Prescott Bush, the father of the forty-third president, embodied this group of men (and they were all white men). After attending Yale, where he belonged to the elite Skull and Bones secret society, he served as an intelligence officer in World War I. His business career briefly took him to Massachusetts, where George H. W. Bush was born. He moved to Greenwich, Connecticut, an affluent suburb of New York City, and built a successful career as a Wall Street investment banker. He was active in Connecticut Republican politics, and in 1950, he was the party's candidate in a special election for the United State Senate. Days before the vote, journalist Drew Pearson said in a radio broadcast that the elder Bush had been a leader of the American Birth Control League, a forerunner of Planned Parenthood. The statement was inaccurate, but Bush had raised money for Planned Parenthood.[9] In heavily Catholic Connecticut, a state law still forbade birth control, and would do so until 1965, when the US Supreme Court struck it down in *Griswold v. Connecticut*. Bush lost narrowly. Two years later, the death of another Connecticut senator prompted another special election, and Bush ran again. The Cold War was a national preoccupation, and Joseph McCarthy's extreme anticommunism was popular among his fellow Catholics. Bush introduced McCarthy at a rally in Bridgeport. Despite the partisan setting and the need to win over Catholics, Bush politely voiced reservations about McCarthy's methods.[10] McCarthy took no offense, but the audience booed Bush. In November, Bush narrowly defeated Representative Abraham Ribicoff, in part because of the coattails of Dwight Eisenhower, who carried the state by a 56–44 percent margin.

Like most establishment Republicans, he supported social welfare programs and civil rights legislation. (Governor Dewey had signed the Ives–Quinn Act, a state-level forerunner of the 1964 Civil Rights Act.) Senator Bush's most consequential vote put him at odds with many conservatives. In 1954, he supported the censure of McCarthy.[11]

Prescott Bush's wealth and social position would help George H. W. Bush get his start in business. His political connections would later give the son entrée to campaign contributors and Washington policy makers. At the same time, his progressive philanthropic activities (in addition to Planned Parenthood, he had raised money for the United Negro College Fund) and his moderate voting record in the Senate would raise suspicions among hard-line conservatives. They wondered if the younger Bush had inherited the old man's attitudes as well as his name and money. In the 1950s, he was sympathetic to his father's position. In a private letter to Senator J. William Fulbright (D-AR), he said: "I realize that anybody who takes a stand against

McCarthy is apt to be subjected through the lunatic fringe to all sorts of abuse."[12] Much later, however, he offered a subtly different interpretation of the elder Bush's beliefs: "He was a conservative who believed that the United States had to take a strong stance against Communist aggression in Eastern Europe and Asia."[13] He wrote those words with coauthor Victor Gold in 1987, when he was launching his 1988 campaign and taking every possible opportunity to identify with the conservative movement.

As a Republican from Connecticut, Prescott Bush was no outlier. Throughout the 1950s, his party held most of the Senate seats from New England and held elected offices up and down the ballot across the Northeast. (The most famous anti-McCarthy speech in the Senate came from Margaret Chase Smith of Maine.) Bush's colleagues in the Republican establishment retained great leverage over presidential nominations. In 1960, Richard Nixon had to make platform concessions to New York governor Nelson Rockefeller, and he chose as his running mate Henry Cabot Lodge of Massachusetts. The conservative South, which would play such a central role in George H. W. Bush's political life, was not yet an effective counterweight in GOP affairs.

DEMOCRATS IN THE 1950S

For nearly a century, the term "Solid South" had referred to the region's monolithic support for the Democratic Party. White Southerners long remembered the ravages of the Union army and rough treatment under Republican Reconstruction governments. To vote for the GOP was to back the party that burned your grandmother's house. Aside from a few scattered pockets, Democrats won practically all elections in the South, from state legislature to the presidency. One exception was the election of 1928, when Democrats nominated Catholic Al Smith for president. Religious prejudice trumped party loyalty, and five of the eleven Confederate states held their Protestant noses and voted for Herbert Hoover. Four years later, Franklin Roosevelt brought the region back to the Democratic fold.

No Southerner had won the presidency since the Civil War. (Virginia native Woodrow Wilson was governor of New Jersey when he ran in 1912.) Nevertheless, the states of the Old Confederacy commanded great power on Capitol Hill. And for decades, the need for Southern support led national Democrats to tread lightly on civil rights. When Harry Truman finally took a strong stand on the issue in 1948, Governor Strom Thurmond of South Carolina bolted from the Democrats and carried four Southern states as a third-party candidate. Four years later, the party's vice presidential nominee was Senator John Sparkman of Alabama. Though not as vocally racist as some other Southern politicians, Sparkman was a segregationist who opposed civil rights legislation. Despite Sparkman's presence on the Democratic ticket, Republicans made a Southern breakthrough that year, with Eisenhower carrying Virginia, Florida, Tennessee, and Texas. Four years later, he added Louisiana to the list.

In other elections, however, the Old Confederacy remained solidly Democratic. During the 1950s, Democrats swept every gubernatorial and senatorial election in the region, and lost just a tiny number of state legislative and congressional seats. Consider Texas. The election of 1950 produced a single GOP member of the Texas House. From 1952 to 1960, Republicans won no seats—zero—in either chamber of the state legislature.[14] The only Texas Republican Congress was extreme conservative Bruce Alger, who won a Dallas-area House seat in 1954.

Both literally and figuratively, the national Democratic Party was all over the map. Alongside the segregationist Southern Democrats stood a growing number of African Americans in the big cities of the North and Midwest. In those urban areas, political machines were in decline but retained some residual power. Organized labor was at peak membership and could mobilize millions of votes in industrial areas. Intellectuals provided the party with rhetoric and policy ideas. In the decade, their champion was Adlai Stevenson, the party's presidential nominee in both 1952 and 1956. Stevenson came across as sedate and brainy, and unlike many previous candidates, he disdained to pander to "the people."[15] In his 1952 acceptance speech, he said: "What does concern me, in common with thinking partisans of both parties, is not just winning this election but . . . to educate and elevate a people whose destiny is leadership."[16] Such language charmed educated professionals, as well as college students such as a Swarthmore undergraduate named Michael Dukakis.

Stevenson lost by landslides in both 1952 and 1956, but his wing of the party grew stronger during the decade. The "programmatic liberals," as political scientist James L. Sundquist called them, renounced machine politics and embraced progressive priorities on social welfare and civil rights.[17] Abraham Ribicoff, who had lost the 1952 Senate election to Prescott Bush, won the governorship of Connecticut two years later. In the same year, Edmund Muskie broke an eighteen-year GOP grip on the governorship of Maine. In 1958, Democrats scored massive victories outside the South, with a net pickup of forty-nine House seats and fifteen Senate seats. A number of Northeastern states were shifting to Democratic dominance. The election flipped the Connecticut delegation in the House from six Republicans to six Democrats. And in Massachusetts, Democrats took over the state senate. From that point at least until the second decade of the twenty-first century, the GOP would never again control either chamber of the state legislature.

Within the Democratic Party, the influx of liberals from the Northeast, Midwest, and West would start to tilt congressional politics in a more progressive direction. As Michael Barone wrote, "Although no one could be sure of it at the time, the 1958 election, not that of 1952, proved the prototype for the future."[18] More evidence of this trend came when Prescott Bush decided to retire from the Senate in 1962. Abraham Ribicoff, who was now serving as John F. Kennedy's secretary of Health, Education, and Welfare, won Bush's seat. The state would reelect him in 1968 and 1974, each time by a wider margin.

THE AGE OF NIXON

After his 1960 defeat, which some pundits blamed on television, Nixon went back to California. In 1962, he ran for governor against the incumbent, Democrat Pat Brown, and lost by a decisive margin. On the day after his defeat, an angry and exhausted Nixon lashed out at Brown and the press, declaring that the occasion would be his last press conference. The image would trail Nixon, and ABC News ran a special that it labeled his "political obituary."

Nixon soon came back and adapted to the ever-increasing role of television in American society. In his 1960 ads, he had spoken directly into the camera about policy issues. This time would be different. He put more of his campaign budget into television advertising and hired ad maker Harry Treleaven, who had made spots for George H. W. Bush in his successful 1966 race for Congress. "Most national issues today are so complicated, so difficult to understand, and have opinions on, that they either intimidate or, more often, bore the average vote," Treleaven wrote in an internal memo laying out his approach to TV campaign. "There'll be few opportunities for logical persuasion, which is all right—because probably more people vote for irrational, emotional reasons than professional politicians suspect."[19]

Nixon avoided unstructured media appearances. Helping him in this effort was a former television talk-show producer named Roger Ailes. In 1968, Ailes demonstrated the skill for image control that he would put to use for Bush two decades later. He specialized in staging "man in the arena" programs where Nixon would take questions from audience members. These shows would give the impression that he was spontaneous and transparent, even though the campaign had selected and prepared the participants. When other campaign staffers objected that he was not letting reporters into the studio, Ailes said, "The audience is part of the show. And that's the whole point. It's a television show. It's our show." If the campaign let reporters in, he went on, they would see a staffer "out there telling the audience to applaud and to mob Nixon at the end, and that's all they'd write about."[20]

The differences between the 1960 and 1968 campaigns went beyond media tactics. As of 1960, Republican presidential candidates could still hope for a substantial share of the black vote. Eisenhower, whose Supreme Court appointee wrote *Brown v. Board of Education,* got about 39 percent of this vote in 1956 and won the endorsement of legendary Harlem congressman Adam Clayton Powell.[21] Eisenhower and Nixon had worked hard to pass the Civil Rights Act of 1957, the first federal civil rights law since Reconstruction. Nevertheless, Nixon did not do as well as Eisenhower, winning about 32 percent of African Americans, which was one reason why he narrowly lost Illinois, Pennsylvania, and New Jersey.[22]

Though not obvious at the time, Nixon's showing would be the GOP's high-water mark. The party was starting an ideological change that would repel African Americans. The modern conservative movement had begun in 1955, when William F. Buckley Jr. started the *National Review.* The movement opposed civil rights bills, and the *National Review* explicitly endorsed racial segregation. The movement's political leader, Senator Barry Goldwater of Arizona, had once desegregated his state's Air National Guard, but he voted against the Civil Rights Act of 1964.[23] In the presidential election that year, Goldwater got only 6 percent of the African American vote, and over the next half century, the GOP would never get as much as 20 percent.

The new conservative movement was not a lineal descendant of the diffuse conservatism of the GOP's past. The older conservatives tended to favor trade protection and certain other forms of government intervention in the economy. Senator Robert A. Taft (R-OH), for instance, sponsored public housing legislation. The newer conservatives advocated free trade and free markets, drawing on thinkers such as Milton Friedman. And whereas the Taft wing tended to be isolationist and leery of the armed forces, the Goldwater wing was zealously interventionist and promilitary.[24] (Goldwater was a brigadier general in the Air Force Reserve.)

The Johnson landslide of 1964 was a setback for the conservatives. In the House, younger and more moderate insurgents seized the GOP leadership from conservative Charles Halleck and replaced him with Gerald Ford. In the off-year elections of 1965, the most prominent winner was John Lindsay, a liberal who became the first Republican to win a mayor's race in New York City since Fiorello La Guardia. Nevertheless, conservatives continued their march through the party ranks, as veterans of the Goldwater campaign remained active and gained influence. Nixon, as always, adapted. Among other things, he hired conservative Pat Buchanan as a speechwriter. Buchanan specialized in fiery prose, and behind the scenes, he served as an ambassador to conservative intellectuals that Nixon had previously shunned.[25]

In 1966 came a new star: Ronald Reagan, who defeated the incumbent governor of California, Pat Brown. During the 1968 Republican presidential contest, Reagan sought to snatch the nomination from Nixon. His effort was late and amateurish, but his conservative stands had great appeal among Southern delegations. Nixon already had the support of senators John Tower and Strom Thurmond (who had switched to the GOP a few years earlier), but he took the Reagan threat seriously enough that he arranged special meetings with the southerners. He assured them that he would not push racial-balance busing to integrate public schools, and that he would not pick liberals for the vice presidency or the Supreme Court.[26] Eight years earlier, he had needed to court Nelson Rockefeller. Now he was genuflecting in a Southern direction, a sign of where his party was heading. In November, he won all the Southern states that he had carried in 1960, plus the Carolinas. He probably would have won more if it had not been for the third-party candidacy of former Alabama governor George Wallace. Nixon and Wallace each carried five states from the Old Confederacy, leaving only Texas to Democrat Hubert Humphrey. The South was the one part of the New Deal coalition that decisively repudiated the Democrats in 1968.[27]

Obviously racial divides were at work. With Lyndon Johnson's presidency, Democrats had become the party of civil rights, and they would never again welcome a John Sparkman to their national ticket. Because of civil rights, Johnson famously told aide Bill Moyers, "I think we just delivered the South to the Republican Party for a long time to come."[28] As president, Nixon hoped to make Johnson's prediction come true. He managed to convince white Southerners that he was on their side, even though he expanded affirmative action and made extraordinary strides in desegregating public schools.[29] In his forty-nine-state 1972 landslide, Nixon became the first Republican in history to carry every Southern state. From this point onward, the white South would remain crucial to GOP presidential candidates.

MCGOVERN'S PARTY

In the late 1960s and early 1970s, the Democrats were shifting too. After the Voting Rights Act of 1965, more and more African Americans could cast ballots. They gained greater influence in Democratic primaries, and their ranks grew among elected officials. In 1972, Representative Shirley Chisholm of New York became the first African American and the first woman to seek the Democratic presidential nomination. Though her campaign made little headway in the short run, it was a sign of increasing African American power in the party, and it set a precedent for even more significant campaigns in the 1980s.

The ideological and demographic composition of the Democratic Party was changing in other ways. John F. Kennedy's militant anticommunism generated little pushback within the Democratic Party, which was still a home for Cold Warriors. Even Adlai Stevenson, dovish by the era's standards, had once referred to the Soviet Union as "the anti-Christ."[30] But by 1968, other voices were emerging. As American casualties mounted in Vietnam, antiwar sentiment deepened. Robert F. Kennedy, who had backed his brother's Vietnam policy as attorney general, was now a senator from New York and a sharp critic of Lyndon Johnson's conduct of the war. In the Democratic nomination contest that year, he competed with another antiwar candidate, Senator Eugene McCarthy of Minnesota. During the 1968 primaries, McCarthy ran strongly in suburbia. Late in the general election campaign, Hubert Humphrey edged away from Johnson's Vietnam stance and scored well in places with concentrations of educated professionals.[31] In his book on the campaign, Theodore H. White again shows his knack for spotting new political forces. He describes "a new type of affluent American . . . an educated, technically trained elite" that voted differently from private entrepreneurs. "Sensitized by the influence media, protected from violence by the suburban belt, aware of a larger world abroad and a crescent scientific world a-borning, they vote as their conditioned intelligence tells them."[32]

After that campaign, Democrats made fundamental changes in their nomination process. Until 1968, both parties chose most their national convention delegates outside the system of primaries and voter caucuses that we know today. Party leaders could deliver delegations, which is why Theodore White spent many pages describing how the candidates courted governors, mayors, and party chairmen. But after Humphrey clinched the nomination without having won a single primary, demands for change came from those who had labored for Kennedy and McCarthy. The party then changed its rules to democratize the selection of delegates and increase their demographic diversity. A number of states then changed their laws to establish presidential primaries, and a side effect was to democratize the Republican process as well.

The first beneficiary of reform was Senator George McGovern of South Dakota, who had chaired the party rules commission and perhaps understood the new system better than any other figure in the party. As a staunch opponent of the Vietnam War, he won the Democratic nomination, to the dismay of party centrists who thought that his positions were too far to the left. During the fall campaign, Nixon ads attacked him as an extremist who would weaken American defenses and break the budget with welfare spending. Amid McGovern's landslide forty-nine-state defeat, only Massachusetts stayed with the Democratic Party.

But as with Barry Goldwater on the Republican side, the landslide defeat masked signs of future strength.[33] Across the country, Democrats made inroads among affluent suburbs and educated professionals.[34] As the ranks of professionals grew in the years ahead, more and more places would come to look like Massachusetts in 1972. And like Goldwater, McGovern left a corps of admirers who would carry on the ideological struggle. Gary Hart, the McGovern campaign manager who would go on to be a senator and presidential aspirant, spoke of a "whole generation of young activists who were motivated by the McGovern campaign and stayed active and have made tremendous contribution to the country."[35] Veterans of the McGovern campaign ran for office and built organizations that became an essential part of the party's grassroots labor force.[36] Within two years of the McGovern race, some of these activists won election to Congress as party of the "Watergate baby" class of 1974.[37]

Amid the movement in ideology and presidential politics, one thing remained remarkably constant in the 1960s and 1970s: Democrats kept control of Congress. For more than two decades after their 1958 midterm trouncing, Republicans had a "glass ceiling" of 192 seats in the House and forty-five seats in the Senate.[38] The South was a major reason for Democratic congressional dominance. Many of the party's white Southern politicians nimbly adapted to the influx of African American voters, changing their positions to support civil rights and adjusting their language to honor the evolving electorate.[39] Andrew Young, who in 1972 became the first African American to win a Georgia congressional seat since Reconstruction, said: "Then you registered 10 percent to 15 percent in the community, and folks would start saying 'Nigra.' Later you got 35 percent to 40 percent registered, and it was amazing how quick they learned to say 'Nee-grow.' And now that we've got 50 percent, 60 percent, 70 percent, of the black votes registered in the South, everybody's proud to be associated with their black brothers and sisters."[40] On the other hand, the white Southern Democrats held onto much of their traditional base by voting a conservative line on other issues.[41]

With the party's resilience in the South, its entrenchment in the big cities, and growth in the suburbs, the Democratic Party was in a strong position to dominate American politics below the presidential level. After Jimmy Carter's defeat of Gerald Ford in 1976, the Republicans seemed to have lost their presidential fortress, and many members of the party fretted about its future. But by the late 1970s, several issue areas would present them with opportunities.

CRIME

From the vantage point of the twenty-first century, the 1960 campaign is notable for the absence of certain issues. There was little discussion of poverty or the environment: Michael Harrington's The Other America and Rachel Carson's Silent Spring, which helped put these matters on the agenda, were two years away from publication. Perhaps the most striking omission was crime. When Kennedy and Nixon mentioned crime, they were talking about labor racketeering, not mugging. They had little reason to focus on street crime because Americans were not obsessing about it as a national issue.[42] Things were different by 1968.[43] Public concern with crime was on the rise, and politicians were orating about law and order. A staff report for a presidential commission observed: "To millions of Americans few things are more pervasive, more frightening, more real today than violent crime and the fear of being assaulted, mugged, robbed, or raped."[44] People came to fear major cities such as New York, where residents barricaded themselves in apartments with deadbolts and police locks.[45]

Concern about crime had a racial dimension. In The Real Majority (1970), among the most influential books of the Nixon era, Richard M. Scammon and Ben J. Wattenberg write about the "typical" voter, a middle-aged white housewife in Dayton, Ohio: "To know that the lady in Dayton is afraid to walk the streets alone at night, to know that she has a mixed view about blacks and civil rights because before moving to the suburbs she lived in a neighborhood that became all black, to know that her brother-in-law is a policeman . . . to know all this is the beginning of contemporary political wisdom."[46]

Where did this fear come from? A series of massive urban disorders started with Los Angeles in 1965 and continued through multiple riots after the assassination of Dr. Martin Luther King Jr. in 1968. The riots, along with sensational coverage in the mass media, reinforced the tendency of white Americans to link crime and African Americans. Local newscasts increasingly focused on violence, giving rise to the cliché, "If it bleeds, it leads." Beyond media hype and racial animosity, however, there really was more crime. Just between 1965 and 1970, the number of murders in the United States rose from 9,960 to 16,000—a 61 percent increase. Robberies went from 138,690 to 349,860—up 152 percent.[47] Criminal justice expert Barry Latzer writes: "As best we can tell—data are sketchy prior to the 1930s—the late-1960s crime rise was the biggest sustained escalation in criminal violence in the United States since the 1870s."[48] Americans had good reason to be afraid.

Barry Goldwater had tried to raise concern about crime in 1964, to little effect. Four years later, the issue loomed larger. In his acceptance speech at the 1968 Republican National Convention (RNC), Nixon said: "Let those who have the responsibility to enforce our laws and our judges who have the responsibility to interpret them be dedicated to the great principles of civil rights. But let them also recognize that the first civil right of every American is to be free from domestic violence, and that right must be guaranteed in this country."[49] Pointing to the hint that civil rights would have to take a back seat to crime control, liberal critics said that Nixon was subtly pandering to racism. But the issue of criminal violence was not inherently racist. Democratic nominee Hubert Humphrey also discussed it in his acceptance speech, albeit with a different emphasis: "We do not want a police state but we need a state of law and order, and neither mob violence nor police brutality have any place in America."[50]

The crime rate continued to soar during the 1970s. The causes were complex, including a demographic bulge of young men that overwhelmed the criminal justice system.[51] Republican politicians reached for a simpler diagnosis, blaming permissive laws and court decisions. They found a receptive audience, as surveys showed public opinion becoming more conservative on crime control.[52] In one development that would be particularly consequential for the 1988 campaign, opinion on the death penalty shifted sharply to the right. Between the mid-1950s and the mid-1960s,

Gallup found declining support for capital punishment, with one survey even showing a narrow plurality in opposition. The numbers turned as the crime rate increased, and by the mid-1970s, the public supported it by a 2-to-1 margin.[53]

TAXES

During their 1960 debates, Kennedy and Nixon did make passing reference to taxation, but neither offered a "no new taxes" pledge. In fact, Nixon said something quite different: "I think it may be necessary that we have more taxes. I hope not. I hope we can economize elsewhere so that we don't have to. But I would have no hesitation to ask the American people to pay the taxes even in 1961—if necessary—to maintain a sound economy and also to maintain a sound dollar."[54] This remark, which would have been controversial for a Republican in the 1980s and beyond, got little attention.

Before this time, the party's economic conservatism had focused more on fiscal discipline than tax reduction. In 1963, when Kennedy proposed sweeping tax cuts to spur demand, Republicans denounced the idea as reckless. Cutting taxes without cutting spending, said the ranking Republican on the House Ways and Means Committee, was "playing Russian roulette with our destiny."[55] House Democrats supported the measure 223–248, but House Republicans voted no by a margin of 29–126.[56] The measure became law in 1964, after Kennedy's death. In its platform that year, the GOP made only a half-hearted effort to outbid the Democrats, calling for "further reduction in individual and corporate tax rates as fiscal discipline is restored."[57] Some prominent Republicans even raised taxes. Liberal Nelson Rockefeller increased a variety of levies, and so did conservatives. In 1967, California governor Ronald Reagan's first major policy initiative involved the largest tax increase in state history.

By the late 1970s, however, the issue was changing. Inflation was bloating tax burdens even for people who did not have real increases in income. In California, where local governments taxed property at a fixed percentage of market value, a combination of inflation and real estate demand was pushing property taxes upward.[58] A pair of grassroots activists responded with Proposition 13, a ballot measure to set property assessments back to 1975 levels and cap annual property tax increases at 2 percent. The measure had little support from the Republican establishment, with the notable exception of Reagan, who had left the governorship in 1974. The measure passed with 65 percent of the vote.

Republicans across the country grabbed the tax-cut issue.[59] Their gains in the 1978 midterm were only modest, but as we shall see, the election did provide a lift to key antitax figures in the Republican Party, including Jack Kemp. The tax-cut issue had staying power because inflation remained troublesome: both 1979 and 1980 would see double-digit hikes in the consumer price index. In addition to its effect on property taxes, high inflation effectively raised income taxes too: In the phenomenon known as bracket creep, inflation pushed taxpayers into higher tax brackets. The result was a larger tax liability without greater purchasing power. Bracket creep affected many Americans and particularly caught the attention of the affluent. At the time, the top marginal income tax rate was 70 percent, though various tax preferences softened the impact for those with good accountants and tax lawyers.

In the meantime, a burgeoning network of conservative think tanks and publications was providing Republican politicians with a rationale. Saying that the old economic paradigm had failed, they argued that Republicans should downplay deficits and instead focus on growth through tax reduction. Some even contended that tax cuts would pay for themselves by generating work, savings, and investment. Mainstream economists— even conservative ones—derided the notion of self-financing tax cuts, but so-called supply-side economics started to enter GOP talking points. Conservative editor Irving Kristol later explained why he provided a platform for these ideas: "I was not certain of its economic merits but quickly saw its political possibilities. To refocus Republican conservative thought on the economics of growth rather than simply on the economics of stability seemed to me very promising."[60]

COLD WAR REDUX

In the first half of the 1970s, Cold War tensions seemed to be waning. In 1972, President Nixon went to Moscow to sign an arms treaty, and in the following year, Nixon and Soviet leader Leonid Brezhnev toasted each other in Washington. In 1975, President Ford signed the Helsinki Accords, which aimed to curb East–West conflict on issues ranging from territorial borders to human rights. During this time, polls showed public hostility toward the Soviet Union was declining.[61] By the mid-1970s, however, Americans could read an English translation of *The Gulag Archipelago,* in which Aleksandr Solzhenitsyn provides a vast amount of shocking detail about the USSR's prison camps. As the decade continued, the arms race sped up and the Soviet Union asserted influence in developing countries. In December 1979 came the invasion of Afghanistan. President Carter, who had once spoken of an "inordinate fear of communism," now said, "This action on the part of the Soviet Union has made a more dramatic change in my own opinion of what the Soviets' ultimate goals are than anything they've done in the previous time that I've been in office."[62] The Cold War had not ended after all.

At the height of Nixon's power, conservative Republicans had grumbled about his policy of détente. Dissatisfaction grew during the Ford administration and helped fuel Ronald Reagan's surprisingly strong challenge to Ford during the 1976 primaries. At the GOP convention that year, conservatives forced the adoption of a platform plank that implicitly criticized the Nixon–Ford approach: "Ours will be a foreign policy which recognizes that in international negotiations we must make no undue concessions. . . . Agreements that are negotiated, such as the one signed in Helsinki, must not take from those who do not have freedom the hope of one day gaining it."[63]

As with economic issues, the conservative wing was gaining strength and drawing ideas from intellectuals. Some prominent anticommunists were still nominal Democrats, but they rejected what they regarded as their party's leftward drift. These neoconservatives, including Jeane Kirkpatrick, would go on to play important formal and informal roles during the Reagan and Bush administrations. And like the tax issue, national security gave the GOP a boost. By 1980, Republicans had a political edge on the issue, as more and more voters voiced skepticism about the USSR and support for a stronger military.[64]

It would be an oversimplification to draw a neat line between GOP hawks and Democratic doves in the late 1970s. Within the GOP there was still some hesitancy about a confrontational foreign policy, especially among members of the Senate. Mark Hatfield of Oregon, whose religious convictions inclined him toward pacifism, would chair the Appropriations Committee after the party's 1980 takeover of the chamber. The Democratic Party was even more deeply divided. Carter's administration reflected the split, with national security adviser Zbigniew Brzezinski favoring a hard line against the Soviet Union and Secretary of State Cyrus Vance emphasizing diplomacy. Brzezinski gained the upper hand after the invasion of Afghanistan. At the 1980 Democratic convention, Carter won approval of a platform supporting deployment of the MX missile, but he had to overcome strong opposition party liberals, who had the support of the rank and file on this issue.[65] During his presidency, Reagan could often win support in Congress from Southern and border-state white Democrats, as well as such old-line hawks as Representative Sam Stratton of upstate New York and Senator Henry Jackson of Washington State. Over time, their ranks would thin out.

CULTURAL ISSUES

Starting in the late 1960s, a diffuse set of social and cultural issues became an important part of national politics. Some of these issues involved patriotism. In response to antiwar demonstrations where a handful of protesters burned the American flag, the Ninetieth Congress enacted the Flag Protection Act of 1968. The statute made desecration of the flag a federal offense. Though the law was the product of a Democratic Congress and bore the signature of a Democratic president, the next administration tried to identify patriotism with the GOP. Nixon started wearing flag lapel pins, and his aides followed suit. Vice President Agnew had the task of suggesting that the administration's critics were less than patriotic. In a 1969 speech in New Orleans, he said: "A spirit of national masochism prevails, encouraged by an effete corps of impudent snobs who characterize themselves as intellectuals."[66] In 1970, he was even more direct, attacking the antiwar chair of the Senate Foreign Relations Committee: "Let Senator Fulbright go prospecting for his future party leaders in the deserters' dens of Canada and Sweden. We Republicans shall look elsewhere." Agnew drew a sharp contrast between the protesters and the patriots in uniform: "Indeed, as for these deserters, malcontents, radicals, incendiaries, the civil and the uncivil disobedients among our young. . . . I would swap the whole damn zoo for a single platoon of the kind of young Americans I saw in Vietnam."[67]

Issues of the flag and patriotism would resurface decades later, and so would another Agnew theme: criticism of liberal media bias. In Des Moines, he delivered a speech written by Pat Buchanan: "The American who relies upon television for his news might conclude that the majority of American students are embittered radicals; that the majority of black Americans feel no regard for their country; that violence and lawlessness are the rule rather than the exception on the American campus. We know that none of these conclusions is true."[68] In the 1970s and 1980s, conservative critics would write books and articles arguing that the news media were stacked against the GOP. Roger Ailes, who served briefly as a consultant to the Nixon White House, pondered ways to get around the purported bias. A memo that Ailes either wrote or approved (authorship is unclear) laid out a plan to supply proadministration video clips for inclusion in local television newscasts. According to the memo, this arrangement "avoids the censorship, the priorities and the prejudices of the network news selectors and disseminators."[69] In the 1988 race, Ailes would help Bush flank the "news selectors," and a few years after that, he would found "fair and balanced" Fox News.

Birth control and reproductive rights were increasingly prominent topics of debate, but the partisan lines were blurry. Moderate Republicans such as Prescott Bush had supported birth control, but so did many conservatives, including Barry Goldwater.[70] In 1968, the Republican platform said: "The world-wide population explosion in particular, with its attendant grave problems, looms as a menace to all mankind and will have our priority attention."[71] In 1969, President Nixon said that "no American woman should be denied access to family planning assistance because of her economic condition."[72] In the years before the *Roe v. Wade* decision of 1973, New York governor Nelson Rockefeller and California governor Ronald Reagan both signed bills liberalizing their states' abortion laws. Though Nixon privately expressed reservations about *Roe,* he made no public statement. Over the next several years, some of the strongest opposition to the decision actually came from Democrats. Reverend Jesse Jackson wrote a 1977 article for *Right to Life News* linking his antiabortion stand to his own life story: "I was born out of wedlock (and against the advice that my mother received from her doctor) and therefore abortion is a personal issue for me. From my perspective, human life is the highest good, the *summum bonum.*"[73]

Many Catholic politicians in both parties publicly agreed with the anti-abortion stance of their church. But it took awhile for evangelicals to enter the fray on abortion and other social issues. For one thing, they initially regarded abortion as a Catholic issue, and some evangelical leaders even voiced pro-choice sentiments.[74] For another, they had generally stood aloof from partisan politics on a national level. As of the mid-1970s, the religious right was not yet part of the Republican coalition, and GOP presidents felt no pressure to engage in God talk beyond the generic language of the American civil religion.

It was a Democrat who brought the evangelical tradition to the attention of the national media. During the 1976 campaign, when Jimmy Carter spoke in public about being "born again," NBC News anchor John Chancellor thought that he had to explain the term to his viewing audience. "Incidentally, we have checked this out. Being 'born again' is not a bizarre experience or the voice of God from the mountaintop. It's a fairly common experience known to millions of Americans—particularly if you're Baptist."[75] Carter enjoyed fleeting support from evangelicals, but he soon disappointed them on several issues, including his endorsement of a bill to extend the ratification deadline for the Equal Rights Amendment.

Abortion was not the issue that initially galvanized them into political action and pushed them toward the GOP. Since the 1960s, many evangelical churches, especially in the South, had set up private schools. Their founders said that public education was becoming too secular in the wake of Supreme Court rulings on school prayer. They seldom acknowledged another motive: white parents wanted to pull children out of newly desegregated public schools. In 1978, the IRS proposed a rule that would have affected the new private schools, which critics called "segregation academies." To keep their tax exemptions, those with low minority enrollments would face tests of their hiring and recruitment practices. Conservative activist Paul Weyrich said that this issue initially had more heft than abortion or the Equal Rights Amendment. "I am living witness to that because I was trying to get those people interested in those issues and I utterly failed. What changed their mind was Jimmy Carter's intervention against the Christian schools. . . . That is what brought those people into the political process. It was not the other things."[76]

Congress responded by blocking implementation of the rule, and the religious right movement kept rolling. Weyrich helped then draw them into the "other things." He joined with Reverend Jerry Falwell to found Moral Majority, a group that would advocate a broad "pro-family" social agenda on issues such as abortion and school prayer. The 1980 GOP platform reflected the movement's influence. It pledged to "halt the unconstitutional regulatory vendetta launched by Mr. Carter's IRS Commissioner against independent schools." It also addressed abortion: "While we recognize differing views on this question among Americans in general—and in our own Party—we affirm our support of a constitutional amendment to restore protection of the right to life for unborn children. We also support the Congressional efforts to restrict the use of taxpayers' dollars for abortion."[77]

Weyrich was a devout Catholic, and his role in founding Moral Majority was one sign of how politics had changed since 1960. Many evangelicals had hesitated to support John F. Kennedy, worrying that a Catholic would put allegiance to the pope ahead of loyalty to the country. His presidency largely put that concern to rest. By the start of the 1980s, evangelicals increasingly saw conservative Catholics as allies against the forces of secular liberalism.

MEDIA, TECHNOLOGY, AND THE 1980S

At the time of the Kennedy–Nixon debates, politicians were still trying to figure out how to use the relatively new medium of television. Twenty years later, it was a central part of national campaigns. Increasingly, political organizations staged rallies and other campaign events not just to motivate the attendees but also to attract and influence television coverage. Lyndon Johnson and Richard Nixon avoided television debates, but after Gerald Ford met Jimmy Carter on the debate stage in 1976, these events would take place in every subsequent presidential race, at least through the next forty years.

Changes in the medium would have an impact in the coming decade of the 1980s. The number of households with cable television was growing rapidly. One result was to give religious figures a new way to get their message to millions, and thus the term "televangelist" became familiar. Jerry Falwell was one such figure, but soon another televangelist would assume an even higher profile. His name was Pat Robertson.

New cable networks emerged to serve the growing audience. In 1979, Brian Lamb started C-SPAN to provide gavel-to-gavel coverage of the House of Representatives. Its programming gradually became more extensive, and politicians figured out that it gave them a means to deliver long-form messages directly to their followers, without the editing and commentary of television journalists. In 1980 came CNN. The established figures of television news dismissed it at first, but its interview programs and live broadcasts of breaking news offered political figures yet another way to bypass the editing room.

The same year saw the introduction of the Nexis service, providing subscribers with archived stories from newspapers, magazines, and newswires. Though expensive, the new service provided campaign researchers with faster and more effective access. It was now easier than ever to gather material for attack ads, which in turn would become a convenient topic for cable news producers needing to fill air time

Television and computing had existed in limited, fairly primitive form in the 1940s. Still, these developments probably would have astounded the GIs returning from World War II.

2

REAGAN, BUSH, AND THE REPUBLICANS

In their 1991 book *Generations,* William Strauss and Neil Howe define the GI Generation—or what Tom Brokaw would later dub the Greatest Generation—as those born between 1901 and 1924. Some would quibble about the boundaries at either end of this range, but few would disagree that this age cohort left a deep mark on American public life. Strauss and Howe calculated each generation's "national leadership share," the simple average of its share of governors, senators, and House members. From the mid-1950s to the mid-1970s, this generation's share was always over 50 percent. But the silent artillery of time did its work, and by 1979, it was 37 percent. In 1987, it was just 18 percent.[1] This figure roughly tracked with the generation's share of the electorate, which was about 20 percent in 1988.[2]

Americans who served in the war were dying off. In 1970, 13.9 million World War II veterans were still living. By 1988, that figure was down by about a third, to 9.4 million.[3] And by definition, the remaining veterans were all old. The youngest members of the cohort were in their sixties. For an ever-growing proportion of the population, the formative experiences of these vets were a matter for history, not firsthand memory. The era of the World War II junior officers would soon end. Nevertheless, their generation still had some missions ahead.

THE MAKING OF GEORGE H. W. BUSH

In accepting the 1988 Republican presidential nomination, George H. W. Bush said: "My life has been lived in the shadow of war. I almost lost my life in one."[4]

He was born in Milton, Massachusetts, on June 12, 1924. The next year, his father accepted an executive position In New York City and moved the family to Greenwich, Connecticut. Bush attended Greenwich Country Day School until the age of twelve, when he entered Phillips Academy Andover, a boarding school catering to the Eastern elite. He was a natural fit for the school, and he was active in sports and student government. As millions were suffering from the Great Depression, his father had become a partner in Brown Brothers Harriman and Company. Amid their wealth and privilege, the Bush family taught an ethic of public service. It was more than talk. After graduating from Yale, Prescott Bush had enlisted in World War I, seeing combat in France. With American involvement in World War II, the younger Bush followed his lead. When he graduated in 1942, Secretary of War Henry L. Stimson gave a commencement address urging the class to go to college before entering the military. Bush ignored the advice and enlisted in the navy. Ten months later, he got his commission as an ensign, becoming the nation's youngest naval aviator at the time.[5]

On September 2, 1944, Bush, by then a lieutenant, piloted a torpedo bomber in an attack on a radio installation on Chi Chi Jima Island, about 150 miles north of Iwo Jima. Even after Japanese antiaircraft hit his plane, Bush kept going and bombed his targets. He flew several miles away and bailed out successfully, but his two crewmates died. On a raft without a paddle, Bush drifted close to the Japanese garrison, which was infamous for its brutal treatment of prisoners.[6] After several hours, the submarine USS *Finback* surfaced nearby. Not only did the crew save him from torture and death, but it also provided him with something that would become a political asset many years later. An ensign took movie footage of the rescue, which would find its way into Bush campaign ads.

During a leave from his naval duties, he married Barbara Pierce, whom he had been seeing since his student days. After his discharge, he followed his father's path to Yale. Even as an older, married student living off campus, he was active in college activities, serving as captain of the baseball team. In this capacity, he scored another bit of photographic luck during a ceremony at Yale Field, where he got a picture with Babe Ruth. He also won election to the most prestigious of Yale's secret societies, Skull and Bones. His membership in the group would both extend his vast network of friends and—much later—provide grist to conspiracy-minded adversaries. The Bushes' New Haven years produced their first child, George W. Bush, whose birth in Connecticut would prove a handicap in his early Texas campaigns.

Bush took an accelerated program and graduated in three years. He shunned the obvious path of accepting a job offer from a relative. "I am not sure that I want to capitalize completely on the benefits I received at birth—that is on the benefits of my social position," he wrote a friend at the time.[7] At the same time, his family ties came in handy. A friend of his father was head of Dresser Industries, a supplier of equipment and services to the oil industry. At his suggestion, Bush took a job with a Dresser subsidiary in Texas. Bush and a partner later struck out on their own, starting a small oil development company. He raised a lot of the money in the East, where his name opened doors that would have been closed to other start-ups. When Bush's company split in 1959, he became president of Zapata Off-Shore, and he moved with its headquarters to Houston.

As Prescott Bush immersed himself in politics, his son was focusing more on his family and his business than politics. If his career goal had been elected office, the political alignments of the time would have kept him in Connecticut. Nevertheless, as he rose in the Texas oil business, friends encouraged him to turn to politics. "These were Democrats talking, but some were influential figures in Texas politics, like Lyndon Johnson's friend George Brown, of Brown & Root Company," Bush wrote. "They mentioned several possibilities, including a chance at a US Senate seat, if I crossed over and became a Democrat."[8] Bush said that he declined to switch because he was philosophically a Republican, although he would have been a good fit for the conservative faction that dominated Texas Democratic politics. More important, as the 1960s began, he saw that a Republican could now have a political future in the state.

Instead of immediately seeking office, Bush ran for chairman of the Harris County Republican organization. Establishment Republicans worried that members of the ultraright John Birch Society would take over the local party. The group's founder had suggested that President Dwight Eisenhower and General George C. Marshall had been communist agents, and even in conservative, anticommunist Texas, such bizarre beliefs had limited appeal. A Birch takeover, Bush wrote, "would mean that all the gains Republicans had made in recent years would be jeopardized."[9] Though Bush won the chairmanship, he did not move to purge Birchers from the party organization.

He sought party unity not only for the GOP's sake but for his own. In September 1963, he announced that he would run against incumbent Democratic senator Ralph Yarborough. As a member of his party's liberal faction, Yarborough looked vulnerable. The political ground shifted on November 22, when John F. Kennedy's assassination made Lyndon Johnson president. Whereas polls had suggested that Kennedy might lose Texas, Johnson was a sure winner in his home state, and the rest of the Democratic ticket would benefit. Bush soldiered on. In line with the leanings of the state party, he endorsed the presidential candidacy of Barry Goldwater and took conservative positions across the board, including opposition to the 1964 Civil Rights Act. The latter stand made political sense because Yarborough voted for it and state opinion ran strongly against it. But as he wrote to one supporter, he had misgivings: "The civil rights issue can bring Yarborough to sure defeat. . . . What shall I do? How will I do it? I want to win but not at the expense of justice, not at the expense of the dignity of any man—not at the expense of hurting a friend nor teaching my children a prejudice which I do not feel."[10]

A little more than a year later, he announced that he would run for the US House in a new Houston-area district drawn in response to the US Supreme Court's "one man, one vote" decision. In a constituency with many city dwellers and African Americans, Bush modified his rhetoric. "Too long, Republicans have been oblivious to poverty, the Negro ghettoes, inadequate housing, medical care needs, and a million other pressing problems that face our people," he told the Texas Young Republican Federation.[11] Bush easily won the race.

Thanks to the influence of his father, who had retired from the Senate but still had friends on Capitol Hill, he landed a seat on the tax-writing Ways and Means Committee. Despite this coveted assignment, he was a junior member of the minority party and so had little chance to write major bills. Instead, he joined with other younger members to rebrand the GOP as the party of new ideas. Ray C. Bliss, the chair of the Republican National Committee, set up the Republican Coordinating Committee as a forum for party officeholders and policy experts. Bush served as vice chair of its task force on job opportunities and welfare. Its proposals included a federal income tax credit for training workers in skills in short supply—the kind of idea that would become standard GOP fare but seemed innovative in the mid-1960s.[12]

Like his father, George Bush was a strong supporter of population control, so much that Ways and Means chairman Wilbur Mills (D-AR) nicknamed him "Rubbers." In 1968, he entered a remarkable statement into the *Congressional Record*: Concerned about "rising welfare costs," he said that "the problem is by no means wholly financial; it is emphatically human, a tragedy on unwanted children and on parents whose productivity is impaired by children they never desired. . . . Certainly responsible religions have the right to determine their doctrines, but for those of us who feel so strongly on this issue, the recent encyclical was most discouraging."[13] The encyclical to which Bush referred was Pope Paul VI's *Humane Vitae,* which reaffirmed the Roman Catholic Church's opposition to birth control. Twenty years later, it would have been shocking for any Republican politician to take such a position and to criticize the Catholic Church so directly.

In his statement, Bush discussed the "myth" that "Negroes do not want birth control, believing it to be a form of 'genocide.'" He said it was becoming more popular among African Americans because "our black citizens recognize that they cannot hope to acquire a larger share of American prosperity without cutting down on births, just as the rest of the Nation must do."[14] In fact, large numbers of African Americans did suspect that racism motivated such proposals.[15] Early in his public career, Reverend Jesse Jackson voiced similar concerns. Though approving of contraception in general, he said in 1973: "Abortion is genocide."[16]

Bush got attention for his vote in favor of the Civil Rights Act of 1968, which included provisions banning discrimination in housing. This position was a shift from his opposition to the 1964 bill. In a Houston speech, he linked the issue to the war: "In Vietnam I chatted with many Negro soldiers. They were fighting, and some were dying, for the ideals of this Country, and some talked about coming back to get married and start their lives over. Somehow it seems fundamental that this guy should have a hope."[17] He got a standing ovation, which suggests that the audience was already sympathetic to him. Even in a cosmopolitan district, though, there was opposition to the measure, and he got a great deal of mail attacking his vote.

During the 1968 nomination race, Bush endorsed Richard Nixon even as many Texas Republicans preferred Ronald Reagan. At the Republican convention in August, Nixon considered Bush as his running mate. Senator Strom Thurmond of South Carolina, the onetime Dixiecrat who had become a Republican and was now a key Nixon supporter, put Bush's name on a short list of acceptable candidates.[18] Nixon never explained why a freshman House member would rank alongside better-known politicians, but it is possible to make a guess. Nixon was always straddling ideological divisions. In the 1968 election, he needed to win several Southern states and to hold onto white voters who might otherwise support firebrand third-party candidate George Wallace. He also needed moderates who would help him in the GOP heartland. In this light, Bush's appeal becomes more obvious: he was a Yalie turned Texas oilman who had taken both hard-line and moderate issue positions. His relative youth (age forty-four) and location in the Rim South would have provided some balance to the fifty-five-year-old Nixon, who had roots in California and now lived in New York.

Nixon instead picked another split-the-difference candidate. Spiro Agnew was the governor of Maryland, a slave state that had remained in the Union during the Civil War. He had won in 1966 as a racial moderate against a segregationist Democrat. But after riots broke out in Baltimore after the assassination of Martin Luther King Jr., he took a hard line and accused African American community leaders of abetting the violence. Nixon talked a great deal about crime during the campaign, though he was hazy about what the federal government could do about it. In this context, picking a seemingly tough-on-crime running mate seemed like a smart political move at first. Agnew, however, quickly embarrassed the campaign with a string of gaffes. Ironically, this purported crime fighter proved to be a criminal himself. Several years later, it would come to light that he was taking bribes from state contractors. His 1973 resignation would bend Bush's political trajectory.

During the autumn of 1968, Bush had plenty of time to campaign for the GOP ticket, because he was unopposed for reelection. After Nixon's victory, Bush took the next logical step, looking for a 1970 rematch against Senator Ralph Yarborough. Eager to oust an antiwar Democratic senator, Nixon encouraged Bush and funneled campaign money in his direction. Bush was the favorite until former House member Lloyd Bentsen defeated Yarborough in the Democratic primary. As a pro-business moderate conservative, Bentsen was an excellent match for Texas at a time when it still leaned Democratic in state and local elections. In some ways, Bentsen ran to Bush's right, criticizing his support for Nixon's proposed guaranteed income. "I think I could have beaten Yarborough," Bush later recalled, "Bentsen proved much tougher and was also aided by a 'liquor by the drink' vote that brought out Democratic voters in rural Texas in record numbers."[19] The final tally was 53.7 percent for Bentsen, 46.3 percent for Bush.

INTERSECTIONS

Although the Lyndon Johnson landslide had provided a ready excuse for the 1964 result, Bush's 1970 defeat was conspicuous because the GOP had scored a net gain in Senate seats. As a Nixon favorite, though, he still had a future in appointive office. The president was unsure about what job to give him, finally settling on ambassador to the United Nations. Bush's international experience was light, consisting of his military service plus some foreign travel as a business executive and House member. He explained why Nixon gave him the job: "Nixon viewed the UN as a forum for world opinion. To him, the US ambassador's job was as much a political as a diplomatic assignment. That made my political experience an asset, not a liability in his eyes."[20] There was also little chance that a newcomer to diplomacy would upstage Nixon's foreign policy adviser, Henry Kissinger.

If the selection was expedient for Nixon, it was valuable for Bush. It would lay the foundation for later appointments that would make him a plausible presidential candidate in 1980. Much of Bush's work at the UN revolved around the Cold War. He wrote that Soviet ambassador Yakov Malik continually "quotes back to me things that are wrong with our country, things that he has read in the paper. The *Times* is quoted all the time."[21] His biggest setback was the General Assembly vote to expel Taiwan in favor of mainland China. A few months after the vote, however, Bush invited mainland diplomats to brunch at his boyhood home in Connecticut, a gracious gesture that the Chinese government would remember.

After the 1972 election, another job loomed, and Bush's life would intersect with Bob Dole, who would be a bitter rival and necessary ally for decades to come.

Like Bush, Dole had been a junior officer in World War II. While serving in Italy near the end of the war, he suffered grievous wounds that cost him the use of his right arm. Despite his disability, he went on to earn a law degree and became county attorney for Russell County, Kansas. The local congressman decided to retire in 1960, and Dole ran for the open seat. In this Republican district, the GOP primary was the real contest, which Dole won by a mere 982 votes. He easily won in November, and he would serve three more terms in the House. Along with most of his GOP colleagues—but unlike Goldwater—he voted for the 1964 Civil Rights Act. In 1968, the years of Nixon's comeback, he won a Senate seat.

Since 1971, Dole had served part time as chair of the Republican National Committee. Nixon was unhappy with Dole's dour public image and his poor fundraising. Always skittish about personal confrontation, Nixon sidestepped his real concerns and instead told Dole that the committee needed a full-time chairman. He floated Bush's name as a replacement. When Dole agreed, Nixon told him that Bush wanted to stay at the United Nations, so he should go to New York to persuade Bush to take the job. In fact, Bush had already accepted Nixon's offer, in part because Nixon had hinted that a Cabinet post might await him in the future.[22] After speaking with Dole, Nixon phoned Bush:

Between you and me, you have a very sensitive problem with Dole. I'll let you in on it in a nutshell. . . . He'd like to stay on for three, four months because he likes the car, he likes, you know, the rent paid, and all that, I mean, which of course, that's crappy stuff. But then also he says it would help him in Kansas if he didn't leave right after the election. I said, Bob, if you don't leave right afterward and then the sentiment builds up that they need a full-time chairman, it's going to look as if you were forced out. I said you've got to take the lead. . . . The thing is, what we need to do to get this properly positioned and to save Dole's face is to let Dole now have a little talk with you.[23]

Dole later found out that the whole exercise had been for show.[24] After growing up poor and suffering life-shaping injuries in wartime, Dole had plenty of reasons to resent the scion of a rich family who had served in the navy without scars. Now he had another reason.

As Bush settled in to RNC headquarters at 310 First Street SE, Dole's dudgeon was the least of his worries. Over the first few months of 1973, the Watergate scandal gathered momentum, forcing Bush to defend conduct that later proved indefensible. After the 1974 release of an audiotape proving that Nixon had obstructed justice, Bush and other GOP leaders urged him to resign. "The man is amoral," Bush wrote in his diary. "He has a different sense than the rest of people. . . . I don't want to increase the agony of his family. And yet I want to make damn clear the lie is something we can't support. But this era of tawdry, shabby lack of morality has got to end."[25]

In the meantime, the OPEC oil embargo led to gasoline lines and helped start the worst recession in decades. The scandal and the slump slammed the Republican Party, which suffered a net loss of forty-eight House seats and five Senate seats in the 1974 midterm election. In Colorado, a two-term GOP incumbent lost by a huge margin to George McGovern's campaign manager, Gary Hart. In Kansas, Bob Dole's reelection worries proved well founded. Despite the state's Republican leanings, he barely squeaked by. Republicans lost ground in gubernatorial races, including big states such as New York and California, and they came out of the election with just thirteen governorships. Some party figures worried about the party's prospects for survival, and serious conservatives talked about ditching the GOP altogether and starting a new party. All in all, it was an unpleasant time to chair the RNC.

Bush did derive a couple of long-term benefits from his job. First, it enabled him to build a national network of political contacts who could later offer him endorsements and campaign contributions. Second, it brought him into contact with a young man named Lee Atwater. There had been a disputed 1973 election for chair of the College Republican National Committee, and Bush oversaw an investigation to settle it. In the end, the winning candidate was Karl Rove, who would go on to be George W. Bush's political adviser. Atwater had led the campaign for Rove, who made him executive director of the College Republicans. Bush invited Rove and Atwater for a long, friendly meeting, and as the two young men started to leave, Atwater asked if he could borrow Bush's boat for a date. Rove recalled: "He allowed that he was familiar with boats, mentioning the specific kind the chairman had, and pledged to return it fully fueled. He'd done his homework. The request was unexpected, out of left field, edgy and chancy. It impressed Bush."[26] Atwater got to use the boat and ended up marrying the young woman.

At the end of Watergate, Bush almost got a promotion. A bribery prosecution had forced Vice President Agnew from office, and Nixon replaced him with House GOP leader Gerald Ford. Upon Nixon's resignation, Ford became president, and he needed a vice president of his own. Conservatives hoped for Ronald Reagan, then in his second term as governor of California, but Ford and Reagan disliked each other.[27] Ford settled on three finalists: Bush, NATO ambassador Donald Rumsfeld, and former New York governor Nelson Rockefeller. Bush made the short list for the same reason as in 1968: he seemed to bridge the party's ideological and regional divides. Moreover, the UN post had provided him with the foreign policy experience that he had once lacked. Rumsfeld had served with Ford in the House and had backed Ford's 1965 election as party leader. Rockefeller had the most impressive background, but conservatives thought that he was too liberal. Just before Ford made his choice, *Newsweek* raised ethical questions about the campaign money that Nixon had funneled to Bush in the 1970 Senate campaign. Though the Watergate special prosecutor later cleared Bush of wrongdoing, the story may have been enough to scuttle his chances, and Ford picked Rockefeller.

As a consolation prize, Ford named Bush to head the US liaison office in Beijing, although without the title of ambassador, because the United States did not yet have full diplomatic relations. During a 1975 administration shake-up, Ford brought Bush back to the United States as the director of Central Intelligence. Accepting the appointment, Bush wrote: "I do not have politics out of my system entirely and I see this as the total end of any political future. . . . In all candor I would not have selected this controversial position if the decision had been mine, but I serve at the pleasure of our President and I do not believe in complicating his already enormously difficult job."[28] Bush probably believed what he wrote, because revelations of past misconduct had put the CIA in a bad light. Knowing that Bush had twice been on vice presidential short lists, however, congressional Democrats worried that Ford might put him on the GOP ticket in 1976. (With a nudge from Ford, Rockefeller had said that he would retire at the end of the term.) In a letter to the chair of the Senate Armed Services Committee, Ford ruled Bush out for the vice presidential nomination.[29] He appeared to be off the electoral track.

THE FORTUNATE FALL

Bush's CIA tenure came to an end when Jimmy Carter defeated President Ford in 1976. The election was closer than the political community had expected. A switch of 5,559 votes in Ohio and 3,687 votes in Hawaii would have reversed the result, giving Ford a bare majority of 270 electoral votes.[30] Yet had Ford won, Bush might never have had a path to the presidency. He would probably have stayed at the CIA, where he could not engage in partisan politics. Under the Twenty-Second Amendment, Ford could not have run for a second full term in 1980. Either Reagan or Bob Dole, Ford's 1976 running mate, would have been the likely GOP nominee.

In reality, Dole had his problems on the 1976 campaign trail. He got poor marks for his performance in the first-ever television debate between vice presidential nominees. He said that 1.6 million Americans had died in "Democrat wars," a line that had long been a staple of the GOP Lincoln Day dinner circuit, but one that appalled Americans who did not think of World War II as a partisan conflict. Addressing the Urban League a year after the election, he said that African American voters had sent a message to both parties. "We got ours. We got ours in spades."[31] Such gaffes undercut his standing as a mainstream alternative to Reagan, leaving space open for Bush.

It turned out that Bush's stint at the CIA was not the political liability that he had assumed; within the GOP at least, it was an asset. Republicans were turning more hawkish, and Bush's time at Langley reinforced his credentials as a Cold Warrior. Conservative critics of détente with the Soviet Union had been calling the agency to bring in hard-line outsiders to provide a second opinion. Unlike the previous CIA director, Bush approved the idea, and "Team B" took a predictably harsh view of Soviet intentions and capabilities.[32] Though many scholars and members of the intelligence community regarded the group's report as flawed, it did reassure conservative activists and intellectuals that Bush was open to their ideas on national security.

In early 1977, Bush went home to Houston. By doing some business consulting and joining several corporate boards, he was soon able to make a handsome living and still have plenty of time for politics. His Texas friends James Baker and Robert Mosbacher set up committees to give money to GOP congressional candidates and to fund Bush's 1978 campaign travel, which covered forty-two states.[33] He was doing what Richard Nixon had done in done in the 1966 midterm: strengthen relationships with Republicans across the country and build the base for a presidential campaign two years hence. He stayed on the road after the midterm, explaining in a letter to Nixon: "I start with no name identification and realize that. I will, however, continue to keep a 'low profile.' I am traveling with no press secretary, no advance text and no fanfare. I am determined to organize, and organize well, before escalating the candidacy to high levels of public attention."[34]

Bush's party was coming back to life. In 1977, the Republican National Committee had chosen former Tennessee senator Bill Brock as its chairman. Brock modernized the national party's organization, finances, candidate training, and image building. He was eager to reestablish the GOP as the party of ideas. He founded a quasiacademic policy journal called *Commonsense* and invited an eclectic array of speakers to address the committee.[35] One of them was Jesse Jackson. Since Martin Luther King's assassination in 1968, Jackson had risen as a prominent civil rights leader and head of Operation PUSH. "Mutual need is the basis of an alliance," he told the RNC's 1978 winter meeting. "Black people need the Republican Party to compete for us so that we have real alternatives for meeting our needs."[36] The committee gave him a standing ovation—and at the same meeting, it rejected an African American candidate for party co-chair.[37] The party was continuing to send mixed messages to the black community.

THE TAX ISSUE AND JACK KEMP

In June 1978, California voters stunned the national political community by passing the tax-cutting Proposition 13. Across the country, Republican politicians took the outcome as a sign that tax cuts were a hot issue. And as Proposition 13 was providing a political motive for backing tax cuts, Jack Kemp was touting an economic rationale.

Jack French Kemp—who had the same initials as a tax-cutting president, John F. Kennedy—had up to this point achieved his greatest fame as a football player. Though he had fallen short of NFL stardom after graduating from Occidental College in 1957, he became a standout quarterback in the fledgling American Football League. He signed up with the Los Angeles Chargers, which relocated to San Diego. During a league championship game in Houston, it stunned him to learn that there was separate seating for the families of black players, who could not stay in the same hotel as white players. In 1961, he insisted that his black and white teammates stay together.[38] During the same year, his army reserve unit went into active service during the Berlin crisis, but Kemp got a medical exemption. "Jack had a legitimate injury," a teammate remembered years later. "He would have 10 or so painkilling shots just to play. It sounds weird, but he could play football and not be fit to serve in the Army."[39]

After ending his football career with the Buffalo Bills, Kemp won a House seat in the Buffalo suburbs. He appeared to be an ordinary minority-party backbencher until he latched onto the tax issue. In 1976, journalist Jude Wanniski had introduced him to the work of economist Arthur Laffer, who claimed that reductions in tax rates could pay for themselves by spurring economic activity—a notion at the heart of supply-side economics.[40] Kemp introduced several tax measures, most recently an across-the-board cut, which Delaware Republican William Roth sponsored in the Senate. (Everyone called it the Kemp–Roth bill except for Roth, who called it Roth–Kemp.)

Like Bush, Kemp worked hard for GOP candidates in the 1978 congressional elections. The House GOP class of 1978 included several members who would help define the positions of the House Republicans in the years ahead, including a Georgia college professor named Newt Gingrich. Following Kemp's lead, many of the freshmen had based their campaigns on support for tax cuts. Once in office, they worked with Kemp and Representative David Stockman (MI) to devise the "Budget of Hope," an alternative to what they called the Democrats' "Budget of Despair." The young militants proposed domestic spending cuts and a $20 billion tax cut, which they assumed would shrink the deficit by spurring economic growth.[41] Although it did not pass, it won the support of 187 members, including thirty-nine Democrats. It would prove to be a dress rehearsal for congressional action on Reaganomics two years later.

Some of Kemp's friends urged him to run for president in 1980. He declined, realizing that Ronald Reagan had first call on the GOP's conservative wing and was the front-runner for the party's nomination. Outside Republican ranks, many observers doubted that Reagan could beat President Carter. In the spring of 1979, journalist Richard Reeves published an article in *Esquire* magazine titled "Why Reagan Won't Make It."[42]

THE 1980 CAMPAIGN

Reagan did make it in 1980. To a large extent, national politics during the subsequent decade revolved around him as politicians defined themselves as opponents or supporters.[43] In Bush's case, it was first as one, then the other.

If Reagan was going to be the candidate of the Republican Party's conservative wing, who would represent the traditional moderate wing? For much of 1979, the smart money was on Howard Baker. Largely forgotten by the early twenty-first century, the senator from Tennessee had gained political celebrity as ranking Republican on the Senate's Watergate committee, where he famously asked, "What did the president know and when did he know it?" In 1977, Senate Republicans chose him as their leader. He was a Beltway favorite because of his affable personal manner, his calm demeanor on television, and his willingness to work across party lines. He cemented his Beltway standing in 1978, with Senate approval of the treaty ceding control of the Panama Canal. Thanks largely to Baker's efforts to get fifteen other Republicans behind the agreement, it passed with one more vote than the necessary two thirds.[44] His position carried risks. In 1976, Reagan had harnessed grassroots GOP opposition to the treaty, which helped him come close to toppling Ford for the party's presidential nomination. Years later, Democratic senator Robert Byrd of West Virginia said: "Courage? That's Howard Baker and the Panama Canal."[45]

By 1979, Baker was betting that the canal issue would be cooling off and that he could emerge as the main alternative to Reagan. According to political consultant Douglas Bailey, the assumption was that Reagan had a ceiling of about 40 percent of the primary vote. "I think it was an underlying thesis of the Baker campaign to be the survivor so that when it came down to two people it would be Reagan and Baker."[46] The last-man-standing idea was reasonable, except that the man would be Bush, not Baker.

Just as he had privately told Nixon, Bush had been hitting the party circuit in ways that did not draw national publicity. "There was an effort then to build on Bush's popularity within the party," said pollster Robert Teeter. "He had been chairman of the National Committee; he was well known among the party people and reasonably popular among them." The goal, Teeter continued, "was to win some early caucuses and early primaries. And that alone would break you away. Almost the entire effort was to build some kind of an organization that would allow you to do that, during that period in early 1980."[47]

After several months off the front page, Bush announced his candidacy on May 1, 1979. His first big splash came in November, with a nonbinding straw vote at the Maine GOP's presidential forum. Howard Baker assumed that he would easily win such an event in a state where Republicans tended to be moderate and practical minded, so he timed his announcement of candidacy to come just a couple of days earlier. Journalists were reporting—accurately—that Baker was so focused on his Senate work that he neglected fundraising and campaign organization. He hoped that a Maine victory would change the story. In the meantime, Bush was quietly mobilizing supporters for the forum. To the surprise of the political community, he won. Bush's victory was narrow, involved just a few hundred attendees, and had no direct bearing on the selection of delegates to the national convention. Nevertheless, the media portrayed it as a noteworthy development.[48] Bailey acknowledged "that one event probably doomed Baker's candidacy more than anything else because rather than changing perceptions, it confirmed perceptions and made, for the first time, I believe, Bush a credible candidate even to his own people."[49]

There were other candidates. Like Baker, Bob Dole was concentrating on his Senate duties to the detriment of his presidential campaign. He was also dealing with the bad impressions left over from his 1976 vice presidential candidacy. John Connally was the former Democratic governor of Texas who had served as Nixon's treasury secretary. The administration's ethics problems had smudged him, as he had gone on trial for charges stemming from a milk-price deal. An acquittal enabled him to say that he was the only candidate "certified innocent." The line did not impress GOP primary voters, who knew of his history as a wheeler-dealer and Johnson underling. Two House members from Illinois also ran. A right-wing intellectual, Phil Crane, sought conservative Republicans who did not want Reagan—of whom there were vanishingly few. John Anderson had moved to the left just as his party had moved to the right. Neither Anderson nor any of these other candidates posed a serious threat to front-runner Reagan.

The Bush organization focused on the Iowa caucuses, and from a twenty-first-century perspective, such an emphasis might seem obvious. Although Jimmy Carter had benefited from an unexpectedly strong showing in the 1976 Democratic caucuses, the state had not been crucial in Republican nomination contests. Then as now, the precinct caucuses chose no national convention delegates; rather, they merely began a multistep process that would later result in such a selection. Before 1980, Iowa Republicans had never polled all their caucuses about presidential preferences, so they got little notice. This time, they would conduct their first such poll. Though not binding—again, as has been the case ever since—the poll would enable candidates and the media to treat the caucuses as something like a primary.[50] As Teeter said, the Bush campaign operated on the assumption that "the unique breaking away from the pack would come from the fact that you won the Iowa caucuses."[51]

And Bush did win the Iowa caucuses. From the media's perspective, it did not matter that his margin was only a couple of percentage points, or that the results did not necessarily translate into convention delegates. The "David Beats Goliath" story was big news, and he ended up with a *Newsweek* cover story titled "Bush Breaks Out of the Pack." Money and volunteers started pouring in, and a Harris poll showed Bush suddenly running even with Reagan among Republicans and independents.[52] Bush started talking about his campaign momentum, or as he put it in his awkward phrase, "Big Mo." Did he have it? Not as much as he thought. In campaigns since then, long-shot candidates have often enjoyed brief surges during the primary season. Mike Huckabee, Rick Perry, Herman Cain, Newt Gingrich, Rick Santorum, and Ben Carson all flew up in some polls, only to crash. In 1980, Reagan still had a reservoir of affection within the GOP. His campaign had erred by taking a pivotal contest for granted, and it would not repeat that mistake.

The nomination calendar was less front-loaded than it would be in subsequent election cycles. The New Hampshire primary took place more than a month after the Iowa caucuses, giving Reagan plenty of time to regroup. He used these weeks well, campaigning with a vigor that helped allay concerns about his advanced age. Bush also had an opportunity, which he squandered. Republicans were hazy on who he was and what he stood for, and he could have used this period to tell them. Instead, he kept talking about momentum. In the words of *New York Times* columnist Anthony Lewis: "Bush has come across, so far, as a man campaigning primarily on his ability to campaign."[53] Teeter said: "I don't think it was ever agreed on well at any point what kind of central theme or message there was going to be. I think there were a lot of details but no real central theme."[54] Then came Nashua. Reagan agreed to a one-on-one debate with Bush just before the primary under the sponsorship of the *Nashua Telegraph*. After the Federal Election Commission ruled that the paper could not underwrite a debate that excluded the other candidates, Reagan paid for it himself. His campaign manager then invited the other candidates to show up. At the debate site, Bush objected to the last-minute change, and Reagan disregarded him. Once on stage, Reagan asked the other candidates to come out. Moderator Joseph Breen from the *Telegraph* said that Reagan was violating the ground rules and threatened to cut off his microphone. Reagan responded with a line that has entered campaign legend: "I'm paying for this microphone, Mr. Green!"[55] He got the moderator's name wrong, but he got the moment right. Cameras recorded Reagan radiating strength and passion while Bush was sitting silent and looking peevish. Reagan ended up winning New Hampshire by more than a 2-to-1 margin over Bush.

In the party's collective memory, Nashua was the moment when Bush let Reagan turn defeat into victory. The reality was more complicated. Reagan's pollster found that he was surging several days before Nashua, after a less dramatic debate among all the GOP contenders in Manchester.[56] Reagan was on track to win the New Hampshire primary anyway, and the Nashua confrontation just padded his margin. In the longer run, it hurt Bush's reputation in the GOP political community and planted doubts about his ability to handle himself under the lights.

Bush went on to win a few primaries, but the GOP race was essentially over. If the party's nomination process had still worked as it did through the 1960s, he could have had a chance. In the old system, only a minority of delegates came from primaries and voter caucuses. Party leaders largely determined delegate selection, and they would have smiled on a moderate conservative who had faithfully served GOP presidents and chaired the Republican National Committee. That system was gone. In the 1970s, reforms of the Democratic nomination process had the side effect of changing the Republican process. State legislatures—most with Democratic majorities in those days—accommodated their party's reforms by enacting presidential primary laws, which usually applied to the other party as well.[57] The power now belonged to the people who voted in primaries. Reagan's strong challenge to Ford in 1976 was a clear sign that they wanted conservative leaders.

The Reagan–Bush competition was fairly civil, as the candidates generally refrained from personal attacks. Still, the two camps released some political toxins that would linger. Bush criticized Reagan's economic policies, especially his support for the Kemp–Roth tax cut proposal. "Governor Reagan is promising to cut taxes by 30 percent, balance the budget, increase defense spending and stop inflation all at the same time." He summed it up as "voodoo economic policy."[58] Democrats shortened the phrase to "voodoo economics," and they used it for years to depict Reagan as an economic con man and Bush as a hypocrite. Some Reagan supporters, in turn, spread conspiracy theories about Bush's membership in the Trilateral Commission, an international group of civic leaders. Conservative groups called it "a powerful coalition of liberals, multinational corporate executives, big-city bankers and hungry power brokers."[59] Well into the 1990s, the hard right would repeat the refrain.

At the Republican convention, Reagan had to pick a running mate. Bush was the logical choice because he had high-level experience and would bring geographical and ideological balance. Reagan balked. Nancy Reagan resented Bush's criticisms of her husband, and she would nurse that grudge until the day she died. Reagan himself was less concerned with the attacks than with Bush's behavior in Nashua. "It imprinted on Reagan that Bush was a wimp," a Reagan insider later told journalist Jules Witcover. "He couldn't understand how a man could have sat there so passively. He felt it showed a lack of courage."[60] For a while Reagan toyed with the idea of tapping former president Gerald Ford, but after Ford agreed in an interview that the arrangement might lead to a "co-presidency," Reagan dropped the idea. At the eleventh hour, Reagan called Bush. He asked if Bush would have problems with his issue positions, and Bush assured him that he would back the Reagan platform down the line. That pledge included not just the Kemp–Roth tax cut but also a much tougher stance against abortion than Bush had previously been willing to take.[61]

Reagan triumphed by a 51–41 percent margin over Carter, with most of the remainder going to John Anderson, who had left the GOP to run as an independent. He won forty-four states with 489 electoral votes, even taking Massachusetts by a whisker. Survey evidence suggests that Bush might have been a small net asset to the GOP ticket. The keyword is "small."[62] A recession and the Iranian hostage crisis had put Carter at such a disadvantage that Reagan was likely to win. And he was going to carry Texas with or without Bush. During the fall campaign, Bush had little chance to shine, as there was no debate among the vice presidential candidates. He helped mostly by doing no harm.

After the election, he assured the incoming president that he would stay that course. "I will never do anything to embarrass you politically," he wrote the Reagans on November 10. "I have strong views on issues and people, but once you decide a matter that's it for me, and you'll see no leaks in Evans and Novak bitching about life—at least you'll see none out of me."[63] For eight years, he would keep his word, which would be both a benefit and a burden to him.

THE LANDSCAPE OF THE EARLY 1980S

Many Republicans spoke hopefully of a political realignment. Not only had Reagan scored an Electoral College landslide, but also the party had taken control of the Senate for the first time since the election of 1952. Political scientists tried to douse the notion that 1980 was a realigning election. Because of the geographic distribution of the Reagan vote, they argued, the Electoral College magnified his margin, as his bare majority of the popular vote was only a bit greater than Carter's share in 1976.[64] Geography was the GOP's friend in Senate elections as well. Thanks to equal representation in the Senate, GOP victories in small rural states overmatched Democratic wins in large urban ones. In one of the big states, New York, Republicans caught a lucky break. Al D'Amato won an upset GOP primary victory over incumbent Jacob Javits, who then ran as the Liberal Party candidate in November and siphoned just enough votes from the Democrat to tip the race to D'Amato. Nationwide, Democrats had an edge of three million votes in the aggregate tally, even as Republicans won twenty-two of thirty-four Senate seats.[65] Democrats continued to hold most House seats, state legislative seats, and governorships. They also enjoyed a substantial, if slightly reduced, lead in party identification among voters.[66] Political scientists were right that there was no immediate realignment.

Yet the political landscape was shifting in ways that would become more evident over the years. For one thing, the tax issue was now at the center of Republican Party politics, both in presidential campaigns and on Capitol Hill. By embracing the Kemp–Roth tax cut, Reagan had cemented Jack Kemp's standing as a national political figure. Right after the election, Kemp used his new stature to seek election as chair of the House Republican Conference. In a sign of the GOP's conservative trend, his rival for the job was a fellow supply-sider who was much farther to the right: John Rousselot of California, a member of the John Birch Society. Kemp won by a vote of 107 to 177.[67] With Democrats in the majority, he could not control the chamber's legislative agenda. The post did provide him with staff support, a seat at the leadership table, and entrée to meetings at the Reagan White House.

Reagan had campaigned on Kemp–Roth and followed through by winning congressional approval of an across-the-board tax cut. The measure had near-unanimous support from Republicans in both chambers and got a fair number of Democratic votes. By 1982, however, a combination of tax cuts and increases in defense spending was bloating an already large budget deficit. The trend disturbed Bob Dole, who had become chair of the tax-writing Senate Finance Committee when the Republicans won the majority. Dole was an orthodox conservative who was always skeptical of supply-side economics, and a visit from Federal Reserve chairman Paul Volcker added urgency to his desire to address the deficit. Interest rates were in double digits, with the prime rate topping 21 percent in mid-1982. Volcker told Dole and other members of the committee that if they could curb the inflationary deficits, he would ease up on the money supply. Falling interest rates would then help the ailing economy. According to Dole aide Rod DeArment, "that's what was the real motivator" for the Tax Equity and Fiscal Responsibility Act (TEFRA) of 1982.[68] With the support of deficit hawks on the White House staff, Dole persuaded President Reagan to back the bill, which would close loopholes to raise nearly $100 billion in tax revenue during the next three years. Most Senate Republicans sided with Dole. House Republicans were more sharply divided, with Newt Gingrich complaining: "The fact is, on this particular bill, the President is trying to score a touchdown for liberalism, for the liberal welfare state, for big government, for the Internal Revenue Service, for multinational corporations, and for the various forces that consistently voted against this President."[69]

Dole knew that he was running a risk. "A pathologist in Kansas offered to give me a free autopsy," he said. "The trouble is, he wants to do it now."[70] Also in 1982, Dole backed a nickel-a-gallon hike in the gasoline tax for public works, and in 1983, he joined in a bipartisan Social Security rescue effort that raised payroll taxes. Dole did not stand alone. Many leading Republicans, from President Reagan on down, were willing to support certain kinds of tax increases during the early 1980s. They used euphemisms— TEFRA as a "tax reform" and the gas tax hike as a "user fee." The word games did not fool anybody, but absolute opposition to any new taxes had yet to become GOP doctrine.

In 1982 and early 1983, the economy threatened to cut short the careers of Ronald Reagan and George Bush. The Federal Reserve's tight-money policy fostered a painful recession. In late 1982, the unemployment rate reached 10.8 percent. The country had not seen that level of joblessness since 1940—and would not see it again even during the Great Recession of the early twenty-first century.[71] Manufacturing had already been in trouble for years, and the slump hastened the decline of the Rust Belt. In 1980, Republicans had blamed Democrats for hard times. The National Republican Congressional Committee ran a television spot in which an unemployed factory worker walked through his idle plant and asked: "If the Democrats are good for working people, how come so many people aren't working?"[72]

In 1982, Democrats returned the favor by putting the same man in an ad of their own. In 1980, he said, the Republicans had paid him to go on television, and then put lies on his lips. "Well, since they've been in control, unemployment is the highest since the Great Depression and businesses are closing down every day. Millions of Americans are without jobs, and we've got to do something. I'm a Democrat, but I voted Republican once—and it's a mistake I'll never make again. And I did not get paid to say this."[73] Many voters felt the same way, and in the fall, Democrats scored a net pickup of twenty-six House seats and seven governorships. They gained no ground in the Senate, primarily because they already held twenty of the thirty-three seats up for election that year.

"The stench of failure hangs over Ronald Reagan's White House," said a *New York Times* editorial in early 1983.[74] With Reagan's approval ratings tumbling, Speaker O'Neill belittled his reelection prospects: "My personal opinion. . . . He couldn't win. The man will be 74. My political instincts are that it would be kind of foolish."[75]

IT'S MORNING AGAIN

Even as O'Neill was speaking, however, the ground was shifting again. As 1983 wore on, inflation ebbed, interest rates eased, and the economy started to recover. Accordingly, Reagan's reelection prospects were looking better. All along, in fact, he had greater underlying strength than news headlines were suggesting. The midterm congressional loss was a setback, but because the recession was so severe and because Democrats largely controlled congressional redistricting, it could have been worse for the GOP.[76] Whereas the president's party typically takes most of the blame for an economic downturn, an October 1982 poll found that voters blamed the parties about equally.[77] Under the circumstances, Republicans were in fairly good shape.

Reagan had no opposition for his party's nomination, but there were internal disputes over the issues. Religious conservatives had complained that his one Supreme Court nominee to date, Sandra Day O'Connor, did not have a record of opposing abortion. In 1983, Reagan sought to placate them by issuing a ghostwritten book laying out his position on the issue. At the Republican convention, Reagan forces agreed to toughen the abortion plank, which future platforms would repeat almost verbatim. There was also a dispute about taxes. Reagan White House aides, including deputy chief of staff Richard Darman, proposed this language for the party platform: "Our most important economic goal is to continue the economic recovery.

We therefore oppose any attempt to increase taxes which would harm the recovery and reverse the trend toward restoring control of the economy to individual Americans." Jack Kemp, Newt Gingrich, and other conservatives noticed that the line opened the door to tax increases that would purportedly not hurt economic expansion.[78] That wording was intentional. Reagan had already acceded to several tax increases and believed that presidents should never foreclose policy options. The conservatives disagreed, insisting on a comma after the word "taxes." As columnist William Safire explained, the idea was to turn a defining clause into a nondefining clause, thereby proclaiming that any tax increase would harm the recovery.[79] Wary of a convention floor fight, the Reagan staff yielded on the point. Bob Dole, who supported the original language, shrugged off the change: "We'll just say it was a typo."[80] The comma controversy got only minimal coverage and quickly fell into the shadow of subsequent events. The conservative victory was more significant than it seemed at the time. It was an omen of things to come, a sign that GOP activists were taking a harder line on taxes.

Republicans enjoyed their customary advantage on national security. An iconic moment of the Cold War came in 1983, when Reagan gave a speech calling the Soviet Union "the focus of evil in the modern world." Liberal activists were calling for a mutual freeze on nuclear weapons by the United States and the Soviet Union, and Reagan argued that such a move would lock the United States into strategic inferiority. He devoted much of his speech to the case against the freeze. It is significant that his immediate audience was the National Association of Evangelicals. Although evangelicals had been turning conservative, they had not yet reached the point where he could count on their automatic support. He thought they needed a sermon from the Gipper. He warned of "the temptation of blithely declaring yourselves above it all and label both sides equally at fault, to ignore the facts of history and the aggressive impulses of an evil empire, to simply call the arms race a giant misunderstanding and thereby remove yourself from the struggle between right and wrong and good and evil."[81]

A couple of months later, the House passed a nonbinding resolution endorsing the freeze. The final vote reflected the direction of each party, with Democrats voting for it 218–243 and Republicans voting against it 60–106. Polls appeared to show strong support for the freeze, and the issue of arms control got even greater publicity when ABC aired *The Day After*, a TV movie about the horrors of nuclear war.[82] Democrats thought they were riding a political wave that would carry them back to the presidency. By the summer of 1984, however, no crisis was in the offing. Republicans claimed that the success of the deployment vindicated their policy of "peace through strength" and exposed Democratic weakness on foreign policy. At the convention, United Nations ambassador Jeane Kirkpatrick—still a nominal Democrat—gave a keynote address condemning the "San Francisco Democrats" for their practice of "blame America first." She cast the election as a choice between a party that had confidence in the United States and one that did not. "The American people know that it's dangerous to blame ourselves for terrible problems that we did not cause," she said.[83]

Republicans wanted to corner the market on patriotism. In the video that introduced his acceptance speech, Reagan spoke of a "reawakening of patriotism in this country," and the visuals were full of flags.[84] The soundtrack featured a new song that would become the party's unofficial anthem for decades to come: Lee Greenwood's "God Bless the USA." Four years later, Bush would pick up the theme.

In 1984, real gross domestic product grew 7.3 percent, the fastest clip since 1950—and a rate that the country would not see again for at least the next thirty-two years. The Soviet threat was real, but the United States looked strong enough to keep it in check. With the fundamentals of peace and prosperity so heavily on his side, Reagan would have had to commit a monumental error to put his reelection in jeopardy. For a few days, his campaign worried that his first debate might be such a moment. He stumbled over his lines and sometimes looked confused. Years later, there would be speculation that his poor performance was a sign of the Alzheimer's disease that would eventually kill him. A good showing in the second debate calmed GOP jitters and squelched any faint Democratic hopes of an upset.

What about Bush? He occupied a job with no independent power; a vice president could only do what the president allowed. When a reporter asked Dwight Eisenhower to describe a policy originating with his vice president, Richard Nixon, he replied: "If you give me a week, I might think of one. I don't remember."[85] Kennedy weaponized the quip in a 1960 attack ad. Hubert Humphrey shrank in Lyndon Johnson's shadow, and his efforts to establish independence came too late to save his 1968 campaign. Jimmy Carter did rely on the Washington expertise of Walter Mondale, but his job was to support the administration, not stake out a public identity of its own. And for four years, Bush had kept his word to Reagan and avoided any hint of disagreement. He faithfully carried out ceremonial duties, including attending state funerals. James Baker, the once and future Bush campaign leader who was serving as Reagan's chief of staff, joked that the vice president's motto should be, "You die, I'll fly."

In the fall campaign, he debated Democratic vice presidential nominee Geraldine Ferraro, the first such event since Dole debated Mondale in 1976. The confrontation changed few minds, and a postdebate gaffe got far more attention than their exchanges on the issues. The next day, Bush was greeting a crowd of dockworkers. Not seeing a television boom microphone nearby, he told a union official, "We tried to kick a little ass last night."[86] Commentators faulted his off-color language, and Ferraro's campaign manager said that such remarks "have gone beyond decency."[87] By the twenty-first century, such reactions would sound quaint.

The kerfuffle made no difference in the race, except to remind GOP activists of Bush's uneasy relationship with television. During the final days of the campaign, polls showed Reagan building an insurmountable lead. On Election Day, he won nearly 59 percent of the popular vote, along with 525 electoral votes. Mondale carried the District of Columbia and barely edged out Reagan in his home state of Minnesota, for a total of thirteen electoral votes.

As the title of a 1985 book put it, the result was a landslide without a mandate.[88] Reagan based his campaign on the improving economy. "It's morning again in America," said the voice-over in a famous ad, which closed with a line that tied Mondale to the perceived failures of the Carter administration: "Why would we ever want to return to where we were less than four short years ago?"[89] As for the next four years, Reagan was vague. During his 1984 State of the Union address, he said that he would direct the Treasury Department to come up with a detailed plan for tax reform. When he added that it would be due in December—a month after the election—congressional Democrats laughed in his face.[90] Accordingly, Republicans could not convincingly claim that the voters were endorsing a specific policy agenda.

In elections for the House, Republicans made only slight gains that did not make up for their losses in the 1982 midterm. They kept their Senate majority, mostly because the set of seats up for election in 1984 presented few opportunities to the Democrats. Still, there were changes in the Senate lineup that would affect the 1988 presidential race. In Delaware, Joseph Biden scored a big victory in his bid for a third term. He had won his first term at the earliest possible age, for he had turned thirty shortly after the 1972 election. He was now a senior senator who was still only in his early forties, meaning that he could be an attractive choice for Democrats seeking a candidate who was a fresh face yet an experienced hand. In Illinois, Representative Paul Simon defeated three-term incumbent Republican

Charles Percy. Illinois later became a Democratic fortress, but it had voted Republican in every presidential election since 1968. At least in theory, having Simon on the next ticket might give Democrats a better shot at a large swing state. And in Tennessee, Howard Baker retired, creating an open seat that went to Representative Al Gore. Baker's departure also left a vacancy in the post of Senate Republican leader. Bob Dole wanted the job. It was no sure thing. The fifty-three Republican senators required four ballots to settle on their choice, and Dole defeated Alaska's Ted Stevens by the less-than-thumping margin of 28 to 25.

Winning the post helped put Dole into contention for the 1988 GOP nomination. Party leaders command media coverage and can raise money from interest groups eager to gain access to congressional power. Again, ponder the role of contingency. If just two senators had changed their minds, Dole would have had another embarrassing defeat on his political record. As a longtime national figure, he might still have run, but it would have been harder to position himself as Bush's chief rival.

HALF PAST REAGAN

By the mid-1980s, tax reform ideas had been circulating for many years. Columnist William F. Buckley Jr. had proposed a conservative version back in 1972, and Senator Bill Bradley spelled out a liberal version in a 1984 book.[91] Because of huge deficits, there was a bipartisan consensus that any reform had to be revenue neutral—that is, it would have to close enough loopholes to make up for the forgone taxes resulting from rate cuts. Every loophole had a constituency, so the smart-money bet was that the idea would fizzle out. When congressional Democrats laughed at Reagan's mention of postelection tax reform, they did not expect that he would make a serious proposal. He did. In November 1984, just as he had promised, the Treasury Department issued a detailed plan for cutting rates and ending special-interest preferences. In May 1985, the administration put out a second draft, and Reagan made an Oval Office television address to gain public support.

After more than a year of complicated legislative maneuvering that often careened onto the edge of doom, Reagan signed a tax reform bill in October 1986. "This will reach working-class Americans, Hispanics, blacks, Catholics," White House communications director Pat Buchanan said at the start of the process. "This is a reach for the conservative movement to bring these people into the Republican Party."[92] As the bill neared passage, the Republican National chairman, Frank Fahrenkopf, said that it would remove "the albatross that Franklin Roosevelt placed around our necks—

the idea that all we care about is big corporations and the wealthy."[93] These hopes proved hollow. A couple of weeks after the signing ceremony, Republicans lost their majority in the US Senate and saw their already anemic numbers drop further in the House.

Those results were predictable. The party holding the presidency had lost House seats in every midterm during the previous half century. The class of senators up for election in 1986 included several Republicans who had ridden Reagan's coattails in 1980 but were too politically weak to win on their own. There was no sign that the tax bill had done anything to blunt the party's midterm disadvantage. It had always been unrealistic to expect that the legislation would be of much electoral benefit to the GOP, because its passage had hinged on bipartisan cooperation. Indeed, House Republicans had tried to kill it at one point, and most of them voted against sending it to the Senate.[94] And oddly for a bill with a bipartisan ancestry and broad support from policy experts, it was not popular. In an October poll from Cambridge Reports, 36 percent said that it would raise their taxes, compared with just 16 percent who believed that it would lower them. Over the next three years, the former group would grow to 50 percent.[95]

Other issues were in play. The 1982 TEFRA tax increase had been only partially successful in curbing the budget deficit. In 1985, Majority Leader Dole took another crack at the problem with a plan that would have ended thirteen programs and stopped Social Security cost-of-living increases for a year. To pass the bill, Dole summoned Senator Pete Wilson of California from a hospital room. After Wilson entered the chamber in a wheelchair and voted aye, Vice President Bush broke the tie to pass the measure. Despite this dramatic gesture, the plan died in the House, leaving Senate Republicans with a futile roll-call vote that further damaged their standing in the 1986 midterm.

Congress did manage to pass one significant antideficit bill in 1985: Gramm–Rudman–Hollings. The legislation set limits on the deficit and provided for automatic spending cuts in case Congress breached those caps. Critics said that the act was a cynical ploy that enabled lawmakers to claim credit for fighting the deficit without naming which programs they would reduce or which taxes they would increase.

Until the fall of 1986, Reagan was doing well in the polls, with about two thirds of the public approving his job performance.[96] Now, after several years of good economic news, worrisome stories were starting to blemish the front page. In 1986, oil prices plunged. For drivers who remembered the gas line of 1973 and 1979, this development was welcome. But it was a hardship for people in the oil-producing states of Texas, Oklahoma, and Louisiana. Meanwhile, farm prices also plummeted—good for consumers, bad for farmers in the Midwest. The one–two punch was a blow to financial institutions. There had been too much construction, and when the money stopped flowing from oil and agriculture, banks suffered losses on real estate loans. During 1986, 138 banks failed, mostly in oil and farm states.[97]

There was also controversy about foreign policy. Nowadays we think of Mikhail Gorbachev's 1985 rise to power in the Soviet Union as the beginning of the end of the Cold War. It was not so obvious at the time. Conservatives faulted Reagan for being too friendly toward the new Soviet leader, suggesting that the old man had gone soft. Newt Gingrich was especially harsh. Before Reagan's first summit with Gorbachev, he warned that there would be "more pressure on President Reagan to appease the Soviet Union than there has been in any Western leader since Neville Chamberlain went to Munich in 1938."[98] The following year, he noted the gap between Reagan's Cold War rhetoric and the administration's "pathetically incompetent efforts."[99]

Meanwhile, the superpowers continued to wage Central American proxy wars. In El Salvador, the Soviets supported Marxist rebels against an American-backed regime, and in Nicaragua, Reagan had tried to support rebels against a Soviet-backed regime. The latter effort was unpopular, and Congress enacted strict limits on American aid to the Nicaraguan forces, known as the Contras. Weeks after the 1986 midterm, news broke of the Iran–Contra scandal. It turned out that the Reagan administration had concocted an arms-for-hostages deal with Iran and had used the proceeds to fund the Contras, in apparent violation of congressional limits. This harebrained scheme dominated the news for months, and it would cause trouble for Vice President Bush throughout the 1988 campaign.

For awhile in 1987, there were even some whispers about impeaching Reagan.[100] By fall, Reagan had apologized for the scandal, and the public was starting to lose interest. Then the stock market crashed. On October 19, 1987, the Dow Jones Industrial Average plunged 22.61 percent in one day. By contrast, the steepest one-day drop of the Great Recession (October 15, 2008) was only 7.87 percent. It would later become apparent that the 1987 crash stemmed from market-specific causes—especially program trading—rather than underlying weakness in the economy. But for weeks, Americans had the jitters.

And Democrats had reason for hope. No party had held the White House for more than two consecutive terms since the Roosevelt–Truman years.

The administration was running low on ideas, and Reagan's would-be heirs were squabbling among themselves. Scandal and economic uncertainty made it plausible to think that the electorate was ready for a change. Early in 1988, Fred Barnes surveyed the political scene in an article for the *New Republic*. Its title was "A Donkey's Year."[101]

3

THE DEMOCRATS IN THE 1980s

In 1985, the top choice of Democratic voters was neither a new face nor a champion of new ideas. When the Harris Poll gave them a choice among ten potential nominees, 31 percent chose Senator Edward Kennedy of Massachusetts.[1]

The Kennedy name had much to do with it. The family had circled presidential politics since the 1950s. During the 1956 Democratic convention, nominee Adlai Stevenson let delegates pick the vice presidential nominee. Senator John F. Kennedy ran for the spot, leading on the second ballot before losing to Senator Estes Kefauver on the third. In 1960, Kennedy became president. After Kennedy's death, Lyndon Johnson feared that Attorney General Robert F. Kennedy might snatch the 1964 nomination, but Kennedy instead ran for the Senate from New York. In 1968, he had just won the California presidential primary when an assassin struck him down. Some Democrats then wanted to draft Edward Kennedy, but he declined. The following year, a female companion died when he drove his car off a bridge on Chappaquiddick Island, Massachusetts. The murky circumstances of the incident scarred Kennedy's reputation. Even so, Nixon feared that Kennedy could threaten his reelection in 1972 and put him under surveillance. He chose not to run for president that year, and he spurned George McGovern's offer of the vice presidential nomination. Nixon's fall brought him a measure of revenge, if not redemption, as he played a major behind-the-scenes part in the Watergate investigation.[2]

Kennedy opted out of 1976 race but opposed incumbent Jimmy Carter for the Democratic nomination in 1980. After running an uneven campaign, he lost. At the Democratic convention, he restored some of his luster with a stirring oration that eclipsed Carter's clumsy acceptance speech. Amid personal difficulties, including a divorce from his wife of twenty-five years, he chose not to run against Reagan in 1984.

People still saw the Kennedys as glamorous, but the senator was shrewd enough to know what he was up against. His private life was unsettled, and would remain so until his second marriage in 1992. If Chappaquiddick were not enough, he now had to face stories of drinking and womanizing. On December 19, 1985, he said that he would not run for president in 1988 and instead would seek a fifth term in the Senate. "I know that this decision means that I may never be president," he said in a televised statement. "But the pursuit of the presidency is not my life. Public service is."[3]

Despite his withdrawal, the Kennedy name would continue to have emotional resonance in the Democratic Party. Its candidates would invoke memories of the first chief executive of the World War II generation. And although the party would never again nominate a member of that generation for the presidency, it would end up with an echo of the 1960 campaign: a ticket representing Massachusetts and Texas.

THE DUKAKIS ORIGIN STORY

Born in Brookline, Massachusetts, in 1933, Michael Dukakis spent World War II in elementary school. After excelling at Brookline High School, he entered Swarthmore College in the fall of 1951. The Korean War was under way, but a student deferment kept him out of uniform for the next four years. During the 1988 campaign, Representative Gerald Solomon (R-NY), a Korean War veteran, would accuse Dukakis of evading service during the conflict. Dukakis defused the issue by pointing out that as soon as he graduated, he volunteered for the draft and served in Korea, albeit after the end of combat operations.[4]

It was fateful that he chose Swarthmore, a distinguished liberal arts college in Pennsylvania. As he started his first semester, Democrat Joseph Clark was running for mayor of nearby Philadelphia. In the early twenty-first century, the GOP scarcely exists in most big Eastern cities, but at this time, Philadelphia Republicans ran a powerful and corrupt machine that had held the mayor's office for sixty-seven years straight. Clark promised to sweep out the city's political rot, often brandishing a broom to drive home the point. His reformism appealed to the young Dukakis, as did his sterling credentials: Phi Beta Kappa at Harvard, and a law degree from the University of Pennsylvania, where he had edited the law review. Dukakis organized Swarthmore students for Clark, taking them by train to some of the city's roughest precincts. Clark won—and the city would not have a Republican mayor for at least several decades. Biographers Richard Gaines and Michael Segal observe: "Joe Clark became Dukakis's political role model. Clark was a pol whose values of honesty, integrity and reform, and whose impatient intolerance for corruption and waste, closely mirrored Dukakis's own."[5]

The Clark campaign drew Dukakis toward political life. (A poor grade in freshman physics also squelched his earlier ambition for a medical career.) During his sophomore year at Swarthmore, he organized the campus for Democratic presidential nominee Adlai Stevenson. It is telling that the Stevenson campaign gave Dukakis his first exposure to presidential politics. Swarthmore has a Quaker tradition of social activism. Years later, Dukakis recalled its influence on him:

> In fact, Swarthmore was such a hotbed of anti-McCarthy sentiment during the 1950s that a ticket agent at the suburban train station in downtown Philadelphia used to refer regularly to Media as "the stop after Moscow." But those were the days when McCarthy was running around the country accusing countless Americans of being "pinkos," "crypto-Communists," or, at the very least, "Communist dupes." And I, a young kid from Boston who had been out of New England only once, found myself in a community of scholars, students, and activists that took McCarthy on and, with the help of a lot of other people, beat him.[6]

With his friend Carl Levin—later a Democratic senator from Michigan—Dukakis took part in the campus affiliate of the Americans for Democratic Action, a liberal group that was both anticommunist and anti-McCarthy. He also joined the American Civil Liberties Union, a connection that Bush would use against him in the 1988 campaign. During a 1988 campaign stop in Texas, Dukakis recalled the "1950s when the Republicans cheered in this country as Joseph McCarthy slandered good Democrats and called them Communists and Communist sympathizers." The crowd roared when he added: "And those Republicans haven't changed a bit . . . now they're attacking my patriotism."[7]

On May 14, 1954, toward the end of Dukakis's junior year, the US Supreme Court delivered its unanimous ruling in *Brown v. Board of Education*. The civil rights movement was not as powerful as it would be a decade later, but Americans were taking notice, and Dukakis was a small part of it. More from his Swarthmore recollections: "The barber shops in the borough of

Swarthmore wouldn't cut the hair of a handful of black students who began attending the College. . . . Swarthmore students decided to boycott the barber shops. I became the campus barber and learned an important lesson: One could combine a commitment to social justice with economic opportunity and win on both counts."[8] Layiwola Shoyinka, a Nigerian who attended Swarthmore at the time, confirmed the account. Though Dukakis was not a particularly good barber, Shoyinka appreciated what he did: "Dukakis was a leader, very active in getting people to act, getting students to react to change things."[9]

During the summer of 1954, he had a fellowship to study at the University of San Marcos in Lima, Peru. He was able to travel elsewhere in Latin America, and he developed his fluency in Spanish. He stayed in the middle-class home of Victor and Blanca Nuñez del Acro. "I would take Miguel to the slums of Lima so he could see the misery in which our people lived," Ms. Del Arco recalled in 1988.[10] Dukakis remembered the "troops with the German bucket helmets" ruling Peru. "There was no political freedom of any kind," he said, also noting that "1954 was the year the United States government overthrew the popularly elected government in Guatemala."[11] In an interview with the *New York Times,* he elaborated: "In the United States, virtually nobody knew what was going on, and in Peru everybody knew what was going on. . . . We planted phony Soviet weapons, which were then 'discovered' in a CIA operation. All this came in the context of the most hysterical McCarthyism, the Cold War, Stalin, the Iron Curtain."[12] So whereas Bush had his first major foreign experience as part of a victorious military force, Dukakis witnessed an American-backed dictatorship and saw that other countries did not always see the United States as a liberator.

During his senior year, Dukakis won admittance to Harvard Law School. Before starting his studies, however, he fulfilled his military obligation. Dukakis joined the army on July 19, 1955. After he underwent basic training at Fort Dix, New Jersey, and training as a radio operator at Camp Gordon, Georgia, the army sent him to Munsan, South Korea, just below the demilitarized zone. His service was honorable but uneventful. In 1957, he returned to Brookline, moved back in with his family, and started his legal studies at Harvard. He joined the law school Democratic club, which hosted a 1958 event for Senator John F. Kennedy, who was seeking reelection. During his remarks, Kennedy happened to mention Dukakis's political role model. "I remember him saying, Joe Clark and I are the only two Democrats in the Harvard Corporation, and we stand in a corner and talk to each other at these meetings," Dukakis said in an oral history interview. "I remember that it was an absolutely brilliant performance. Even then I'd seen a fair number of politicians in action, and I hadn't seen anybody quite as sharp, as interesting, as funny."[13]

While doing well in his studies, Dukakis was advancing his ambitions. In 1958, he ran for the Brookline Redevelopment Authority, losing by 127 votes out of several thousand. The following year, he won his first office, a seat on the Brookline Town Meeting, the legislative arm of the community's government. During his final Harvard semester in 1960, Dukakis and some classmates helped engineer a progressive takeover of the Brookline Democratic Town Committee. The progressives then started the Commonwealth Organization of Democrats, or COD. The group embodied an increasingly important phenomenon in American party politics. Unlike classic political factions that motivated members through patronage or ethnic solidarity, COD was about political reform, or what later generations would call transparency and participatory democracy. Its approach was appealing to the younger professionals who were starting to proliferate in Brookline neighborhoods.

Of course, 1960 was also the year of John F. Kennedy's election to the presidency. Although Kennedy had his share of dealings with machine politicians, reform Democrats of Dukakis's generation saw him in a different light. "A lot of us, I think, looked at Kennedy and said, 'Jesus. If he can do it, why can't we? Why can't we transform the Democratic party in Massachusetts into a party which is very much in Kennedy's image?'"[14] During the summer, Dukakis and his law school friend, Paul Brountas, drove all the way to Los Angeles to see the Democratic convention.[15]

Dukakis drew inspiration from John F. Kennedy but was not a Kennedy family vassal. When Edward M. Kennedy sought his brother's old Senate seat in 1962, Dukakis and COD backed another candidate in the Democratic primary, state attorney general Edward McCormack. Dukakis said of the younger Kennedy: "My attitude was that maybe he ought to start a little lower on the totem pole—How about the state legislature first?—so I was with McCormack, who had been a very good attorney general, and I thought a pretty impressive guy. But Ted got elected."[16]

COD was more successful in backing candidates for the state House of Representatives, focusing on affluent suburbs along the Route 128 corridor.[17] One of them was Dukakis himself, who took one of Brookline's three seats. "I was elected in 1962 at a time when this state was one of the three or four most corrupt states in the country, I kid you not," he recalled at a

Harvard forum in 2011. "People would say to me, you look honest. I'll vote for you. I finally called my mother. I said, Mom, thanks for producing a kid that looks honest."[18]

In the Massachusetts House, Dukakis developed his persona as a liberal wonk, focusing on government reform and institutional structure.[19] His major achievement was the nation's first no-fault automobile insurance law. His style was consistent with the data-driven cost–benefit approach of Harvard's public policy program, which in 1966 got a new name: the John F. Kennedy School of Government. As his biographers Charles Kenney and Robert L. Turner explain, his role in the civil rights movement was classic Dukakis. "[He] never went south, didn't march or carry banners. Instead, he worked in the legislature to create the Massachusetts Commission Against Discrimination . . . and to give it strong enforcement powers."[20]

In 1966, he ran for state attorney general. After failing to win the endorsement of the state Democratic convention, he withdrew and instead ran for reelection to the state House. During his abortive run, he did get the first-ever endorsement of the Massachusetts Political Action for Peace (Mass PAX), who called him "the peace candidate."[21] Dukakis was an early opponent of the Vietnam War. In 1968, he supported the presidential candidacy of Eugene McCarthy.[22] In 1970, he voted for a bill saying that no Massachusetts member of the armed forces would have to serve in a foreign combat zone for more than sixty days unless Congress had declared a state of war. The bill passed, and Republican governor Francis Sargent signed it into law. The goal was to prompt judicial review of the Vietnam War's constitutionality, but the Supreme Court declined to take up the case.[23] Dukakis's vote for the measure would reemerge during the 1988 campaign.

This position came naturally. Dukakis's youthful opposition to Joseph McCarthy and his experiences in Peru had turned him into a skeptic of American foreign policy. His opposition to the war also reflected the views of his constituents. Although the Route 128 corridor depended on defense spending, many residents regarded intervention in Vietnam as irrational. Dukakis's Brookline voters were part of a broader trend.

In 1970, Dukakis was the party's nominee for lieutenant governor on a ticket with gubernatorial candidate Kevin White, the mayor of Boston. The Democrats lost, in part because moderate Republican incumbent Francis Sargent had co-opted them on many issues, including the Vietnam bill. Though he had to give up his legislative seat, Dukakis performed well on the statewide campaign trail, and the exposure put him in a good position for a future race.

Until 1966, Massachusetts voters cast separate ballots for governor and lieutenant governor, but now candidates for these offices ran together. Accordingly, most of the blame for the Democratic defeat in 1970 fell on gubernatorial nominee Kevin White, not Dukakis. With his political viability intact, Dukakis went back to the full-time practice of law and found ways to get media attention. He launched the Raiders, a group to monitor Massachusetts government performance and publicize shortcomings in the Republican state administration. He also hosted *The Advocates,* a PBS program featuring policy debates between liberals and conservatives. It was a good vehicle for honing his television skills and remaining visible to the educated professionals who watched the show.

If the mid-1970s were years of angst for Republicans, they were a fine time to be a Democrat in Massachusetts. Through the 1950s, the state had not been a bastion for the party. In 1956, for instance, its vote share for Adlai Stevenson was slightly smaller than his national figure. It then shifted in the Democrats' direction, with John Kennedy, Lyndon Johnson, and Hubert Humphrey all outperforming in the state by double-digit margins. In 1972, George McGovern got only 37.5 percent nationwide, but 54.2 percent in Massachusetts, which was the only state that he carried. With such numbers, Francis Sargent's grip on the governorship was weak. In 1973 and 1974, Watergate and national economic trouble made his Republican label more of a liability than ever. Dukakis, with his ongoing political activism and visibility on television, was a logical successor.

THE RISE, FALL, AND RISE OF A GOVERNOR

The state Democratic Party was moving in his direction, as educated progressives were wielding more and more influence. In 1973, Dukakis said: "All of us in this state—liberals, moderates or conservatives—are acutely aware of the importance of what we now call the McGovern constituency. It's particularly important because that's where the workers are. The people who get out there and ring doorbells for you are the kids with the McGovern buttons. They work like crazy. So nobody wants to antagonize them."[24] The 1974 Democratic gubernatorial primary pitted Dukakis against an old-style party war horse. With major liberal organizations behind him, Dukakis got 58 percent of the primary vote. In the general election, national headwinds and homegrown troubles combined to hobble Governor Sargent. Among other things, chaos in the state's prison system forced him to oust his own corrections commissioner.[25] Like many Democrats across the country in 1974, Dukakis won.

In retrospect, we can see hints of future political difficulty just beneath the surface of his victory. His campaign slogan, "Mike Dukakis Should Be Governor," sounded arrogant. The problems facing Massachusetts should have been humbling. The ranks of educated professionals had grown, but many residents dwelt in declining mill towns that were not sharing in the bounty of high technology. State unemployment was high, hitting double digits in 1975. These economic woes spawned budget shortfalls that Dukakis could not solve through technocratic efficiency. He proposed spending cuts that neither pleased his fellow liberals nor went far enough to close the fiscal gap. The only choice left was to raise taxes. Unhappily for Dukakis, he had made a "lead pipe" promise not to. In words that foreshadowed a famous pledge by his 1988 opponent, he said during the campaign: "I will guarantee there will be no new taxes next year if I am elected."[26] Eventually, he had to break his promise and ask the state legislature for a tax hike.[27] He got his way, which helped reduce the deficit, but his public image was scuffed.

Like other states, Massachusetts suffered from high rates of violent crime in the 1970s. Dukakis's response was reform of the state court system—a worthy idea, but one that did not appeal to the public's hunger for revenge against muggers and killers. Although capital punishment was popular, Dukakis vetoed legislation to restore the death penalty in the state. "I have never seen any convincing evidence that the death penalty is a deterrent to crime," he said.[28] In 1988, he would use almost those exact words in response to Bernard Shaw's debate question about the hypothetical rape and murder of Kitty Dukakis. Another Dukakis veto would also come up during the presidential campaign. In 1972, Governor Sargent had signed a bill establishing a furlough program for the state's prisons, and a court later ruled that the state could not deny furloughs to prisoners serving time for first-degree murder. (In Massachusetts, prisoners under this sentence were not eligible for parole.) In 1976, the legislature passed a bill to exclude these prisoners from the program and to require those convicted of second-degree murder to serve their minimum sentence before being eligible for a leave. Dukakis pocket-vetoed the bill, saying it "would have cut the heart out of our efforts at inmate rehabilitation."[29]

In 1978, Dukakis faced a primary challenge from conservative Ed King and liberal Barbara Ackerman. At first, he thought he had a good chance. Despite the inflation of the 1970s, the state's economy was doing better, and he got strong reviews for his leadership during a big snowstorm. By summer's end, however, King was effectively attacking his record on crime and taxes, and Ackerman was siphoning off liberal support by criticizing his budget cuts. By the time he realized that he was in trouble, it was too late. King won with 51 percent to Dukakis's 42 percent and Ackerman's 7 percent. In the November election, King narrowly defeated liberal Republican Francis Hatch. State voters also approved Proposition 2½, a tax-cutting measure that was part of the tax revolt had had produced Proposition 13 in California. Dukakis had misjudged the issue's appeal. "Massachusetts voters are too smart to fall for such a simplistic proposal," he said.[30]

Dukakis secured an appointment at Harvard's Kennedy School, with the understanding that he might run again. "We knew that he was taking a four-year sabbatical from politics," said the head of the search committee, "but we also knew that he would adopt the mindset of a Kennedy School faculty member."[31] Dukakis took his new job seriously, even as he was laying the groundwork for a rematch against King. The sojourn at the Kennedy School strengthened his ties to the academic community and gave him a chance to think in depth about economic issues such as job creation. And by the time he announced his candidacy, he looked like a winner. Corruption and incompetence had plagued the King administration, and the 1982 recession weighed on King just as the 1974 slump had hurt Francis Sargent. (It did not help in Massachusetts that the conservative King had gained the nickname of "Reagan's Favorite Democrat.") In one memorable ad, Dukakis worked to neutralize the crime issue. He told of a doctor who had been bound, gagged, and robbed in his own office, and a young man who died in a hit-and-run. He then revealed that he was talking about his father and brother. "I know what it feels like when crime touches my family," he said. "I want to make sure it does not touch yours."[32] King fought back hard, with the help of consultant Dick Morris, who would go on to notoriety as an adviser to Bill Clinton and an eccentric television commentator. Circumstances were too tough for King, however, and Dukakis won the primary by 7 points. In the fall, he easily dispatched the GOP candidate. His running mate, who had come out ahead in a multicandidate Democratic primary, was a former antiwar activist and prosecutor named John Kerry.

Timing worked in Dukakis's favor. He reentered the governorship just as the national economy recovery was getting under way, and the Reagan defense buildup was enriching the Massachusetts technology sector.[33] The state started doing well, and Dukakis claimed credit. He also got attention for a major policy initiative, Employment and Training Choices. Its strategy was to provide welfare families with job training and services (e.g., child care) that would enable adults to earn enough to rise from poverty. By 1984, there was already talk of a future Dukakis presidential race. A Reagan victory that year, wrote *Boston Globe* columnist David Farrell, "automatically installs Dukakis as a leading contender for the party's presidential nomination in 1988, assuming his reelection as governor in 1986."[34] In other words, his White House hopes would depend on a Democratic defeat.

THE 1984 RACE BEGINS

In the very early stages of the 1984 nomination contest, things looked much better for Democratic prospects. Thinking that their party had a chance at bringing Reagan down, and believing that the nomination was up for grabs, several Democrats entered the contest. Some candidacies were weightier than others. George McGovern, who had lost his Senate seat in 1980, had little going for him except nostalgia for the antiwar movement. Senators Ernest Hollings of South Carolina and Alan Cranston of California found little support outside the Capitol building and their home states. Reubin Askew, a moderate New South Democrat who had backed civil rights as governor of Florida, came across as the second coming of Jimmy Carter—a bad image in a party that painfully remembered Carter's 1980 defeat. Senator John Glenn of Ohio, a war hero who had become the first American to orbit the earth, seemed more formidable. Adding to his appeal was the fall 1983 premiere of *The Right Stuff,* a movie about the Mercury astronauts in which Ed Harris portrayed him in a highly sympathetic way. Reagan campaign manager Ed Rollins said: "The candidate we were most fearful of was John Glenn, who ran the strongest against the President head to head. On the qualities of patriotism, for instance, which we thought we would want to stress, Glenn did equally well."[35] For all his strengths as a general-election candidate, he was ill-positioned to get through the Democratic nomination process. As his communications director acknowledged, "A lot of political battles, infighting, straw polls, endorsements, fund-raising [were] all the things that John Glenn is least well-suited to do."[36]

By January 1984, Glenn was fading. Walter Mondale, who had served as Jimmy Carter's vice president, was the front-runner. Mondale enjoyed several advantages in the nomination contest. He had served a dozen years as a US senator and been an influential vice president, so there was no doubt about his qualifications. He had strong ties to organized labor, which was still a major force in the party. As a protégé of Hubert Humphrey, he was at home in the party's traditional liberal wing, and his issue positions were acceptable to progressives. An establishment candidate such as Mondale had an extra edge in 1984. Acting on the recommendation of a reform commission, Democrats had restored an element of peer review to the nomination process. They reserved one-seventh of convention delegate slots for superdelegates, members of Congress, and other party figures who would be free to their preferred support candidates. Mondale was already winning commitments from superdelegates before the primaries and caucuses began. The support of political elites brought other benefits. Governors, mayors, and labor leaders had political organizations that could supply money and volunteers in key states.[37]

Mondale had problems too. He was a dull television presence, and his long career as a political insider made it hard for him to campaign as the candidate of change. Backing from labor made him vulnerable to the charge that he was a servant of special interests. And events took the edge off his message. At the start of 1983, he could plausibly argue that the country had been better off during the Carter–Mondale years. By 1984, economic growth had flipped the argument. His administration's record was starting to look weak by comparison.

Two other Democratic contenders would cause trouble for Mondale, and their stories would extend into the 1988 race.

GARY HART

Senator Gary Hart of Colorado was one. A graduate of Bethany Nazarene College in Oklahoma, Hart was attending Yale Divinity School during the 1960 campaign. He had planned to be a minister or a teacher, but had grown uncertain. Kennedy's candidacy sparked his interest in politics. With several classmates, he went to New York to see Kennedy speak. "Gary was in awe of him," said one. "It was in a way Gary's revelation."[38] Hart volunteered in the campaign and decided to switch his career to public service. In the fall of 1961, he began his studies at Yale Law School. The Kennedy assassination took place during his last year there, and he regarded it as if it were a death in the family. After graduating and spending two years at the Department of the Interior, he moved back home to Colorado. In 1968, as soon as Robert Kennedy announced his candidacy, Hart helped set up his state headquarters. Robert Kennedy's assassination hit him as hard as John Kennedy's, and he traveled east to attend the burial at Arlington Cemetery. A couple of years later, he joined with other former Kennedy hands in the presidential campaign of George McGovern.

After winning a Colorado senate seat in 1974 and securing reelection in 1980, he worked to establish himself as a next-generation Democratic leader. Though he disliked the term, Hart was part of a well-publicized if vaguely defined Democratic movement called neoliberalism. The movement was a reaction to the widespread idea that the party had ceded intellectual momentum to the GOP. "We have let ourselves be turned into a party of government, which is not a very smart party," said Senator Daniel Patrick Moynihan of New York. "While that has been happening, the Republicans have become a party of ideas. I don't say *the* party of ideas, but ideas nonetheless. The intellectual base of our party is deeply eroded."[39] The neoliberals responded by giving a face-lift to party ideology. In "A Neo-Liberal's Manifesto," editor Charles Peters explained: "We still believe in liberty and justice and a fair chance for all, in mercy for the afflicted and help for the down and out. But we no longer automatically favor unions and big government or oppose the military and big business. Indeed, in our search for solutions that work, we have come to distrust all automatic responses, liberal or conservative."[40]

Unlike many older liberals, the neoliberals spoke more of economic growth than redistribution. They talked about fostering new business and entrepreneurship, albeit with guidance from the government. Their response to shuttered factories was "industrial policy," an effort to build up "sunrise industries" through cooperation among government, labor unions, and businesses.[41] The neoliberals were enthusiastic about high technology, which is why some called them the Atari Democrats, after the era's top maker of video game consoles. (The company later failed and buried many of its unpopular games in a mass grave.) In social welfare policy, they wanted to move people off the welfare rolls through employment and training programs that would enable them to rejoin the mainstream economy. Neoliberals strongly favored environmental protection, with an emphasis on economic incentives (e.g., pollution taxes) over command-and-control regulations. They were in the good government tradition, preaching transparency, expertise, and rational policy making. Unlike conservatives, they championed progressive positions on civil rights and foreign policy.

Like most programs of new ideas, neoliberalism was not quite as new as its packaging. Woodrow Wilson was writing about administrative efficiency before he became president, and John F. Kennedy's secretary of defense sought to bring corporate management practices to the Pentagon. President Lyndon Johnson, the embodiment of the old-style liberalism that the neoliberals were purportedly transcending, used language similar to theirs: "Investments in human resources are among our most profitable investments. Such investments raise individual productivity and incomes, with benefits to our whole society."[42] In cases where the neoliberals did break from party orthodoxy—supporting reform of entitlement programs and opposing trade protectionism—political pressures would eventually draw them back into the fold.

But in the 1984 campaign, the movement still seemed new and innovative. In 1983, Hart published *A New Democracy*, a book that laid out neoliberal themes for his 1984 presidential campaign. Throughout the book, he suggested that technology and managerial efficiency could achieve liberal goals without painful tradeoffs. Rust Belt industries, he said, "must again be vital elements of the American economy. But they must also be revitalized by the introduction of new technologies."[43] We could slash the defense budget without weakening national defense, he argued. "Our defense focus should be on investment in quality, not just quantity; on buying wisely, not just buying more."[44]

Gary Hart announced his candidacy in early 1983. Although ten years too old to be a baby boomer, and just eight years younger than Walter Mondale, he ran as the candidate of a new generation. (His telegenic features enabled him to get away with it.) He said he was running "because this country needs new leadership, a new agenda, a break with the politics of the past and the old arrangements."[45] He languished in the polls throughout 1983, a situation he had encountered before. Said campaign manager Oliver Henkel: "Well, it was very clear that because Gary had had the experience of running George McGovern's campaign and had really developed the insurgency techniques, he understood better than I think anyone the rhythm of this campaign, the fact that you don't throw all of your guns in 1983, that it's not until 1984 that things become important."[46] Hart had more opportunity than the early polls suggested. Whereas Mondale came out of the old-fashioned Democratic politics that catered to urban machines and industrial labor unions, Hart had greater appeal to suburbanites and knowledge workers. And their numbers were greater than ever before. In 1984, 19 percent of Americans over the age of twenty-five had completed four years of college—more than double the share in the early 1960s.[47] They were much more likely than less educated people to take part in politics, and they were making up a growing share of the Democratic electorate.[48] Such developments had been under way for some time in Michael Dukakis's Massachusetts, and now the rest of the country was catching up.

Hart could also make a case that he was more electable. Mondale had the advantage when it came to high-level government service, but it is difficult to defeat an incumbent president on experience. The challenger needs to run as a candidate of change. On this score, Hart had an edge. With his relatively youthful looks and his talk of new ideas, he could portray himself as the candidate of the future.

News stories about the race referred to Hart as an "outsider."[49] As a theme of American politics, outsiderism is as old as the country itself, stretching back to the Jeffersonians and the Jacksonians. Outsiders attack the privileges of wealthy, powerful elites and claim to speak for the common people who work with their hands. [50] Hart was an outsider insofar as he held himself aloof from other politicians and questioned his party's alliances with various interest groups. Even so, he was no stranger to the country's social and political hierarchy. He had two degrees from Yale (divinity and law), had managed a presidential campaign, and was serving his second term in the Senate. Hart's rural boyhood was something he had put behind him, and his core constituency consisted not of peasants with pitchforks but professionals with Peugeots.

JESSE JACKSON

The true outsider in the campaign was Jesse Jackson, who announced his candidacy on November 3, 1983. He was born out of wedlock and grew up poor in the still-segregated South. In late 1959, eighteen-year-old Jesse Jackson came home to Greenville, South Carolina, during a Christmas vacation from the University of Illinois. He went to the central library and asked for books that he could not find at the small, blacks-only library. Police officers told him to leave. After a difficult second semester at college, he returned to Greenville for the summer. One day, he and some friends sat inside the central library and were arrested for disorderly conduct. His mother was ironing at home when she happened to see television coverage of his release. It was his first civil rights protest, and his first time on television.[51] He would later transfer to historically black North Carolina A&T, attend divinity school, and become a minister. He continued his civil rights activism, and he was with Martin Luther King Jr. at the time of King's assassination.

Unlike every president up to that time, Jackson had neither held public office nor served in the military. (Decades later, Trump would become the first president without such credentials.) Though he had long been prominent as a national spokesman for civil rights, leaders of the movement eyed him with suspicion. Among many other things, they resented his efforts to get media coverage for himself in the days after King's death.

Because of the 1965 Voting Rights Act, African Americans now made up a large share of the Democratic primary electorate, especially in Southern states. But no African American had sought the party's presidential nomination since the mostly symbolic candidacy of New York representative Shirley Chisholm in 1972. One reason was that the ranks of black officials were thin at the top. Since Reconstruction, there had been only a single African American senator: Republican Edward Brooke of Massachusetts, who had lost his seat in 1978 to Paul Tsongas. No state had ever elected a black governor, and would not do so until Douglas Wilder won his 1989 race in Virginia. There were important African American House members, but they were obscure to the general public. The most famous black elected official was Los Angeles mayor Tom Bradley. At age sixty-six, and with a losing gubernatorial race just behind him, he had little interest in a presidential campaign. The door was open for Jackson.

In fact, the shortage of high-ranking black elected officials was a rationale for his entry into the race. Historically, outsiders had represented groups of Americans who had not gotten recognition or respect. William Jennings Bryan championed the farmers who were losing out in an industrializing America. Huey Long spoke for the forgotten victims of the Great Depression, promising to make "every man a king." In this vein, Jackson said that he represented African Americans and others who had given their votes to the Democratic Party but did not get a seat at the table of power. "Our time has come" was a constant refrain in his speeches. At the Democratic convention, he would say: "My constituency is the desperate, the damned, the disinherited, the disrespected, and the despised. They are restless and seek relief. They have voted in record numbers. They have invested the faith, hope, and trust that they have in us. The Democratic Party must send them a signal that we care."[52]

There was plenty of other fuel for the Jackson campaign. Despite the economic recovery, African Americans endured high unemployment rates, and many saw Reagan as a foe of civil rights. Among other things, he had balked at establishing a Martin Luther King holiday, wondering aloud whether King might have been a communist.[53]

Jackson faced doubts about his qualifications. He lacked political experience and could claim few measurable accomplishments for his antipoverty organization, Operation PUSH. He acknowledged his indifference to management, calling himself "a tree-shaker, not a jelly-maker."[54] A few weeks into the campaign, he quickly gained credibility from an unexpected source. In December 1983, Syrian forces in Lebanon shot down an American naval aircraft and captured its navigator, Lieutenant Robert O. Goodman. Weeks passed, and Jackson suggested that the administration was not trying very hard to win Goodman's release because he was black.[55] Without official approval, Jackson flew to Syria for talks with President Hafez al-Assad. A diplomat from a developing country told columnist Mary McGrory: "As I see it, Syria has a choice of embarrassing Jackson or embarrassing Reagan. I think they have greater reason to embarrass Reagan."[56] Syria chose the latter course and let Goodman fly home with Jackson. Reagan had no choice but to thank Jackson, who could now claim a diplomatic triumph.

Just as Jackson was trying to bulk up his résumé, he was also trying to become acceptable to the increasingly liberal Democratic primary electorate. In the 1970s, he had sometimes strayed from party orthodoxy. During the 1984 campaign, he took liberal positions across the board and flip-flopped on abortion. At an Iowa debate, he used religious language to explain: "I'm not for abortion; I'm for freedom of choice. Even theologically God gives us choice. We must live with the consequences of that choice, whether to go to heaven or hell, but at least we are not robots; we're people that have choice within the law."[57]

Jackson's credibility campaign suffered a setback in mid-February. In the Washington Post, reporter Rick Atkinson published a long article about Jackson's tense relationship with the Jewish community. It related the Syria episode to Jackson's past support for Arab causes, and it reminded readers that he had once said, "I am sick and tired of hearing about the Holocaust." Almost as an aside, Atkinson added: "In private conversations with reporters, Jackson has referred to Jews as 'Hymie' and to New York as 'Hymietown.'"[58] Such a comment would instantly go viral today, but in the pre-Twitter era, it took several days for the political community to notice and react. Jackson first denied the comment, then complained that he was "being hounded by certain members of the Jewish community."[59] Jackson later admitted the slur and expressed remorse. Louis Farrakhan, leader of the Nation of Islam and a key Jackson supporter, stepped on Jackson's efforts at reconciliation when he said at a rally: "I say to the Jewish people who may not like our brother, when you attack him you are attacking the millions who are lining up with him. You are attacking all of us. . . . If you harm this brother, I warn you in the name of Allah, this will be the last one you do harm."[60]

Jackson would keep trying to mend the damage, but in the short term, the episode hindered his progress. He had hoped to demonstrate broad support by doing well in heavily white New Hampshire, and in early February, one poll showed him getting 16 percent in the state's Democratic primary.[61] He finished with just 5 percent. Jackson adviser Lamond Godwin explained the drop-off: "A lot of it was because of the 'Hymie' controversy and the way it hurt Jesse's credibility, especially among the young people who viewed him as sort of a civil rights hero, and in that sense New Hampshire was a problem for us."[62]

MONDALE EDGES HART

New Hampshire proved to be a much bigger problem for Walter Mondale. On February 20, he easily won the Iowa caucuses, where John Glenn's humiliating sixth-place finish scuttled his campaign. Gary Hart placed a surprising but distant second, and immediately started getting more attention from the national media. Hart thus became the repository for voters who either disliked Mondale or had previously backed Mondale only because they thought they had no alternative.[63] Public and private surveys showed that Hart was gaining ground in New Hampshire, and on February 28, he pulled off a memorable upset by beating Mondale 37–28 percent. The state's election law allowed registered independents to vote in either party primary. With no GOP contest, they voted mostly on the Democratic side, and for Hart. College-educated voters also broke in his direction.[64]

The national impact was stunning. Before New Hampshire, Gallup found that Hart was the choice of just 2 percent of Democrats nationwide, compared with 49 percent for Mondale. In its first poll after the primary, Hart had shot up to a statistical tie: 35 percent to Mondale's 37 percent. A couple of weeks after that, Hart led, 39–30 percent.[65] In July, however, the Democratic convention nominated Mondale on the first ballot. What happened?

The standard explanation in political science is that party insiders have great influence over the nomination process. Mondale was the insiders' candidate, and their support was crucial to his success.[66] They supplied the money and volunteer labor that kept Mondale going even when the polls were looking dicey. More important, he won the support of 79 percent of the party's superdelegates. Without this bloc, he would have had a narrow and vulnerable majority at the convention.[67]

Nevertheless, we should be wary of assuming that the "insiders rule" idea is enough to explain the 1984 Democratic contest. This theory rests on a small number of cases. The 2016 campaign proved that a candidate can win a presidential nomination without the initial support of party elites.[68] Contingencies matter. The 1984 primaries were a close-run thing, with Hart winning twenty-six primaries and 36 percent of the aggregate vote to Mondale's twenty primaries and 38 percent. Hart might have been the nominee if a few things had played out differently.

The first was the Jackson phenomenon. The controversy over anti-Semitism slowed Jackson down, and even after he started to recover, Farrakhan continued to scare away support. Not until late June, after Farrakhan had called Judaism a "dirty religion," did Jackson break with him.[69] Suppose that Jackson had been more careful in his language and that he had kept a greater distance from Farrakhan all along. He could not have won the 1984 nomination, but he surely could have picked up a few points in the polls and primaries, and his gains would have come mostly at Mondale's expense.[70] A bigger Jackson vote could have tipped Georgia, Illinois, and perhaps some other primaries into Hart's column.

Second, the Mondale campaign did a better job of spinning the news media. Knowing that Mondale was likely to lose most of the Super Tuesday primaries, his campaign director cleverly sold reporters on the notion that Georgia was the make-or-break state. On primary night, he packed a room full of supporters. Chris Matthews tells what happened next:

> The video stage was set for what may have been the greatest election-night postmortem con job in history. Mondale lost seven contests out of nine. But that was just the arithmetic. At a few minutes past ten, campaign director Robert Beckel walked into what looked like a crowded ballroom to tell the faithful that Mondale had just carried Georgia. To the NBC viewing audience, the event played like a victory statement.[71]

Hart did an interview with CBS, expecting to talk about all the states he had won. Instead, reporter Roger Mudd flummoxed him by asking about his failure to "get rid" of Mondale.[72] The narrative of a Mondale comeback took hold, and it restored morale to the shaken campaign. If the Hart team had been savvier and more aggressive about managing media expectations, the story might have been about a fatal blow to Mondale.

Third, Hart was unready for the scrutiny that comes with front-runner status. Even before Super Tuesday, news stories revealed that he had changed his name (from Hartpence), deliberately altered his signature, and fudged his birthdate to make it seem as if he were a year younger. A Hart aide said: "[We] didn't take seriously the whole name and age business. I don't think Hart or the rest of us felt it was a major problem. . . . I think that was a mistake on our part."[73] Hart also drew criticism for some inconsistencies in his issue positions and for purportedly unfair attacks on Mondale. Surveys suggested that these problems may have hurt Hart more than issues such as the name change.[74] Either way, voters developed doubts about Hart's character, which Mondale linked to Cold War concerns. A Mondale television ad showed a ringing red telephone with a flashing light, with this voice-over: "The most awesome, powerful responsibility in the world lies in the hand that picks up this phone. The idea of an unsure, unsteady, untested hand is something to really think about."[75] (In 2008, Hillary Clinton would use a similar spot in her primary campaign against Barack Obama, with less effect.) With some greater self-awareness and public candor about his life story and shifts of issue positions, he could have done much to blunt the attacks.

Both Jackson and Hart would learn from the 1984 campaign. The next time around, Jackson strove to build a broader coalition, and he worked to defuse the anti-Semitism issue by naming a Jewish campaign manager. Hart got an earlier start on fundraising and management but—spoiler alert—he did not cure his personal vulnerabilities.

Despite the troubles in his 1984 campaign, Hart fared much better than nearly anybody had expected at the start of the cycle. His performance reflected social and economic change within the Democratic Party and provided a sign of where the party was headed. Among blue-collar union members, Mondale led Hart 42–25 percent, but among their white-collar colleagues, he was ahead by only 36–31 percent. Young urban professionals (yuppies, as popular culture dubbed them) supported Hart 35–32 percent overall, and 40–22 percent among those who used computers at home or work.[76] In the years ahead, the constituencies that supported Hart would get much bigger.

Democrats met in San Francisco during July. Speaking with reporters during the convention, Speaker O'Neill urged Mondale to hit Reagan in the gut. "The evil is in the White House at the present time," said O'Neill. "And that evil is a man who has no care and no concern for the working class of America and the future generations of America, and who likes to ride a horse. He's cold. He's mean. He's got ice water for blood."[77] Accepting the nomination, Walter Mondale focused more on policy than personality: "Whoever is inaugurated in January, the American people will have to pay Mr. Reagan's bills. . . . Let's tell the truth. It must be done, it must be done. Mr. Reagan will raise taxes, and so will I. He won't tell you. I just did."[78] The line got loud applause in the convention hall, and for a moment, Democrats could convince themselves that economic candor was a winning message. One public poll put Mondale slightly in the lead, although private GOP polls continued to show that Reagan was ahead.[79]

DEFEAT AND AFTERMATH

Mondale lost big. Soon after the 1984 election, Democrats started pondering what had gone wrong for them. Scholars pointed out that it would have been extremely difficult to beat any incumbent president who could boast of peace and a roaring economy. But some Democrats looked inward, saying that the party had to rethink its approach to policy.

Dukakis offered a neoliberal alternative, though, like Hart, he tended to avoid the label. During his second term, Massachusetts went from bust to boom, with plunging unemployment and rapid development of the high-technology sector. He told political scientist William Schneider what he had done:

> The policy entails very direct as well as indirect subsidies. We have an industrial-science agency that has made over three billion dollars' worth of loans. We have the only state development-action-grant program in the country. There isn't much we won't do for a company that's willing either to expand or to relocate in one of our target areas—heavy investments in older downtowns, direct stuff in addition to financing. A lot of money. At any one time we'll have a hundred and fifty or two hundred of these projects going.[80]

His programs got good reviews in the media, and voters responded. Dukakis won reelection in 1986 with nearly 60 percent of the vote. He was now drawing attention as the kind of practical problem solver that the party needed. A few weeks after the election, he went to Florida to speak to a national group of Democratic county officials. The governor was "a heck of a prospect," said the president of the National Association of Counties. "I've worked with him closely for a year and a half. He's an effective governor, and what we need is some effective leadership."[81]

It is debatable whether his policies were responsible for the Massachusetts Miracle. The presence of Harvard, MIT, and other top universities had given birth to the Route 128 high-tech corridor long before Dukakis started his political career there. In a report for the liberal Economic Policy Institute, David Osborne wrote: "When pressed, Dukakis administration officials admit that they have had little impact on overall growth rates in the state. They do claim credit, however, for creating changes in the regional patterns of growth. . . . Again, the claim is difficult to evaluate."[82]

Another movement was growing alongside the neoliberals. In the early 1980s, House Democratic Caucus Chairman Gillis Long (D-LA) had set up a Committee on Party Effectiveness to enable colleagues to tinker with new ideas. Al From, a Democratic aide at the time, recalled:

> It was the first beginnings of a new economic policy for the Democrats, and the key philosophical point was that our twin goals had to be growth and fairness. Now that seems like a pretty silly thing, but through the '70s, growth wasn't part of the Democratic litany. It was all fairness. We gradually moved away from fairness to opportunity over the year because fairness meant to people, We're going to take from you to give to somebody else. Opportunity meant that everybody had a chance to get ahead.[83]

After the Mondale defeat, Long huddled with moderate Democratic elected officials about starting an outside Democratic organization. From drafted a memo laying out the case for such a body, arguing that that party had to reach beyond its liberal base. "The fact of politics in 1984 is that the party that seizes the idea initiative dominates the political process. We lost the idea initiative in 1978—and ever since the Republicans have set the political agenda."[84] Long died of a heart attack shortly afterward, and From took the initiative in bringing the organization to birth. On February 28, 1985, the Democratic Leadership Council (DLC) got underway. Representative Richard Gephardt of Missouri, who had worked with Long on the Committee on Party Effectiveness and succeeded him as House Democratic Caucus chair, was the new group's chairman and public face. Noting that many Democratic officials in the South and West saw the national party as a liability, Gephardt said: "We view the council not as a rival to any other party entity but as a way station or bridge back into the party for elected Democrats."[85]

Some well-established figures signed on, including the man who had defeated Bush in 1970, Senator Lloyd Bentsen of Texas. DLC also provided a platform for a new generation of Democratic leaders, including Governor Bill Clinton of Arkansas. The DLC Democrats shared a good deal of common ground with the neoliberals, particularly in their effort to find a third way between Reagan conservatism and Mondale liberalism. There were differences too. Many represented conservative constituencies, so they tended to downplay social issues such as abortion. They favored more punitive measures against crime, and some of them supported the death penalty. (Years later, Governor Clinton would allow the controversial execution of a man with serious brain damage.) Some, like former governor Bruce Babbitt of Arizona, were willing to touch the much-feared third rail of American politics by discussing reforms of Social Security and Medicare. Others, like Senator Al Gore of Tennessee, took a more hawkish view of national security even as they criticized Reagan's stewardship of the Pentagon.

In the meantime, changes in the nomination process were in motion. The Southern Legislative Conference, a group of state legislators from sixteen Southern and border states, worked to create a de facto regional primary. If most of these states voted at the same time, the thinking went, they could maximize their leverage and tip the nomination to a moderate Democrat who would be more acceptable to the region. John Traeger, a Democratic state senator in Texas, put it this way: "We feel that under this new southern primary effort, our region of the country stands a much better chance of keeping its concerns out front."[86] The project succeeded, and legislatures in fourteen of the sixteen states scheduled primaries for March 8, 1988—Super Tuesday. At the time, most of the lawmakers in these states were Democrats, who had their party's interest in mind.[87] As the next chapter explains, Super Tuesday had consequences for Republicans as well.

Since 1968, the only Democrat to win a presidential election was Jimmy Carter, a centrist from Georgia. The last Democratic victor from outside the South was John F. Kennedy in 1960. And like Harry Truman in 1948, Kennedy got less than half of the popular vote. The last Northern Democrat to win a popular majority was Franklin Roosevelt in 1944. In fact, Roosevelt was the only Northern Democrat in American history to win more than 51 percent of the popular vote—a distinction that would last until Barack Obama in 2008. Accordingly, there was political logic in the drive to nudge the party toward the center and to empower its Southern wing.

There was a catch. A candidate must appeal to the rank-and-file voters who take part in primaries and caucuses, and these voters care about things other than electability. In the 1984 primaries, the moderate candidates (Senator John Glenn of Ohio, Senator Ernest Hollings of South Carolina, and former governor Reubin Askew of Florida) all flamed out early, resulting in a race among two liberals (Mondale and Jackson) and a neoliberal (Hart). If Carter's 1976 nomination proved anything, it was that a Southern centrist might win the nod—provided that such a candidate had strong support from African Americans. This caveat would prove fateful in the 1988 campaign.

THE REPUBLICAN NOMINATION CONTEST

On matters of ideology and competence, George H. W. Bush was a blur. He was a moderate who became a Goldwater delegate to the 1964 convention, an opponent of the 1964 Civil Rights Act who voted for the 1968 Civil Rights Act, a critic of "voodoo economic policy" who espoused Reagan's fiscal plans. As a junior member of the minority party in the House, he could never pass a major bill. In his subsequent posts in government, he always displayed competence as an understudy, never as the leading man. The vice presidency gave him little chance to bring his ideas into public focus. Bush typically kept mum about his opinions during White House meetings, even small ones, saving his advice for his private lunches with Reagan.[1] James Baker, Bush's 1980 campaign manager and Reagan's White House chief of staff, said: "I've often said he was a perfect vice president, because he never let himself get caught speaking out."[2] He meant that as a compliment.

Today it is commonplace to speak of the bubble that separates major politicians and other celebrities from everyday life. Richard Ben Cramer first used the word this way in his classic book, *What It Takes*—and he was referring to the bubble surrounding Vice President Bush. Between the government employees and political aides devoted to his service, wrote Cramer, Bush could "leave his office, board an airplane, travel halfway across the nation, land in another city, travel overland 30 miles to a ball park and never see one person who was not a friend or someone whose sole purpose it was to serve or protect him. This is living in the bubble."[3] The job had not always come with a bubble. Decades earlier, with limited staff and security, vice presidents enjoyed a fairly normal existence. They had no official residence until the mid-1970s, so they had to rent or buy their living quarters. Viewers of the 1962 movie *Advise and Consent* saw nothing odd about a scene showing the vice president (Lew Ayres) flying by himself on a commercial airliner. By Bush's time, staffs were larger, Secret Service protection was tighter, and traveling with the rabble was out of the question. Such a life came with a cost. As Cramer put it, "The bubble imposes its own special blindness, like one-way glass—you might see out, darkly, but you can never see how it looks from the outside."[4]

When Bush looked in the mirror, he could see a war hero whose glittering résumé had earned him the right to run for president. When ordinary Americans beheld him, they saw something smaller. To Bush's annoyance, the title of a *Newsweek* cover story got to the heart of the problem: "George Bush: Fighting the Wimp Factor." Some of it was the vice presidency, and some of it was the path of compromise and appointive office that got him there. Some of it was Bush himself. "He does not project self-confidence, wit or warmth to television viewers," wrote Margaret Warner in the *Newsweek* piece. "He comes across instead to many of them as stiff or silly. Even his most devout backers can sense his unease on the tube. 'I die for him when he gives a speech. I want it to be right, and I know he's just not comfortable with it,' says lifelong friend Betsy Heminway."[5]

For much of Reagan's second term, Bush was an iffy prospect to win the 1988 general election. He was heir to Reagan's legacy, whose value was in doubt. In March 1987, amid weeks of Iran–Contra news, a CBS/New York Times poll found that Reagan's approval rating was at a four-year low. Bush's ratings dropped too. Since January, the ranks of those having no opinion about Bush rose from 34 to 48 percent, suggesting that his public image was getting blurrier.[6] Keeping a GOP White House or a third straight term would be hard enough, but Republicans had to wonder if another candidate would be more electable.

Bush could hardly seize the nomination through his commanding presence and overwhelming public support. He could not assume that the party would bestow it in a natural line of succession. In the twentieth century, Nixon and Humphrey had been the only two sitting vice presidents to become the standard-bearer. No party faction would automatically rally to him. Hard-shell conservatives had distrusted him at least since his 1980 nomination campaign against Reagan, who would stay conspicuously neutral throughout the 1988 GOP race. He was the most natural fit for mainstream party regulars, but they had an attractive alternative: another war hero turned Washington insider who had served as RNC chair and vice presidential nominee. And Bob Dole was not fighting a wimp factor.

GEORGE BUSH AND ANNA BANANA

Bush had assets as well as liabilities. As an incumbent vice president with a vast political network that he had been tending for decades, he could amply fill his war chest and build an effective national organization. In 1985 and 1986, his vehicle was a PAC called the Fund for America's Future. This organizational form stemmed from the legal constraints of the time. A quarter of a century before the *Citizens United* decision, a candidate could not raise unlimited funds through a super PAC. The law forbade direct corporate and labor contributions to presidential candidates and capped individual contributions to their campaigns at $1,000. (Congress later raised the limit.) There was a loophole. A potential contender could establish a multicandidate PAC whose ostensible purpose was to support party organizations and other candidates for office. The individual contribution cap for such a group was $5,000 instead of $1,000, and the group's spending would not count against the expenditure limits that applied to candidates accepting federal matching funds.

In an advisory opinion, the Federal Election Commission said that the Fund for America's Future would meet the legal criteria for a multicandidate PAC, as long as it did not explicitly promote a Bush candidacy.[7] The fund followed the letter of the law in its public activities, but its real purpose was obvious.[8] Among many other things, it bankrolled Bush's travel on behalf of GOP candidates, which enabled him to speak to Republican voters and put GOP politicians in his debt. Research director James P. Pinkerton said: "We sat there and just did nothing but sort of plot and scheme to get Bush elected in '88. They say, look now, you've got to remember the allocable rules, if you start spending money on helping Bush get elected in '88, it counts against his '88 totals and so we've got to be careful about that. So okay, fine, we'll call it something else, we'll call it Anna Banana."[9]

Keeping up the public fiction about the Fund's aims, Bush said: "The Fund's staff is now set for an aggressive and strategic effort on behalf of Republicans in 1986."[10] Lee Atwater would head the fund and unofficially serve as campaign manager in waiting. As noted in an earlier chapter, Bush had known Atwater since his days at the RNC, but they were not close. Unlike James Baker (Princeton '52), who managed Bush's 1980 effort and would become Atwater's superior in the fall 1988 campaign, Atwater (Newberry College '73) was hardly a social peer. Despite their early encounter, he was not part of Bush's political orbit either. He was a protégé of Senator Strom Thurmond and had run campaigns in South Carolina, where he built a reputation for playing rough. While running one congressional race, he had mocked an opponent's long-ago electroshock therapy by saying he had been "hooked up to jumper cables."[11] During the 1980 nomination race, he took sides against Bush by running Reagan's primary campaign in South Carolina. His reward was a job in the White House political office under Ed Rollins. In 1984, Rollins managed the Reagan reelection campaign, with Atwater as his deputy. Their relationship ended in a feud, with Rollins blaming Atwater for leaking a nasty story about him to NBC, and then for freezing him out of the 1988 Bush operation to seal his own primacy. "With Lee, it was never enough to win," Rollins later wrote. "He always needed to drive one more spike through someone's heart."[12]

Between the Reagan and Bush campaigns, Atwater was a principal in the political consulting firm of Black, Manafort, Stone, and Atwater. Two of his partners, Charles Black and Roger Stone, were advising Jack Kemp. Between his partners' connections and his 1980 work for Reagan, Atwater got a cool reception from Jeb Bush and George W. Bush. The latter asked: "How can we trust you?" Atwater responded: "Why don't you come up here and watch? And if I am disloyal, you can do something about it."[13] George W. Bush eventually took him up on the offer, moving to Washington to serve as Atwater's minder and his father's enforcer.

Atwater was an odd match for the courtly vice president, but the choice was smart. Precisely because Atwater was so different from Bush and had spent most of his career working for other politicians, he knew what the world looked like outside Bush's bubble. A candidate with a wimpy image needed a tough campaign manager. A refined WASP needed a fan of rock music, Tabasco sauce, and the *National Enquirer*. A man who bombed Chi Chi Jima needed a baby boomer to help him connect with voters who were too young to remember World War II. Most of all, a transplant from New England needed a bone-deep Southerner.

The South had been part of GOP math since the 1950s, but it would be critical in the 1988 nomination contest. This status was a side effect of Democratic maneuvers. The goal of Super Tuesday was to help nominate an electable moderate. The national strategists and Democratic state legislators who devised it gave barely a thought to the GOP contest. In most of the Super Tuesday states, though, moving the Democratic primary to March 8 also meant moving the Republican primary. Together with the March 5 South Carolina primary, Super Tuesday three days later would be a bonanza to any Republican candidate who could consolidate support in the South. Atwater saw it as a firewall against possible early losses in Iowa or New Hampshire.[14] He explained: "What I outlined very early was that I thought could be done with the Super Tuesday configuration, particularly if we were able to position South Carolina appropriately. You would then have a fully united party by the convention. So it wasn't just a lucky break that we had something. That was one of the single, original strategic concepts we had in operating the campaign."[15]

Many of the Southerners who had moved to the GOP during the Reagan years were evangelical Christians. As a mainline Episcopalian, Bush did not speak their religious language. Luckily, an interpreter stood close by. George W. Bush had undergone a religious awakening in the 1980s, and his faith deepened when he quit drinking. He had steeped himself in small-group study and other features of contemporary evangelical Christianity. Doug Wead, who was helping Bush with religious outreach, noticed that the vice president was heeding his advice, and he concluded that someone who knew the movement was vetting his memos. He learned that it was the younger Bush. He recalled: "George W. said, 'I've been reading your memorandum. Good stuff, Wead. I'm taking you over. You report to me. I'll be your boss.'" Wead explained why their joint effort mattered: "It was important that the vice president be speaking directly to [evangelicals], saying to them what he believes. I didn't want to influence what he believed, but I wanted to make sure he was communicating. So a lot of it was language and communication, and 'What does this mean?' and 'What do you mean when you're saying this?'"[16] Accordingly, Bush started using evangelical constructions in his speech. "I happen to believe in Jesus Christ as my personal savior," he said.[17]

Bush needed to plant his ideological flag. Atwater believed that the party's old liberal wing had mostly disappeared as Reagan pulled the GOP center rightward. Reagan, in turn, was less doctrinaire than either his left-wing critics or his right-wing boosters had once expected.[18] As a result of the party's movement and Reagan's practicality, Atwater said, the new nominating wing was "the mainstream conservative wing of the party, which would be about 70 percent of the vote."[19] If Bush could win this bloc, then other candidates would have to compete for the remainder that was even farther to the right. So Bush courted the support of conservative activists and writers such as Russell Kirk. Sometimes the courtship created a backlash. On December 11, 1985, Bush spoke at a Washington dinner honoring William Loeb, the New Hampshire publisher who had earlier criticized him in crude terms. A few weeks later, George Will wrote: "The unpleasant sound Bush is emitting as he traipses from one conservative gathering to another is a thin, tinny 'arf'—the sound of a lapdog."[20]

Aside from embracing Reagan and Reaganites, Atwater said, Bush needed to act on two policy areas. Although the Cold War was nearing its end, Republican remained wary of the Soviet Union. Bush thus had to be "hard-core on the anti-communist cluster of issues."[21] Between his tenure as CIA director and his loyalty to Reagan's foreign policy, he was well positioned as an experienced hawk. The campaign mantra of "peace through strength" came naturally to him. Nevertheless, his claim to national security expertise entailed problems. If he was such a maven on foreign and military affairs, reporters and opponents could ask, what was his role in the Iran–Contra scandal? If he knew that this fiasco was unfolding, why did he not try to stop it? If, as he said, he was "out of the loop" on the issue, was he really a player in foreign policy? These questions would linger.

The second issue was taxation, and it was a heavier burden for Bush. Reagan had acceded to tax increases over the years, but his opening position had been so strong that tax-cut conservatives tended to forgive him. Bush lacked such political immunity. He would never entirely live down the "voodoo economic policy" crack from the 1980 race, so he needed to offer antitax activists a clear sign that he was on their side. That sign would be the product of a group called Americans for Tax Reform. Started in 1985 by Grover Norquist, a former staffer at the US Chamber of Commerce, Americans for Tax Reform began as corporate-financed group that mobilized support for President Reagan's tax reform. In the 1986 congressional elections, Norquist started a Taxpayer Protection Pledge. By signing the pledge, which has been a staple of GOP politics ever since, candidates would go on record against any tax increases. Bush policy advisers were skittish about having the vice president sign pledges, but Pinkerton devised a workaround:

> So Grover is a pretty good friend of mine, so I said, If Bush writes you a letter, using exact identical, comma for comma, word for word language of the tax pledge, will it count as if he signed the pledge card? And Grover said, Sure. So finally we got Bush to write a letter to Bob Dornan, then Congressman, circa April '86 saying, Dear Bob, and then he just used, as you know, I am a fervent opponent of the tax increase, and used line for line, the entire thing. It was just a paragraph. Bush signed that, we mailed out probably fifty million copies of that, conservatively, to anybody we could think of who would help on the Republican activist thing.

It just became part of, it became the core, really, of the New Hampshire campaign.[22]

Having made politically shrewd choices on campaign personnel and policy, Bush was ready for a fight, and he would get one.

KEMP'S CAMPAIGN

Jack Kemp loomed as a significant early rival. He never served in the House majority or sat on the tax-writing Ways and Means Committee, but he had been the driving force behind the Reagan tax cut of 1981. And although he played only a peripheral role in writing the 1986 tax reform bill, his advocacy of tax simplification had helped rally Republican support for the idea. Conservative intellectuals liked him because he paid attention to their arguments and adopted many of their policies. Junior Republicans in the House revered him as a role model. Newt Gingrich called him "the first Republican in modern times to show it is possible to be hopeful and conservative at the same time."[23] (Gingrich seemed to forget that Ronald Reagan was still president.) In Washington political circles, Republicans and Democrats alike thought that Kemp could expand the GOP's base by appealing to blue-collar workers and ethnic minorities. Referring to a football career that brought him into regular contact with African Americans, Gingrich said: "Jack literally showered with guys that most Republicans never meet."[24]

Early in 1985, Kemp won a presidential straw poll at the twelfth annual Conservative Political Action Conference, a national gathering of conservative activists. His margin was surprisingly narrow: 39 percent to 35 percent for Bush.[25] Later that year, the conservative Free Congress Foundation commissioned a survey of voters who had supported Reagan in 1984. Only 56 percent recognized Kemp's name, compared with 98 percent who knew Bush. Kemp's favorable–unfavorable ratio was a respectable 6–1, but Bush's was 12–1.[26]

Why did Kemp fail to gain altitude outside the Beltway? For one thing, the House of Representatives is not a hatchery of presidents. The only sitting House member ever to win a presidential election was James A. Garfield in 1880. House members tend to get less press coverage than senators.[27] They also have fewer resources at their disposal; even senators from small states have larger personal staffs than their counterparts in the House. Like Richard Gephardt, Kemp was a member of his party's leadership and thus had some funding for additional staff. But because he was in the minority party, that payroll was meager, consisting of a few aides working in a cramped office on the dingy sixth floor of the Longworth House Office Building. Those aides were excellent, however, and he relied on their help.

Because his football career had unfolded when players earned modest salaries, he was not wealthy and he needed his congressional paycheck. Accordingly, he took time out from his as yet unannounced presidential campaign to seek reelection to the House in 1986. The race was bumpy. His Democratic opponent waged a spirited campaign to undercut his standing as a champion of working people. In their sole debate, he hammered Kemp for living in suburban Maryland. "When Bethlehem Steel closed, and Republic Steel closed and Westinghouse, they were my relatives and my friends and my neighbors who were laid off—they weren't Mr. Kemp's relatives because Mr. Kemp doesn't live in western New York."[28] Later, a *Washington Post* reporter followed up by asking him for his voting address in the district. He had to take out his driver's license to check.[29] He won 57 percent, an anemic showing by the standards of House incumbents, and his smallest vote share since his initial election in 1970. Even worse, the race consumed precious time and money. His reelection committee ended up deep in debt.[30]

Fundraising was going to be a challenge anyway. Belonging to what seemed to be a permanent minority party in the House, he was in a weak position to raise money from special interests. (Democrat Gephardt, by contract, collected a tidy sum from lobbyists and political action committees.[31]) Kemp's attitude toward the money chase was unhelpful. "Jack did not like to make fundraising calls," said campaign manager Charles Black. "He didn't mind calling people to ask them to host a fundraiser, so we'd get him to call a few people to be on the committee for the fundraiser, and then we could do that."[32] He had some success with fundraisers, as well as bad luck. John Buckley, his press secretary, said that "sometimes you know when a campaign is snakebit." He recalled that Kemp's biggest New York fundraising event took place in a Manhattan disco—on what turned out to be the day of the stock market crash. "And so all the people who were to come to write their checks, they were showing up looking like their dog had been shot."[33]

Kemp did better with direct mail fundraising, which supplied more than half of his contributions.[34] Even here, he had a problem. Direct mail, like the internet fundraising that became prevalent during the early twenty-first century, depends on personal anger and ideological fervor. Kemp was ill-equipped to stoke either. He disliked going negative, and although he would passionately describe policy differences, his speeches seldom included personal attacks.[35] On his signature issues of tax reduction and reform, he was a victim of Reagan's victories. The president often said that there was no limit on what people could do it they did not care who got the credit.[36] He liked that phrase because he got the credit. The public thought of the 1981 and 1986 measures not as Kemp initiatives but as the Reagan tax cut and the Reagan tax reform.

Kemp also found other candidates seizing issue territory that he sought for himself. "Bush did an excellent job of positioning himself as the heir to Ronald Reagan," Kemp wrote after the campaign. From his stand against further tax increases to his tough talk on foreign policy, "Bush took 'right' positions and narrowed the opportunities for his opponents to use these issues to overcome his advantages as vice president."[37] Kemp had been vocal on abortion and other issues of concern to social conservatives, but another candidate blocked his path to the hearts of the religious right. Charles Black said that "as the first evangelical leader with a national following to attract that constituency, [Pat Robertson] turned out, in fact to be more dangerous to Jack's chances than Bob Dole did."[38] And in some press accounts, Pete du Pont was the "new ideas candidate," though his campaign amounted to little in the end.

Apart from his rivals' issue maneuvers, Kemp had trouble with the GOP base. Some of his enthusiasms appealed only to a tiny niche. His support for the gold standard, for instance, only fired up people who enjoyed infomercials for bullion. Other parts of his message could potentially attract new voters in a general election but offered nothing to the people who took part in GOP primaries and caucuses. In his formal announcement of candidacy on April 6, 1987, Kemp said that the party should be a "good shepherd" to the weak and those who had fallen behind. "We must enact free enterprise zone legislation to reach into the most stubborn pockets of urban and rural poverty with a helping hand of job creation; and we won't rest until we pass urban homesteading legislation, so that families in public housing who work hard and save will got the chance to become homeowners."[39] The rhetoric was both uplifting and ineffectual. For the typical GOP voter, those pockets of poverty were places to avoid, not reach into. Few Republicans had lived in public housing, and most would recoil at the prospect of having people from the projects move in next door.

He spoke to the Republican Party as he wanted it to be, not as what it was. Covering a campaign stop in Wisconsin, R. W. Apple reported that many of Kemp's GOP listeners looked quizzically at one another as he proclaimed that it was not the Grand Old Party anymore:

"We've got to be the party of labor," the Buffalo Republican continued, and there were more puzzled glances. "Economic growth doesn't mean anything if it leaves people out. If we trust our ideas we have to take them into the ghetto, into the barrio and into the trade union hiring hall. Franklin Roosevelt made his party the party of hope, and now we must do the same thing for the party of Lincoln." To judge from their comments afterwards, the Republican loyalists gathered that snowy night in Oconomowoc, west of Milwaukee, had expected something a little different—"stuff on abortion and school prayer and a strong defense," one man said.[40]

For the kind of people who showed up to Lincoln Day dinners, organized labor was an enemy, and for those of a certain age, Roosevelt was the first presidential candidate that they had voted against. "Jack has a way of antagonizing people," said *Human Events* editor Allen Ryskind. "He likes to divorce himself from conservatives."[41] He hoped to be the candidate of a Republican rainbow coalition. Unhappily for him, it existed only in his hopes.

PAT ROBERTSON'S CHRISTIAN SOLDIERS

One reason why Donald Trump could emerge as a presidential candidate in 2016 was that millions of Americans had come to know him through *The Apprentice,* the Golf Channel, and other television venues. Many bought his ghostwritten books and his branded products, including courses from the ill-fated "Trump University." Most journalists and academics had never watched his programs or purchased his wares, so his political rise shocked them.

Something roughly comparable had happened in the 1980s with Pat Robertson. Marion G. "Pat" Robertson, the son of a segregationist Democratic senator from Virginia, filed incorporation papers for the Christian Broadcasting Network (CBN) in 1960. Robertson had attended Yale Law School, but after flunking the bar exam, he got a divinity degree from the New York Biblical Seminary. His new "network" did not go on the air until the fall of 1961, and at first it consisted of a single UHF station in Portsmouth, Virginia. During the 1970s, the spread of cable television would expand its reach. In 1977, Robertson had turned the CBN into a basic TV cable network, and he now invited school activists and Christian lawyers to appear on his flagship program, *The 700 Club.*[42] He had spent years developing the CBN as a place for devotional programming. As he later acknowledged, that format put a low ceiling on its audience. "We started out on cable all-religious, but we learned after about 10 years that all-religious programming just doesn't reach people," he told UPI. "They want comedy, they want sports, they want news."[43] In 1981, CBN broadened its lineup to include entertainment shows, including reruns of old westerns and wholesome comedies. *The 700 Club* included more news from its own reporters and political commentary by Robertson himself. By the middle of the decade, CBN was reaching ten million homes each week. Compared with the established broadcast networks, the audience was small, but it was enough to advance a political movement. CBN viewers liked what Robertson was saying, and they took him just as seriously as any of the other talking heads on national television. As Trump would do years later, Robertson reinforced his electronic image through books and articles. And as with the Trump phenomenon, these developments took place outside the notice of most political reporters.

During the first Reagan term, the most prominent leader of the Christian right was Jerry Falwell, head of the Moral Majority. Falwell often let loose with controversial comments, such as calling South African archbishop Desmond Tutu a "phony."[44] Among Americans who knew enough about him to have an opinion—about half of the public—his ratings were 2–1 unfavorable.[45] After the 1984 election, Ed Rollins acknowledged that Democrats had used Falwell against the GOP: "Jerry Falwell, no question, is a very high negative."[46] Falwell's influence waned as many Republican leaders started keeping their distance. One exception was Bush, who sought and got Falwell's endorsement before Robertson entered the race.

With his Phi Beta Kappa key and (unused) Yale law degree, Robertson was better educated and more polished than Falwell. Having grown up as the son of Senator Willis Robertson (D-VA), he knew politics. "I've laughingly said, 'Right after I learned to say 'Mommy' and 'Daddy' I learned to say 'constituent,'" he told writer Garrett Epps in 1986. "We discussed the issues and strategy—this stuff was just part of our lives back then."[47] Just as CBN was expanding its grassroots audience, Robertson was building up his political presence through an organization called the Freedom Council. The group lobbied for proposals such as a constitutional amendment to permit prayer in public schools, and it increasingly focused on promoting Robertson himself. It dissolved in 1986 amid legal questions about its connection to the Robertson candidacy.

Robertson argued that American had lost its moral compass. Time and again, he said that he was crusading to "restore the greatness of America through moral strength."[48] In a way, he bore a likeness to the other Baptist minister in the race. Jesse Jackson spoke for people who had chafed under the power of the elites—"the desperate, the damned, the disinherited, the disrespected, and the despised." Robertson's followers were nearly all white and had not undergone anything comparable to Jim Crow. Yet they noticed that elite culture was hostile to their religious tradition: books and movies such as *Elmer Gantry* had long portrayed them as ignorant yahoos. Robertson played to this perception when he attacked progressive groups as "anti-Christian atheists."[49] The Robertson campaign, wrote conservative columnist Charles Krauthammer, was "a revolt of the culturally disenfranchised against a national ethos that has become progressively more secular and liberal."[50]

Like Jackson, Robertson struggled to reach beyond his base. As campaign manager Marc Nuttle explained, his challenge was to portray himself as "a statesman with a religious background rather than a religious man with a statesman background."[51] To allay fears about breaching the separation of church and state, he resigned from the ministry before beginning his race. Nevertheless, Americans continued to see him as a televangelist—a job description that was taking on a bad odor. In 1987, Oral Roberts made a unique fundraising pitch: if supporters failed to send in at least $8 million, God would "call me home." During the same year, Jim Bakker of the PTL (Praise the Lord) Club fell suddenly in the wake of scandals involving money and sex. One of his critics was preacher-singer Jimmy Swaggart, who got caught with a prostitute early in 1988. Robertson was not directly involved in any of these cases, but they tended to undermine the credibility of televangelism.

Robertson did not help himself by making a baseless suggestion that the Bush campaign had somehow set up Swaggart.[52] The news media, probably with help from opposition researchers, found many other misstatements in Robertson's record. The most embarrassing revelation was that he had fudged his wedding date to avoid acknowledging that his first child resulted from premarital sex. Despite years in the public eye, he was unready for the level of scrutiny that comes with a presidential campaign. "I have never had this kind of precision demanded of me before," he said.[53] Robertson also made odd comments about policy issues, such as his claim that the Soviet Union had put nuclear missiles back in Cuba. Campaign manager Nuttle acknowledged "a series of statements that cost us credibility, not only with the public but with our own base."[54]

For all of Robertson's shortcomings, his base—like Jesse Jackson's— was passionate. His supporters were willing to show up for tedious meetings, arriving early and staying late. As on the Democratic side, this kind of dedication would be particularly important in states that chose delegates through caucuses instead of primaries.

BOB DOLE

In the years before Trump blew up generalizations about the electoral process, a myth had developed that Republicans usually pick the candidate who is next in line. Like many myths, this one rested on a small number of cases. For instance, no one could claim that Eisenhower was the next in line for the 1952 GOP nomination, since he had never taken part in partisan politics. Moreover, the definition of "next in line" was fuzzy and retroactive. The label supposedly applied to Nixon in 1968 because he had run in 1960. But in the years since, Nelson Rockefeller had sought the party's nomination and had twice won statewide elections. Had he wrested the nomination from Nixon in 1968, hindsight might have dubbed him the next in line.

In 1988, Bob Dole had a reasonable claim to the title. In 1976, he had been the party's vice presidential nominee, and he had run for the presidential nomination four years later. He could argue that he done more than Bush to earn the political inheritance from Reagan. As chair of the Senate Finance Committee during Reagan's first term, he had helped enact Reagan's policies on taxes, trade, and entitlements. As GOP party leader in the second term, he had even broader responsibilities. To the extent that the Reagan program succeeded on Capitol Hill, much of the credit belonged to Bob Dole. Bush, by contrast, could offer little more than public cheerleading and private advice.

More than any of Bush's other rivals, Dole was in an excellent position to raise money. Although Senate Republicans had lost their majority in the 1986 midterm, Senate rules and norms still gave the minority leader a great deal of influence. Special interests knew that they would have a tough time passing any measure through the Senate over Dole's opposition, so they had an incentive to give generously to his campaigns. His decades in Washington had enabled him to build a far-reaching network of fundraising contacts. His wife, Elizabeth, had contacts of her own, stemming from her experience as a member of the Federal Trade Commission, as a Reagan White House aide, and as a secretary of transportation.

Americans admire leaders who have overcome hardship, which is why so many presidential contenders have tried to play up humble origins.[55] On this point, Dole had a big advantage over Bush. Though Bush sometimes spoke of difficult times in his life (the shoot-down over Chi Chi Jima and the childhood death of his daughter), his Northeastern upper-class background was hard to hide. Bob Dole, by contrast, had grown up on the edge of poverty in the middle of the country. After suffering his war wounds, he had willed himself to succeed in a world that did not yet accommodate people with useless right arms. Journalist Joe Klein once wrote that the handshake is the threshold act of politics, but for Bob Dole, it was a constant challenge. He had to keep a pen in his withered right hand to discourage people from grasping it. Longtime Dole press secretary Walt Riker said: "What I think that means for voters is that they can understand that Bob Dole has gone through tough times. He can relate to people who are also going through tough times."[56]

Unable to perform many of the physical stunts of the campaign trail, he had to sell his knowledge and experience. He had a detailed grasp of the issues and had developed a reputation as an effective legislative leader. "I offer a record, not a resume," he said in his announcement speech, drawing an implicit comparison with Bush. "A track record of nearly 11,000 votes in Congress and 27 years of leadership that says, 'I can make a difference, I have made a difference, I will make a difference.'"[57]

Dole's weaknesses were obverse side of his strengths. His hard life had given him a hard edge, and he sometimes acknowledged that his struggles had left him bitter.[58] He did not need to raise his voice to show ill temper. In a memorable 1996 description, journalist William Saletan wrote: "Dole's anger wouldn't seem so dark if his appearance weren't so menacing. His left eyebrow hangs thick and low, so that when he tilts his head down and gazes forward, a dark pupil floats up to the shaggy ridge, glaring out of the hollow of its socket. His gravelly voice, an uninflected baritone, churns like a chain saw in low gear."[59] A happy Dole would still look dour, and an irate Dole would be downright scary. This facet of his character was an opportunity for the Bush campaign. Lee Atwater loved to quote Sun Tzu's The Art of War, which explained how to defeat an enemy: "Anger his general and confuse him." He reckoned that the Bush campaign could bait Dole into showing his dark side.[60]

Dole's membership in the Washington establishment undermined his efforts to stress his humble roots. He and his wife had befriended many lobbyists and corporate leaders. Archer Daniels Midland CEO Dwayne Andreas had helped Dole with campaign finance and provided him with preferential treatment in buying an apartment in Bal Harbour, Florida.[61] The Bush forces needled Dole accordingly. Referring to the historic, high-end complex where Dole lived when he was in Washington, Bush deputy manager Richard Bond called him "the barefoot boy from the Watergate Hotel."[62]

Dole was a son of Russell, Kansas, who had become a creature of the United States Senate, which was a problem: no sitting party leader in the Senate had ever won a presidential election. The leader's desk is not a good springboard for a national campaign. Whereas presidential candidates need to be inspirational, leaders of the Senate must be transactional. Trent Lott, who later succeeded Dole as Senate GOP leader, likened the job to "herding cats." The task involves bargaining, compromise, and other practical tasks that voters disdain. Columnist Maureen Dowd said that Dole was "fluent in the arcane language of cloture and second-degree amendment," but could not offer a concise statement of what he believed.[63] The 11,000 roll call votes that he touted in his announcement encompassed many hard-to-explain tactical maneuvers that opposition researchers could exploit to paint him as inconsistent or unprincipled. And whereas other senators running for president could play hooky from the chamber for long stretches, a conscientious party leader was glued to the floor. Campaign strategist William Lacy explained that Dole "did his Senate job extraordinarily well, but we didn't have very much time for him to do his presidential job, and that was always a challenge."[64]

In addition, Dole's presidential campaigns were just not very good. His 1980 race had been an embarrassment. Early on, it was clear that his 1988 organization would have its own ailments. Bill Brock, the former RNC chair who had become Reagan's secretary of labor, announced in the fall of 1987 that he would leave the Cabinet to head the Dole campaign. He later recalled what he had found on arrival: "The campaign was a mess. A lot of the money had been spent, with no discernable impact."[65] Brock brought his own staffers, whom the existing staffers saw as a *Star Trek* enemy. Lacy said: "You know, we'd go down the hall and when the Brock people weren't looking and we saw one of our allies, we'd say, 'Live long and prosper, avoid the Klingons.'" More seriously, Lacy blamed the campaign's woes on the Brock forces, saying that they "basically spent the campaign into bankruptcy" and "created all kinds of ill will with all of Dole's supporters everywhere."[66] So gobs of money went to waste, and the opposing factions pointed at each other. In the end, it does not matter which side was more at fault because Dole was ultimately responsible for his own factionalized, inefficient organization.

The intramural tong wars loomed large in contemporaneous accounts of the Dole campaign, and for good reason. But one should not attribute his defeat to the infighting. Every presidential campaign has its feuds and factions, and some notoriously troubled organizations have gone on to win. (In 1980, Reagan fired his campaign manager on the day of the New Hampshire primary.) The story of Bush's victory and Dole's defeat was more complicated.

ALSO-RANS AND NOT-QUITE-CANDIDATES

Other contenders took part in the campaign despite long odds. Pierre S. "Pete" du Pont IV had served as a House member and governor of Delaware. With his degrees from Princeton and Harvard, along with his membership in the famous du Pont family, he was one of the few people in the country who could make Bush look almost plebeian by comparison. Even more problematic for GOP nomination politics, he had a reputation for moderation. Accordingly, he tacked hard to the right. On April 26, 1986, du Pont spoke to the moderate Republican Mainstream Committee to tell them how conservative he was.[67] "Frankly, America is finding a clarity in the candor of the conservative movement," he said, openly disagreeing with the group's positions on tax increases and American policy in Central America.[68]

Like Democrat Bruce Babbitt, he was casting himself as a bold truth teller. According to campaign manager Allan Hubbard, the strategy was that being the "innovative idea guy" would get him recognition.[69] His ideas included phasing out farm subsidies and supplementing Social Security with private savings accounts financed by tax credits.[70] The ideas had been circulating for years among libertarian and conservative policy wonks. But because GOP candidates were usually leery of these issues, they did set du Pont apart.

Distinctiveness and popularity are two different things. Ideas that appeal to intellectuals often fail to gain traction among the rank and file. Like other Americans, Republican voters had long ago accepted the Social Security system and were not hankering for change. Years before, Reagan had stumbled over the issue, and years later, George W. Bush would find scant grassroots support for a private-account plan. As for farm subsidies, the issue was never a top priority for GOP voters—except for those who benefited from them.

Alexander Haig, a general who had served as Richard Nixon's last chief of staff and as Ronald Reagan's first secretary of state, was the least probable contender. A dozen generals had served as president, and with his robust ego, Haig thought that he was in their league. If the Cold War had still been at its most intense, he might have had a better shot. Unfortunately for Haig, it was not 1952 anymore. To the average American, his most memorable moment came right after the assassination attempt on Reagan. Haig barged in on a White House press briefing to claim that "I'm in control here," even as his quavering voice suggested the opposite. His tenure ended badly in 1982, with a forced resignation. His prickly personality had alienated most of the people around the president, especially Mrs. Reagan. Though he claimed to be a Reagan torchbearer, he was critical of Reagan's economic and foreign policies—not a path to success in a party that still revered the Gipper.

Despite their slim chances, both du Pont and Haig took part in presidential debates and would have some scrapes with the bigger candidates. Other Republicans thought of running, then chose not to. Howard Baker, whom Bush had eclipsed as the more moderate alternative to Reagan in 1980, had left the Senate in 1984 to keep his options open for 1988. When Reagan tapped him as chief of staff in 1987, he ruled out a race. Senator Paul Laxalt of Nevada, Reagan's best friend on Capitol Hill, launched an exploratory committee and hired staff, only to withdraw after money ran short. Two administration officials, communications director Pat Buchanan and United Nations ambassador Jeane Kirkpatrick, disappointed conservatives when they said that they would not be candidates in 1988. Buchanan would instead run in the next three elections, seeking the GOP nomination in 1992 and 1996 and serving as the Reform Party candidate in 2000.

And then there was Donald J. Trump. In the summer of 1987, Roger Stone urged him to run for governor of New York. He had no interest in that office, but he liked Stone's idea of using print advertising to raise his political profile.[71] That fall, Trump spent about $95,000 to publish an issue ad in several major newspapers. The headline read: "There's nothing wrong with America's Foreign Defense Policy [sic] that a little backbone can't cure." The ad previewed themes from his 2016 race: "For decades, Japan and other nations have been taking advantage of the United States. . . . Why are these nations not paying the United States for the human lives and billions of dollars we are losing to protect their interests? . . . The world is laughing at America's politicians as we protect ships we don't own, carrying oil we don't need, destined for allies who won't help."[72] His immediate motive may have been to draw attention to his new book, *The Art of the Deal*. Michael Dunbar, a GOP activist in New Hampshire, took the ad literally and seriously. He arranged for Trump to address the Rotary Club in Portsmouth. According to an account in the *New York Times*, Trump "drew a bigger audience than have any of the Republican candidates, including Senator Bob Dole, the Rev. Pat Robertson or Representative Jack Kemp, according to club officials. As he spoke, a group of college students armed with 'Trump for President" placards rallied outside."[73]

Trump did not enter any primaries, but he kept talking about his issues. A December appearance on Phil Donahue's show earned him a glowing letter from Richard Nixon: "I did not see the program, but Mrs. Nixon told me you were Great on the Donahue show. As you can imagine, she's an expert on politics and she predicts that whenever you decide to run for office you will be a winner!"[74] On April 23, 1988, Oprah Winfrey had him on her program, and she asked him if he would ever run for president. "Probably not. But I do get tired of seeing the country get ripped off."[75] So why did he stay out in 1988? Though he was famous enough to go on talk shows, he had not yet achieved the television stardom that would later come with *The Apprentice*. Online social media, which would propel his 2016 campaign, did not yet exist. And as he suggested in his reply to Oprah, a Trump candidacy would depend on bad news. In 1988, the decline of manufacturing jobs and the rise of blue-collar despair were emerging as issues, but they had not yet reached the point where millions would take a chance on someone like Trump.

Late in the primary season, Trump would chair a fundraising reception for Bush, saying, "He's a great man. He's a man I support."[76] Earlier in the campaign, he had also given to Gephardt, Simon, Babbitt, Gore, Kemp, and Dole.[77] In the spring and summer, his friends floated the idea that Bush was considering him for the vice presidential nomination. After Bush picked Dan Quayle, Trump told Larry King that he would not have considered the job if Bush had offered it to him.[78]

EARLY SKIRMISHES

The GOP nomination process started on August 5, 1986, when voters in Michigan's midterm Republican primary selected thousands of precinct delegates. This election had a convoluted relationship to the selection of the nominee. The precinct delegates would go to county conventions, which would then pick delegates to a state convention that in turn would choose national convention delegates. Given the degrees of separation between the 1986 voting and the 1988 outcome, Dole stayed out. Bush, on the other hand, made a serious effort. "It has a defensive value in 1986 in protecting Bush's flanks," said deputy manager Rich Bond. "And it'll have an offensive value in 1988 when Bush takes off by winning delegates."[79] Kemp and

Robertson also worked hard in Michigan, hoping that a solid showing in an early contest would bolster their credibility.

Bush seemed to come out ahead. A survey of primary voters found that he was the choice of 40 percent, with Kemp and Robertson getting 9 percent each.[80] The names of the presidential candidates were not on the ballot, and allocation of national convention delegates would not be proportional to precinct delegates, so the poll figures were a goalpost made of smoke. Uncertainty did not keep Atwater from claiming victory: "Today's vote shows that the vice-president's support is a mile wide and a mile deep."[81] Robertson later claimed that he had won, which the Bush camp disputed.[82] Amid the murky results, a few things were clear. Bush had organizational clout, as expected. Robertson was stronger than the political community had anticipated. And Kemp was already faltering. Kemp co-chair Clark Durant explained that the Robertson forces had a better ground operation, which enabled them to many precincts, each with a small number of votes. "So the Robertson people were able to mobilize the churches very effectively, and did catch everybody off-guard by it too. . . . We should have raised money in Michigan and not played in Michigan."[83]

For the next year, the candidates traveled across the country and made formal announcements of candidacy. The Bush campaign did get a jolt in September, with an unscientific straw poll in Iowa, whose caucuses would be an early test. Among the 3,800 Republicans who gave $25 apiece to take part in the poll, Robertson finished first. Bush came in third, behind Dole. It was another sign that Robertson supporters were willing to spend time and money on their candidate. Bush's showing was an embarrassment because his earlier career in presidential politics had hinged on his 1980 upset victory in that very state.

In October, the candidates had their first televised debate, in the form of a special episode of William F. Buckley Jr.'s interview program, *Firing Line*. One topic was the intermediate-range nuclear forces (INF) treaty with the Soviet Union—long forgotten by most people today, but still an issue in the waning years of the Cold War. Kemp, Haig, Robertson, and du Pont opposed the agreement. Dole was cautious: "I don't think we ought to be out here cheerleading for any treaties until we know precisely what's in them."[84] Bush was the only one who backed the treaty. Du Pont criticized Bush's position, saying it lacked specifics. The comment gave Bush an opportunity, and his response is worth quoting at length:

Pierre, let me help you on some of this. One, I think it's a nutty idea to fool around with the social security system and run the risk of the people that have been saving all their lives. We've made the social security trust fund solvent and it's solvent. So that's not maybe a new idea, but it's a dumb one. On the question of the INF Treaty, I told you all these European leaders were for it, I'm for it, the president is for it, the joint chiefs are for it. . . . It's fine when you're outside, carping, criticizing a president, criticizing—And it's different, I've found out it is very different when you're in there having to make the tough calls.[85]

Du Pont wanted people to call him "Pete" because he knew that his given name had a thick air of privilege. Journalist David Broder wrote: "Bush, who has known him for decades, would never call him Pierre in private conversation. As a gentleman and a friend, Bush would respect du Pont's wishes. But with that single sentence, and the public intonation of the name Pierre, he signaled . . . that it was 'no more Mr. Nice Guy' for the veep."[86] Bush's discussion of Social Security veered from the topic of the INF treaty, but it did hit du Pont at a weak spot: the recent stock market crash had rendered his proposal for private Social Security accounts politically toxic. And the invocation of the president's INF position was a reminder that foes of the treaty were siding against Reagan, who was still popular among Republicans. Because of his experiences in 1980 and 1984, Bush did not have a reputation as a good debater. But he could score when he was on his game.

Haig tried to needle Bush by recalling his silence during early discussions of the treaty: "I didn't hear a wimp out of you." His use of the "w" word was just as intentional as Bush's namecheck of du Pont. Haig might have drawn blood, except he was an unsympathetic messenger. At one point, he talked about seeing "our young people shipped home in body bags." Bush research director James P. Pinkerton attended a dial group during the debate and noticed the reaction to that line: "That knob just went below zero."[87]

In the fall of 1987, Bush clung to a lead among Republican voters nationwide.[88] The Bush organization knew that Bob Dole of Kansas would have a natural advantage in the Midwestern farm state of Iowa, whose caucuses would take place on February 8. Accordingly, Atwater had lined up support from three governors whose political organizations could help deliver their states' primaries: John Sununu of New Hampshire (February 16), Carroll Campbell of South Carolina (March 5), and Jim Thompson of Illinois

(March 15).[89] Even with a setback in Iowa, Atwater figured, these states could enable Bush to snap back quickly.

Or so the plan went. One threat was Robertson's nontraditional base in evangelical churches. "He's outside the system, so it's hard to track what he's doing," said Bush campaign aide Mary Matalin.[90] A gaffe by a family member made things worse for Bush. Vice presidential son Neil Bush likened Robertson supporters to "cockroaches issuing out from underneath the baseboards of the Bible Belt."[91] The younger Bush soon apologized, but the damage would persist. A Bush had insulted evangelicals—and had done so at an old-line WASP bastion, Dartmouth College. "That hurt us," said Bush evangelical adviser Doug Wead. "Most evangelicals weren't going to vote for Pat Robertson, for the same reason that non-evangelicals weren't going to vote for him, but when the Robertson people uploaded all this information into the churches . . . we lost support we could have had."[92] In places such as Iowa, some ditched Bush for Dole.

Iran–Contra was another danger zone. By the fall of 1987, Reagan had apologized for the mess, and his approval rating was heading back to the 50 percent line. Yet the affair stayed with Bush like a low-grade infection. In November, a joint report of House and Senate committees damned him with faint praise: "There is no evidence that the Vice President was aware of the diversion. The Vice President attended several meetings on the Iran initiative, but none of the participants could recall his views."[93] A few weeks later, Senator Warren Rudman—a Dole supporter—persuaded the committees to release a newfound memo written by Reagan's national security adviser. It showed that Reagan advisers disagreed about the arms sales, "but most important, President and VP are solid in taking the position that we have to try."[94] Bush claimed that he had broadly supported efforts to release hostages and had never endorsed illegal activity. Not everyone believed him. Dole urged him to make a full disclosure, and during a January debate, Haig said that issue would keep dogging Bush: "I think the American people do want to know what you said and sooner or later you are going to have to do it. If you can't answer your friends, what in heaven's name is going to happen next November if you are our standard bearer and the Democrats get after you on the subject?"[95]

Bush soon got chance to reframe the issue. CBS asked him to do an interview with anchor Dan Rather on its evening news program. Typically a television network would videotape such an interview, then cut it for broadcast. Fearing that CBS would edit the segment to make the candidate look bad, the Bush campaign insisted on a live interview. It was to take place a few hours before President Reagan's 1988 State of the Union address. Bush needed to be on hand for the speech, so CBS agreed to conduct the interview remotely, with Rather in New York and Bush in the vice presidential office in the Capitol. In addition to keeping CBS from editing the interview, this arrangement gave Bush another advantage: media adviser Roger Ailes could stand just out of camera range and prompt Bush with notes.

In Ailes's telling, a CBS source had tipped him off that the network was planning to introduce the interview with a highly critical story about Bush's role in Iran–Contra. (Ailes called it an ambush, but CBS maintained that it had told the Bush camp that there would be a focus on the scandal.) Ailes recounted a conversation with Bush: "He didn't believe that it was going to be a political execution or an attempt at a political execution. I said, 'Why don't we plan for it just in case?' Basically we decided we weren't going to take it lying down."[96] At the start of the interview, Bush accused CBS of misrepresenting its purpose. "I'm asking for fair play, and I thought I was here to talk about my views on education, or on getting this deficit down."[97] When Rather kept pressing Bush on Iran–Contra, Ailes held up a note: "WALKED OFF CAMERA." Rather had once stormed out of a newscast when the network shortened it to air the end of a tennis match. Ailes had briefed Bush about the incident, calculating that he could use it to rattle Rather. On cue, Bush said: "And I don't think it's fair to judge a whole career, it's not fair to judge my whole career by a rehash on Iran. How would you like it if I judged your career by those seven minutes when you walked off the set in New York? Would you like that? I have respect for you, but I don't have respect for what you're doing here tonight." Rather was speechless for a moment, and shortly afterward, he appeared to cut off the interview abruptly.

Bush operatives were giddy, saying that the exchange proved Bush's toughness.[98] Atwater explained: "The strategy that we had across the board in debates, in these confrontational situations was this: That George Bush is a counter-puncher. . . . Dan Rather threw the first punch. Pete du Pont threw the first punch in the 'Pierre' incident . . . it was based on the fact that if the other guy acts unfairly, dish it back to him."[99] For all the high fives among campaign people, survey data showed little direct impact on the nomination race, with Bush's national lead neither growing nor shrinking.

So was the confrontation an overhyped trifle? Hardly. Ponder how it would have turned out if Bush had not scrapped with Rather. When he was talking about his Iran–Contra activities, he was evasive. Without all the back-and-forth about the network's fairness, subsequent coverage of the interview would have zeroed in on Bush's failure to offer a complete account of his role. Even among Republicans, 32 percent thought he was lying about Iran–Contra, and just 42 percent said he was telling the truth. But only 25 percent of Republicans thought that Dan Rather had treated him fairly, compared with 61 percent of Democrats.[100] So the extent that people were talking about CBS bias instead of his part in an arms-for-hostages deal, Bush dodged what could have been a damaging story. The incident reinforced a tactic that Nixon, Agnew, and Ailes had developed in the 1960s: cast political arguments as battles with the press. In the years to come, as public views of the press got darker and darker, Republicans would increasingly run against the media. For now, however, the Bush camp's euphoria would prove to be short-lived. The vice president would find that Iowa could be very cold in February.

THE EIGHT DAYS OF LIVING DANGEROUSLY

In the days after the Dan Rather fight, Bush seemed to be rolling. One good sign came from Michigan, where Pat Robertson had once been a threat. The Robertson campaign had earlier partnered with the Kemp forces, and together the two sides briefly held the upper hand in the state. But then Bush's Michigan campaign reportedly started making secret deals to win over Kemp supporters.[101] The Kemp–Robertson alliance soon became a Kemp–Bush alliance. Kemp campaign manager Charles Black explained: "We were afraid Bush was still going to have a little over 50 percent, with a disciplined group of delegates, and we might be shut out. So . . . the second way to go was to have Kemp and Bush make a deal, and it was obvious that Jack's support plus Bush's support would guarantee the election of the slate."[102] Black and Atwater had recently been business partners, so they were accustomed to dealing with each other. Bush came out of the state convention with thirty-seven delegates to Kemp's thirty-two. Robertson, who got only eight delegates, cried foul and held his own rump convention.

The Iowa caucuses took place on February 8, and the results were alarming for Bush. It surprised no one that farm-state favorite Bob Dole came in first, though his 37 percent was higher than expected. The shocker was that second place went to Robertson, with 25 percent, Bush finished a humiliating third, with 19 percent. True, these votes did not translate directly into the state's delegate allocation, which would take place later. But since 1976, candidates and reporters had treated the straw vote results as the equivalent of a primary, which why Bush's 1980 Iowa victory had made him Reagan's top GOP rival. For months, the Bush machine had been the talk of the political community. Even if it could not overcome Dole's cultural affinity with the state, the thinking went, surely that machine would earn Bush the silver medal.

What happened? Dole would have enjoyed an edge under any circumstances—and the circumstances of 1988 were bad for Bush. The boom of the mid-1980s had bypassed the farm economy, and the period had been tough on the many Iowans whose livelihoods hinged on agriculture. Accordingly, about a quarter of the state's Republicans disapproved of Reagan's performance— a high share by GOP standards. While the majority who approved of Reagan were evenly divided between Bush and Dole, a January poll showed Dole winning 2 to 1 among those who disapproved.[103] Bush's efforts to court farmers were cringeworthy. "Right now the farm program is like a plane that's way up in the air," he said in a policy statement. "If it just tries to stay aloft, it's going to run out of gas. But the answer is not simply to put the nose down and crash. The answer is to find a safe glide path for the landing."[104] Iowa farmers probably did not want to hear about the best way to lose altitude.

Robertson, as Bush operatives had feared, had worked outside normal GOP channels and mobilized supporters who had been invisible to party regulars. About three fifths of his Iowa caucusgoers were taking part in the process for the first time.[105] Like fellow preacher Jesse Jackson, Robertson tended to do best in caucuses, where the most passionate voters predominated. As the season moved to primaries, he was not likely to do as well. That prospect scarcely consoled Bush, who was now at risk of losing the nomination to Dole. "I know just how the press will play it," he wrote in his diary. "There were already columns about Bush being a hemophiliac, and if he finishes third, he's through, etc., etc. But that hasn't always been the case. It feels like you've been hit in the stomach. It's really gloomy."[106]

The gloom was justifiable. In the *Los Angeles Times,* William Schneider wrote what Bush had predicted: "When Bush is wounded, he bleeds. Right now he is hemorrhaging. He may soon bleed out."[107] The February 16 New Hampshire primary, which had once looked solid for Bush, was now in doubt. A poll for the *Washington Post* showed Dole scoring a net gain of 6 points in New Hampshire, leaving Bush with just a 39–33 percent lead.[108] Another poll showed an even tighter margin for Bush, 29–27 percent.[109] By the weekend before the primary, a *New York Times* survey had Dole up by a point, 31–30 percent.[110]

Despite Atwater's talk of a Southern firewall, a New Hampshire defeat would have made it hard for Bush to prevent his campaign from flaming out. A narrow loss in the 1976 primary was crucial in keeping Reagan from overtaking Ford. Four years later, Bush's surge halted when Reagan beat him in the state. It is impossible to know what would have happened if Bush had suffered a New Hampshire defeat in 1988. Perhaps he could have pulled through. It seems more plausible, though, that his campaign's morale would have crashed, and contributors would have stopped their checks to Bush and started writing ones to Dole. Most Republicans would have found it easy to switch sides; both candidates were seasoned public servants with similar mainstream GOP views. Bush thought that losing New Hampshire could end his campaign. "If I don't make it, I have no excuses," he wrote in his diary four days before the primary. "Just go about my life, which will be an exciting one. I would have no politics, no head table, no Republican Party, a total hiatus, shifting directions of my life."[111]

Bush still had several things going for him. One was his connection to Reagan, who was much more popular in New Hampshire than Iowa. A last-minute endorsement from Barry Goldwater added bulk to his conservative credentials. Bush was still energetic at age sixty-three, and in the eight days before the primary, he engaged in a frenetic series of photo opportunities, which included operating a forklift and driving a tractor-trailer. Because of his disability, Dole could not keep up. Bush's campaign was more disciplined than Dole's, and it made a shrewd decision at a critical moment. On the Friday before the primary, Dole got a burst of favorable publicity when Haig pulled out of the race and endorsed him. Knowing that he needed to make a dramatic move, Bush approved a tough television ad that Roger Ailes had made for him:

> George Bush and Bob Dole on leadership. George Bush led the fight for the INF treaty for Ronald Reagan. Bob Dole straddled until Iowans pushed him into supporting INF. George Bush is against an oil import tax. Bob Dole straddled, but now says he is for an oil import tax. George Bush says he won't raise taxes period. Bob Dole straddled, and he just won't promise not to raise taxes, and you know what that means. George Bush, ready on day one to provide presidential leadership.[112]

With hours ticking down before the vote, the Bush camp now had to get the ad on the air. In the future, it would be standard procedure to put such a spot online and let it go viral. But there was no World Wide Web in 1988, so it was necessary to buy time on local television. Here is where another Bush asset came into play. Governor John Sununu, whom Atwater had courted at an early date, was putting his campaign network behind Bush. At his direction, Bush had visited key political and media figures through the state, and now one of those contacts paid off. As Sununu said:

> [All] the TV stations, particularly channel nine in New Hampshire, had closed their books for the weekend. Well, I picked up the phone and called David [Zamatch], the general manager, who had brought his grandchildren in to have their picture taken with the Vice President and whom the Vice President spent time talking to, and giving out vice presidential pens or whatever it is to the grandchildren and so on. I called David and said, We've got to re-open the books and put on a new ad on television, can you? And David got in his car, drove down to the TV station, allowed us to put the ads on Channel 9, which was the most important television station for this weekend.[113]

The Bush campaign had already riled Dole by putting out negative information about his wife's finances. "Straddle" further infuriated Dole, who had dug deep into his political capital to enact Reagan's priorities on taxes. His ill-organized campaign could not translate his anger into effective action. Dole aide William Lacy said that his campaign understood the Ailes–Atwater approach and had foreseen such an attack. "We knew what they were going to hit us on, and they still caught us unprepared. We violated what had become a fundamental rule, I think, of strategy: You must always react in some way, not necessarily respond, but react to any kind of an attack. And we didn't do that."[114]

During a Sunday debate, du Pont handed Dole a written a pledge never to raise taxes. Dole brushed it off, saying: "I have to read it first. Maybe George will sign it." The line got a laugh—at a cost. New Hampshire voters took tax pledges seriously, and Dole's dismissal reinforced the message of the "Straddle" ad. Atwater gloated: "I was stunned that a very quick-witted fellow (like Dole) couldn't answer du Pont's challenge to sign the tax pledge."[115]

On primary day, Bush won by a surprisingly large margin, 38 to 29 percent. Dole won among voters who wanted to change the course from Reagan policies, but they made up only a quarter of the GOP electorate. Among the 75 percent who wanted to stay the Reagan course, Bush won 39 to 25 percent. He ran ahead among those who cited taxes as a key issue.[116] Dole took his upset defeat hard. As soon as the results were in, NBC's Tom Brokaw interviewed Bush and Dole back to back. The vice president wished his rival well, and then Brokaw asked Dole if he had response. He said: "Yeah, stop lying about my record."[117] That line reinforced Dole's reputation for meanness. The following night, Lee Atwater went on the *MacNeil/Lehrer NewsHour* and could barely contain his glee.[118] He knew that he had Dole on the run, and that the next primary would be in his home turf of South Carolina.

WINNING

South Carolina governor Carroll Campbell, first elected in 1986, was only the second Republican to win the office since Reconstruction. By happy coincidence for Bush, Lee Atwater had helped in that race. Accordingly, Atwater had an inside track in gaining his support for Bush's presidential candidacy. Campbell proved to be as valuable as Sununu. Between them, he and Atwater knew practically everyone in South Carolina Republican politics. After months of painstaking work—supplemented with personal calls from Bush himself—they managed to enlist most local activists in the campaign. By the time Dole got started in South Carolina, the competition for endorsements was already over.[119] Dole did have the support of Senator Strom Thurmond, who could do him little good. Because they live and work in Washington, senators do not have the same kind of state political infrastructure as governors. Eight years earlier, Thurmond had endorsed the presidential candidacy of John Connally, who lost the primary to Ronald Reagan by 24 percent. Now aged eighty-five, Thurmond was more a relic than a political force.

Robertson might have been able to build substantial support among evangelicals in the state, but unflattering news stories weighed him down. A former congressman had said that Robertson's father, Senator Willis Robertson, had pulled strings to shield him from combat duty during the Korean War. Robertson sued, which only brought more attention to the accusation.

In the March 5 primary, Bush won big, with 49 percent, compared with 21 percent for Dole and 20 percent for Robertson. The early work by George W. Bush and Doug Wead to court religious conservatives proved providential. Bush ran about even with Robertson among those who told exit pollsters that they were born again or evangelicals, and he took just about every other demographic group.[120] Atwater called South Carolina the "cueball" for Super Tuesday, and three days later, the Bush campaign got a near-perfect break. He swept sixteen states, losing only the Washington State caucuses to Robertson. Dole came close in only a few states. Kemp, who had once had a place in the top tier of candidates, got only low single digits. Two days later, he quit the race. Effectively, the nomination race was over.

Dole hung on for a while. Even before Super Tuesday, the campaign's infighting had broken into the open when Bill Brock abruptly fired two top aides and kicked them off the campaign plane at the Orlando airport. Dole then went to a campaign event at the nearby Universal theme park. Years later, such a venue would have meant a large crowd. In 1988, the theme park was still under construction, so no tourists were there. In the *Washington Post*, Edward Walsh described the scene: "As a cold wind whipped across the barren landscape and bulldozers rumbled nearby, the Senate minority leader was photographed there with four people dressed as movie characters—Woody Woodpecker, Mae West, Charlie Chaplin and Frankenstein's monster." One of the fired aides called the event "a good example of Chairman Brock's leadership."[121]

After Super Tuesday, the Illinois primary loomed as Dole's last chance. He played up his status as Midwesterner. "Dole is a middle American. He is one of us," said his state campaign chairman.[122] But as in New Hampshire and South Carolina, Lee Atwater had long ago won over the state's governor. While the Bush forces rolled on with ruthless efficiency, the Dole campaign stumbled. On the Saturday before the election, Dole tried to air a half-hour program on Chicago television. It was a technical botch. A few minutes in, the screen froze as he kept talking. Then the transmission ended and a biographical film started rolling off-cue.[123] The following Tuesday, Bush won the Illinois primary by nearly 20 points, 55 percent to 36 percent. Dole quit the race two weeks later.

In early May, the nomination race wrapped up more or less officially. Robertson withdrew, and after months of silence, Reagan finally endorsed Bush as his successor. The president's brief statement came at the end of a speech at a fundraising gala. Some reporters described the endorsement as perfunctory, and they noted that Reagan mispronounced Bush's name as "Bosh."

A presidential campaign organization cannot concentrate on November until the nomination is secure. So before Bush put Dole away, his operatives could scarcely glance at the likely Democratic candidate, Michael Dukakis. After Illinois, they shifted focus. Bush research director James P. Pinkerton later recalled reading about a Democratic debate just before the New York primary in April: "I'm reading along, reading along to this transcript, it was on Nexis or something, and Gore is sitting there talking about weekend passes."[124] He followed up, and helped make the Massachusetts furlough program a major issue in the general election campaign.

In the meantime, Bush had to make his biggest decision as the party's presumptive nominee: the choice of a vice presidential candidate.

QUAYLE

On three occasions, George H. W. Bush had seen the vice presidency dangle before him. In 1968, his name came up as a running mate for Richard Nixon, who settled on Spiro Agnew. Six years later, Gerald Ford gave him serious consideration, only to opt for Nelson Rockefeller. In 1980, Bush was the obvious choice, but when Reagan toyed with picking Ford, he assumed that he had lost his chance. Only after talks with Ford broke down did Reagan call Bush.

Now that it was his turn to do the choosing, he chose to do it differently. The process unfolded with stealth and deliberate misdirection. Nodding to various factions and personalities, campaign officials put out the word that several familiar figures were on the list. They backed up the bruited names by creating the appearance of a serious vetting operation, which Pinkerton compared with "the entire mythical first army on Operation Fortitude on D-Day that's going to invade Calais, as opposed to Normandy."[125] Meanwhile, Washington lawyer Robert Kimmitt was doing the real vetting. Kimmitt's list was shorter and included Dan Quayle, the forty-one-year-old junior senator from Indiana. In an oral history interview, Quayle recalled: "As it came down, I knew it was between Dole and myself. I knew it wouldn't be Kemp."[126] Why not Kemp? He had badly underperformed during the nomination campaign, and the GOP Washington community saw him as a gasbag. Dole had a stronger reputation, and despite their past conflicts, Bush respected him. But as Quayle explained, Bush doubted that Dole would add much appeal. "I think, to George Bush's credit, he wanted to do something different. It was a generational selection. I was the first post–World War II candidate for Vice President."[127]

By the customary standards of ticket balancing, Quayle made some sense. Whereas Bush's age group was nearing the end of its dominance, Quayle's cohort was the talk of the political community. "In 1988, the baby boom generation could become half of the electorate," journalist Ron Brownstein had written. "No group will be more important in selecting the next President."[128] Quayle was a Midwesterner, a complement to a man with roots in the Northeast and a residence in the South. Bush's expertise was in foreign policy. Quayle had done journeyman work in domestic legislation and was the author of a well-regarded law on job training.[129] Quayle also had a conservative reputation that might reassure the GOP right.

To heighten the drama, Bush waited until Tuesday of the mid-August New Orleans convention to announce his pick. The launch went badly. Because the choice was such a closely held secret, the aides who would normally have prepared talking points were as surprised as everyone else. Without any other materials at hand, they had to rely on photocopied pages from *The Almanac of American Politics,* an excellent off-the-shelf reference, but hardly enough to field sharp questions about a vice presidential candidate. At a rally aboard the paddleboat *Natchez,* Bush introduced Quayle to America, and the first impression was one of immaturity. Jack Germond and Jules Witcover described the scene: "Quayle was absolutely giddy with happiness, grabbing his benefactor by the shoulder and repeatedly hugging his arm, gamboling around the platform like the jackpot winner on a television game show."[130] Things got worse at a press conference the next morning when a reporter asked why he served in the National Guard instead of going to Vietnam.

> Well it's, growing up in Huntington, Ind., the first thing you think about is education. You think about what any small-town person would think about, eventually growing up, raising a family. I was fortunate enough to be able to go on to law school, meet my wife. We have, I'm blessed with my three beautiful children. We're very happy, very content and looking forward to a very exciting campaign. I did not know in 1969 that I would be in this room today, I'll confess.[131]

The "confession" was both candid and hurtful. With few exceptions, the government did not call up guardsmen and reservists for service in Vietnam. Young men saw service in the Guard and reserves as a way to avoid the draft, and it was common knowledge that those from privileged backgrounds could jump the line.[132] In subsequent interviews, Quayle gave vague and inconsistent accounts of how he got into a Guard unit.[133] Though no hard evidence emerged that Quayle had broken any laws, the campaign soon acknowledged that members of his prominent family had intervened in his behalf.[134] Worse still was his fear-struck demeanor in these interviews, which helped make the phrase "deer in the headlights" part of the vernacular.[135]

The Bush campaign could have curbed the damage by anticipating the National Guard questions and preparing Quayle with better responses. If he had offered a straight story from the start, and spoken with an air of gravity and confidence, the story might have died down quickly. Instead, he became a target of national derision, and would remain so for the rest of his career.

How did such an effective campaign organization get into such avoidable trouble? For starters, as Quayle himself noted, he was the first of his generation to appear on a national ticket, so there was no direct precedent to draw from. Still, it should not have been hard to spot his potential vulnerability. Just about any baby boomer would have noticed that his military experience consisted of writing press releases in Indiana instead of dodging bullets in Vietnam. Kimmitt, himself a Vietnam veteran, asked Quayle about his National Guard service, but he did not pursue the issue once he determined that Quayle had stayed within the letter of the law. "The problem was that Kimmitt is not a strategist," one anonymous adviser told the *New York Times*. "He was a lawyer, not a politician."[136] Other young Bush staffers, who might have seen the political danger, had no chance to weigh in because the selection process involved so few people.

The Bush campaign failed to grasp how much preparation Quayle would need. He had won tough elections in Indiana, but a national campaign involved greater challenges. Perhaps Bush did not appreciate Quayle's problem. By the time Reagan picked him for vice president, he had served in high-level posts requiring Senate confirmation, and he had run for president himself. In 1980, Bush did not need tutoring. In 1988, Quayle did. Several years later, Quayle said, "I just miscalculated. . . . And did not have a good understanding of what the national political scene was going to demand of me. I didn't handle things as well as I should have."[137]

READING LIPS

Bush needed to change the conversation with a strong acceptance address. Fortunately for him, his writer was Peggy Noonan, who had written some of Reagan's best rhetoric. The speech wove together a reference to Bush's World War II heroism and his status as Reagan's successor: "I am a man who sees life in terms of missions—missions defined and missions completed. And when I was a torpedo-bomber pilot, they defined the mission for us. . . . But I am here tonight, and I am your candidate, because the most important work of my life is to complete the mission we started in 1980. And how do we complete it? We build on it."[138]

The speech deftly turned Dukakis's wonkery against him, warning against "the creed of the technocrat who makes sure the gears mesh but doesn't for a second understand the magic of the machine." Under the liberal technocratic vision, "the country waits passive while Washington sets the rules. But that's not what community means, not to me." Drawing on communitarian writers, Noonan's text contrasted that vision with one that relied on voluntary associations:[139]

> This is America: The Knights of Columbus, the Grange, Hadassah, the Disabled American Veterans, the Order of Ahepa, the Business and Professional Women of America, the union hall, the Bible study group, LULAC, Holy Name, a brilliant diversity spreads like stars, like a thousand points of light in a broad and peaceful sky. Does government have a place? Yes. Government is part of the nation of communities, not the whole, just a part.

The speech went through a litany of issues, framing Bush's side as the positive, Dukakis's as the negative. On school prayer, capital punishment, gun rights, and protection of the unborn, he repeated: "My opponent says no, but I say yes." A single line alluded to the furlough issue: "I'm the one who believes it is a scandal to give a weekend furlough to a hardened, first-degree killer who hasn't even served enough time to be eligible for parole."

A little later came the words that would echo throughout Bush's presidential term: "My opponent won't rule out raising taxes, but I will, and the Congress will push me to raise taxes, and I'll say no, and they'll push, and I'll say no, and they'll push again, and I'll say to them, 'Read my lips: no new taxes.'" Bush had long been making the "no new taxes" promise, which had been part of the "Straddle" ad against Dole. But for the millions of voters who had not obsessed over the nomination contest, this was the first time that they had heard it. The "read my lips" part made it especially memorable. Noonan recalled that staffers kept striking the phrase from early drafts "on the grounds, I believe, that lips are organs, there is no history of presidential candidates making personal-organ references in campaign speeches, therefore. . . . Anyway, I kept putting it back in. Why? Because it's definite. It's not subject to misinterpretation. It means: I mean this."[140]

5

THE DEMOCRATIC NOMINATION CONTEST

When an election is tight, it is reasonable to speculate that losing side could have won by doing things differently. If Hillary Clinton's 2016 campaign had done better polling in key industrial states, she might have been able to head off the last-minute swing toward Trump. The 1984 election was not such a case. Because of the fundamentals behind Reagan's landslide—peace and prosperity—no other Democrat could have done much better than Mondale. And on the merits, Mondale was a good candidate. He had superb qualifications, a steady temperament, and issue positions that were well within the mainstream of American politics. No matter; a time-tested tradition in American politics is the roasting of the scapegoat. After every presidential election, political operatives and media commentators dwell on the defeated candidate's faults and flaws. Disgruntled campaign staffers grumble about all the brilliant advice that their superiors disregarded. Next time, party elders vow, we will not run such an awful candidate or mount such an inept campaign. So it was after the 1984 election.

Democratic leaders thought that their 1988 candidate should not be another Walter Mondale. Apart from ruling out liberal Washington insiders with an excitement deficit, an upper Midwestern base, and a Norwegian family tree, that criterion did not provide much guidance. After Edward Kennedy announced that he would not run in 1988, many Democrats looked toward Albany. Like Mondale and Kennedy, New York governor Mario Cuomo was an apostle of the old-time liberal religion. But unlike Mondale, he was an electrifying orator: his passionate "tale of two cities" keynote at the 1984 Democratic convention instantly made him a national star. And unlike Kennedy, he had a spotless personal life. He could speak movingly about the family values that he had practiced, and he could connect with working people and immigrants by talking about his father, a grocer who had come to the United States from Italy. For reasons that were never quite clear, he stayed out of the race.

The noncandidacies of Kennedy and Cuomo worked to Michael Dukakis's benefit. Cuomo would have dominated the "ethnic Northeastern governor" bracket. He was more charismatic and famous than Dukakis, and he would have had access to New York money. Likewise, a Kennedy run would have made a Dukakis campaign practically impossible. Dukakis was not especially close to Kennedy, who remembered that he had opposed his nomination to the Senate in 1962. But the family was so powerful in the state that no other Massachusetts Democrat could have gotten off the ground if Kennedy were in the race. In a Kennedy-free environment, by contrast, the governor had a chance to gather early money and organizational support.

Two other Democrats gained even more than Dukakis did. Columnists Rowland Evans and Robert Novak suggested that Kennedy's withdrawal made Gary Hart and Joseph Biden early front-runners for the 1988 Democratic nomination.[1] They would also be early also-rans.

THE TRAGEDY OF GARY HART

Before December 1985, Gary Hart faced a complicated situation. On the one hand, he was trying to transcend the old-fashioned liberalism that Edward Kennedy embodied. On the other hand, he revered Kennedy. During the 1984 campaign, he often spoke of the late president and copied some of his mannerisms. "Gary overevokes the Kennedy image," one aide warned in a memo. "People resent it because Gary does not seem authentic."[2] Whatever their differences on policy, an imitation Kennedy would pale next to a real one.

With Kennedy out of the race, Hart could instead focus on being the un-Mondale. He had a good claim to that title because he had been Mondale's main rival in 1984. Where Mondale was proudly dull, Hart had a touch of glitz. (Screen idol Hugh Jackman would play him in a 2018 movie.) Where Mondale clung to organized labor and other elements of the Washington establishment, Hart touted his independence. Where Mondale preached the New Deal, Hart spoke of new ideas. During the 1984 campaign, Mondale questioned whether Hart's ideas had any substance. Quoting a popular fast-food commercial of the time, he asked in a debate: "Where's the beef?"[3] The wisecrack stung—and stuck. After the election,

Hart was determined that nobody could ever again get laughs by questioning his depth. In a postelection conference, Hart strategist Susan Casey said: "His message in the campaign really was, despite how naïve it sounds, based on issues, on developing a framework in foreign policy and domestic policy and on laying a foundation for governing that would be successful in a general election."[4]

Hart wanted to discuss how American foreign policy should adapt to change in the Soviet Union. After Reagan and Gorbachev failed to reach an arms-control breakthrough at their 1986 summit at Reykjavik, Hart went to Moscow for meetings with Gorbachev and other high Soviet officials.[5] With these meetings, Hart showed that he was an important Democratic voice on foreign policy. By giving Hart so much attention, the Soviet leaders suggested that they took him seriously as a potential president.

Hart had chosen not to run for a third term in the Senate, thereby leaving 1987 and 1988 wide open for presidential campaigning. On April 13, 1987, he announced his candidacy. "This election in 1988 is not a question of whether our country should move left or right," he said. "It's an issue of recapturing our basic principles, beliefs and values, and, as we did in 1932 and 1960, moving this country forward."[6] On May 3, the *New York Times Magazine* published a Hart profile by E. J. Dionne Jr. "For an agonizing week after announcing his candidacy, Hart found that in Presidential politics, 'character' can indeed overwhelm 'substance' and 'issues,'" Dionne wrote. "The day after he announced, he was drawn into conversations with reporters about a whispering campaign concerning his alleged womanizing, giving currency to the very rumors that infuriate him." In the article, Dionne discussed Hart's religious and philosophical views at some length, then returned to the rumors that he had cheated on his wife. He quoted Hart's response: "'Follow me around. I don't care,' he says firmly, about the womanizing question. 'I'm serious. If anybody wants to put a tail on me, go ahead. They'd be very bored.'"[7]

Before this remark got into print, reporters for the *Miami Herald* had already done something similar. Acting on a tip, they looked into a relationship between Hart and a woman who had done professional acting and modeling. They staked out Hart's Washington townhouse and saw the woman enter. Hart confronted the reporters and denied any impropriety. The paper published the story on the same day as the Dionne article, leading many readers to the false conclusion that the reporters were acting on Hart's dare to follow him around. A media frenzy ensued. Campaign contributors, who were already queasy about the rumors surrounding Hart, were turning their backs.[8] Hemorrhaging support, and facing the likelihood that other news stories about his private life would soon torment him, Hart withdrew on May 8.

Matt Bai's *All the Truth Is Out* provides abundant detail about the episode, and there is no need to dwell on the chronology here. But it is important to consider its historical context. Gary Hart was hardly the first American politician to engage in questionable personal behavior, so why did it hurt him so much? As Bai explains, technology enabled the story to spread more rapidly than it would have a decade or so earlier. Reporters, press aides, and opposition researchers used a relatively new device—the fax machine—to share news reports and statements. "In effect, fax technology did in a limited and rudimentary way what blogs and social media would do twenty years later," Bai wrote. "It enabled large numbers of people outside the elite media to get and exchange information, and it vastly reduced the amount of time it took for that information to get around."[9] In the past, television news crews had relied on bulky film cameras that required frequent reloading. Now they had handheld video cameras that could record for hours, turning television producers into stalkers. And satellite dishes had improved to the point where the three broadcast networks, along with the brand-new Cable News Network, could air live updates from practically anywhere. Bai noted: "What might have been a minor story in years past could now explode into a national event, within hours, provided it had the element of human drama necessary to keep viewers planted in their seats."[10]

Bai said that the Watergate scandal had encouraged reporters to get more aggressive.[11] Recent revelations about John F. Kennedy also brought more attention to the private lives of public officials, especially would-be presidents. During Kennedy's tenure, reporters knew that he carried on with women, yet they thought that such information was out of bounds. In 1975, a news story cracked Camelot's protective wall. A woman had testified to a congressional committee that she had had relationships both with Kennedy and high-ranking Mafia figures.[12] This story, along with subsequent accounts, raised the possibility that Kennedy's private conduct had exposed him to blackmail and other grave security risks. Such revelations supplied journalists with a rationale for digging into the sex lives of presidential contenders.

Hart's withdrawal had an immediate effect on another potential candidate. Bill Clinton was preparing for an announcement when the events of early May forced him to confront his own Gary Hart problem. Adviser Dick

Morris said it "loomed large in his consideration. It loomed very large."[13] Betsey Wright, another adviser, grilled him about a list of purported paramours. At the end of the conversation, she advised him not to run. In July, he made it official. When he did compete in the Democratic primaries four years later, he confronted a sex scandal involving his previous relationship with an Arkansas lounge singer—and he survived it to win the White House.

Clinton's 1992 experience raises a question about Hart in 1988: could he have overcome his scandal if he had just toughed it out, as Clinton did? A couple of days after the Hart story broke, Gallup found that 64 percent of the public thought that press had been unfair to him and that 70 percent disapproved of undercover media surveillance tactics. Moreover, 40 percent of Democrats still supported him for the nomination.[14] Then again, one of the considerations that drove him from the race was the awareness that the *Washington Post* was preparing a story about yet another alleged affair. It is hard to reckon how such news would have moved public opinion, or whether Hart would have handled it with the deftness that Clinton later showed. Hart rejoined the race in December, by which time his campaign money and organizational support had migrated to other candidates. Despite a brief burst of support in polls, he never reached double-digit percentages in any primary.

Another explanation for the divergent fates of Hart and Clinton is that attitudes changed after 1988. Ten years later, Americans sided with Clinton in his impeachment fight, even after they learned that he had had sex with an intern in a government office on government time, and then had given misleading testimony about it. And eighteen years after that, millions of voters shrugged off the *Access Hollywood* tape and multiple accusations of sexual harassment against Donald Trump. The public became more forgiving—albeit too late for Gary Hart.

"LOOK, I'M A BIG BOY"

Joseph Biden thought about running for president in 1984 but ran for reelection to the Senate instead. His youthful vigor and Irish Catholic background gave rise to Kennedy comparisons, which he encouraged. "I think 1988 is going to be about 1960, about our country and not causes, about idealism and not ideology, about the future and not the status quo," he told the *New York Times*. "It's almost as simple as 'Let's get America moving again.' My generation is really ready, and I want to be a part of it."[15] Without Edward Kennedy in the race, he was free to sing the Kennedy soundtrack.

In particular, he constantly invoked Robert Kennedy in his speeches. Sometimes he would use the late senator's words without attribution, a practice that would eventually contribute to political trouble.

Biden formed a multicandidate political action committee, the Fund for '86, to give midterm money to Democratic congressional candidates and to finance his travels on their behalf. Though the committee did not raise as much as other candidate PACs, it was more than enough to maintain his visibility as a Democratic presidential candidate. Campaign manager Timothy Ridley explained Biden's basic strategic assumption: "In 1988, Democrats would be hungry for a nominee who could move the country forward with a compassionate message delivered with great passion. There was only one other candidate who could rival Joe Biden on this score—Reverend Jackson."[16] A Cuomo candidacy would have undercut this assumption.

Biden represented Delaware, a border state that was not as reliably Democratic as it would later be; it had gone Republican in every presidential election since 1968, except for 1976, when it supported Jimmy Carter from Georgia. Although he had a generally liberal voting record, he did bow his constituency by taking some conservative positions, including opposition to racial-balance busing. He joined the DLC and told a North Carolina gathering of the group: "You in the South have been where the Democratic Party was, and now the Democratic Party must be where you are."[17] In both the presidential primaries and the general election, he was hoping to make inroads in the region.

The 1986 Democratic takeover of the Senate complicated both his schedule and his ideological brand. Kennedy was the senior Democrat on the Judiciary Committee, but he chose instead to chair Education and Labor. Biden got the Judiciary chair, along with the time-consuming tasks of hiring staff and managing the committee's business. He declared his presidential candidacy on June 9, and three weeks later, Justice Lewis Powell announced his retirement. In addition to his ordinary duties, Biden would now have to run Supreme Court nomination hearings. President Reagan chose Judge Robert Bork, whose legal career was distinguished and whose judicial philosophy was conservative. Biden had voted to confirm Bork as an appellate judge and had suggested that he would be acceptable for the Supreme Court. "Say the administration sends up Bork and, after our investigation, he looks a lot like another Scalia," he said before assuming the chair. "I'd have to vote for him, and if the groups tear me apart, that's the medicine I'll have to take. I'm not Teddy Kennedy."[18] Months later, answering to mostly liberal Democratic colleagues and facing the potential wrath of liberal advocacy groups, Biden followed Kennedy's lead and came out against Bork.

The flip-flop would undoubtedly have come up during the primary campaign. But as with Hart, something other than issues brought him low, and technology again played a big part. Dukakis campaign manager John Sasso prepared a video juxtaposing Biden's closing remarks during an August debate with a television ad by British Labour Party leader Neil Kinnock. The video showed that Biden had blatantly plagiarized Kinnock. Sasso and another aide provided it to several news organizations, including the *New York Times,* which reported:

> In the commercial, the Briton began, "Why am I the first Kinnock in a thousand generations to be able to get to university?" Then pointing to his wife in the audience, he continued: "Why is Glenys the first woman in her family in a thousand generations to be able to get to university? Was it because all our predecessors were thick?"
>
> Senator Biden began his remarks by saying the ideas had come to him spontaneously on the way to the debate. "I started thinking as I was coming over here, why is it that Joe Biden is the first in his family ever to go to a university?" he said. Then, pointing to his wife, he continued: "Why is it that my wife who is sitting out there in the audience is the first in her family to ever go to college? Is it because our fathers and mothers were not bright? Is it because I'm the first Biden in a thousand generations to get a college and a graduate degree that I was smarter than the rest?"[19]

Sasso saw the attack video as a one-shot tactic that might leave some flesh wounds. Another Dukakis aide explained that "we were, when we put together the two pieces of tape, interjecting ourselves into a much larger controversy than we ever anticipated."[20] As it turned out, the story inspired journalists (probably with an assist from other candidates' opposition researchers) to track down and publicize other instances in which Biden had been careless with his language. A few days later, the *New York Times* reported that Biden had plagiarized portions of a speech by Robert F. Kennedy. Reporter Maureen Dowd wrote that a Reagan White House aide had noticed the copying while watching a Biden speech on C-SPAN.[21] (The aide was Jeffrey Lord, who would later achieve short-lived notoriety as a cable news defender of Donald Trump.) Then came a more serious discovery: Biden had committed plagiarism in law school and had to repeat a course because of it. He admitted his mistake, hinting that other campaigns had shopped the information to the media. "'Look, I'm a big boy,' Biden said. 'I've been in politics for 15 years. This is not my style. If they want to do it this way, so be it.'"[22] Finally, *Newsweek* reported on an exchange that had aired on C-SPAN in April but got no attention at the time. In response to a skeptical question at a small gathering in New Hampshire, Biden snapped, "I think I have a much higher IQ than you do," and went on to make inaccurate claims about his academic record.[23] Biden withdrew on September 23.

Once Biden was out, media stories probed the origins of the attack video. At first, speculation incorrectly focused on Gephardt, whose campaign suffered some short-term turbulence as a result.[24] Dukakis, unaware of what his subordinates had done, denied that his camp had anything to do with it. When a news story revealed the source, Sasso admitted to Dukakis that he had made the video. Dukakis then fired Sasso and his collaborator, Paul Tully.

Except for misleading his boss, Sasso had done nothing wrong. The video depicted a public statement of a public figure. Sasso's work did not inject false claims, invade anyone's privacy, or appeal to prejudice. It was hardly unheard of for American politicians to use each other's words against them, as any reader of the Lincoln–Douglas debates will notice. Dukakis, however, made a point of disdaining negative campaigning, so the story clashed with the high-minded image that he was seeking to convey. Sasso's replacement was more consistent with that image. Susan Estrich was a Harvard law professor who had been elected the first female president of the institution's law review—a position for which she defeated classmate Merrick Garland. She had experience as a congressional staffer and policy adviser to Democratic campaigns, though she had never run a campaign at this level.

Technology had much to do with the incident that had led to the shake-up. A decade earlier, there would have been no attack video because video equipment was costly and rare outside of the television industry. Between 1980 and 1987, the number of video cassette recorders increased from about one million to forty-three million.[25] Until 1979, the year of C-SPAN's birth, there would have been little useful video to record. Apart from special occasions such as the State of the Union address, television seldom aired more than snippets of speeches and other political events—the very reason that Brian Lamb founded C-SPAN.[26] At first, the cable network merely carried the live video feed of the House chamber. It then added a call-in program. In 1982, it expanded its broadcasting to twenty-four hours a day, which enabled it to cover events such as the Iowa debate in which Biden plagiarized Kinnock and the California speech in which he plagiarized Robert Kennedy. In 1987, it launched the "Road to the White House" series, which featured video not only of speeches but also of informal encounters, such as the one in which Biden misstated his academic record. Without VCRs and C-SPAN, Biden's verbal missteps would have been lost in time, like tears in rain.[27]

Ironically, withdrawing from the race may have saved Biden's life. In February 1988, he underwent emergency surgery for a dangerous aneurysm in an artery supplying blood to the brain. The surgery occurred just a few days before the New Hampshire primary. If he had stayed in the race, he would have been under pressure to ignore his symptoms—and any further delay in the procedure could have killed him.

THE FIELD

Between the departures of Hart and Biden, seven significant Democratic candidates had entered the race: besides Biden and Dukakis, there were Bruce Babbitt, Richard Gephardt, Al Gore, Jesse Jackson, and Paul Simon. Compared with noncandidates Kennedy, Hart, and Cuomo, the field appeared to lack stature, and reporters started calling them "the seven dwarfs." The term was problematic in a couple of ways. It hardly fit Jackson, who had been a conspicuous civil rights figure for nearly two decades. And at a time when the disability rights movement was still at the outskirts of public attention, the media never bothered to ask little people what they thought of using the word "dwarf" as a sneer.

Nevertheless, the label became irresistible when the possibility of a female candidate arose. Now journalists could talk about "Snow White and the Seven Dwarfs." The would-be contender was Representative Pat Schroeder of Colorado. She had been national co-chair of Gary Hart's campaign, and she thought about running herself after he pulled out. Her gender made her stand out in the political world of the time. In 1987, there were only twenty-three women in the House and two in the Senate (compared with eighty-three and twenty-one in 2017).[28] In addition to sponsoring prominent legislation, she had gained a reputation as a media-savvy phrasemaker. Among other things, she had noted that political problems never stuck to Reagan; she famously dubbed him "the Teflon President." She also had disadvantages. Unlike Jack Kemp and Richard Gephardt, the other House members running for president that year, she did not have a party leadership position and the additional staff that came with it. Despite her seniority, she did not chair a full committee, so she was not a money magnet for access-hungry interest groups. Of course, she also had to contend with sexism. She said: "'I get the question, 'Why are you running as a woman?' all the time and I simply answer, 'Do I have an option?'"[29] By September, it was too late to begin an effective campaign in Iowa or New Hampshire. On September 28, 1987, she announced that she would not run. Her eyes moistened during her emotional statement, which touched off a round of op-eds about whether a woman politician should cry in public.

By October, the shape of the Democratic nomination contest was nearly set. Six significant candidates were still in the running, and by one measure, Dukakis was a step ahead. There was some media speculation that the attack video controversy might hurt him, but it was an inside-baseball story that few voters followed. Dukakis's edge was financial. In 1987, he raised about $10 million, more than twice as much as any other Democrat.[30] Some of it came from the Route 128 corridor, where high-tech corporate managers kept writing checks to Dukakis, as they had throughout his political career.[31] Richard Berke of the *New York Times* explained that Dukakis profited from being the only sitting governor in the race: "Donations came from real estate developers, investment bankers, lawyers, bond counsels and insurance executives whose companies do business with Massachusetts. Beyond Massachusetts, contributors include executives of many Wall Street firms with whom the state has floated bonds."[32] His surname helped too. About one sixth of his 1987 haul came from Greek Americans around the country. "Being the first person in the Greek community running for the Presidency is an obvious advantage," said former senator Paul Tsongas of Massachusetts. "The next Greek that runs for President will not have this success because the fervor will not be there."[33] (Tsongas would prove himself right. He was the next Greek to run for president, and in his 1992 nomination race against Bill Clinton, the fervor was not there.) Finally, Dukakis had an effective fundraising operation. Campaign treasurer Bob Farmer worked the business and financial communities, which appreciated the generous subsidies that Dukakis had championed as governor.[34]

Massachusetts roots helped Dukakis in another way. Much of next-door New Hampshire lies in the Boston media market, so voters in the first primary were already familiar with his record. His status as the state's favorite son-in-law meant risk as well as opportunity. Another favorite from a neighboring state, Senator Edmund Muskie of Maine, won the 1972 New Hampshire primary, but his margin was so disappointing that it effectively scuttled his candidacy. With Muskie in mind, Dukakis's rivals were eager to build up expectations for Dukakis. "I think his lead here is enormous," said Gephardt. "I think he'd be very hard to beat. . . . My hope would be to come in second."[35]

Gephardt had a home-field advantage of his own. Missouri borders Iowa, and the states have economic and cultural affinities. As soon as Hart withdrew, Gephardt became the candidate to beat in the Iowa caucuses, which in turn meant that he could not afford a defeat there. "From that point on every resource and the entire focus of the campaign was weighed against our 'must' victory in Iowa," said Gephardt campaign manager William Carrick.[36] In addition to spending time and money in the state, Gephardt also sought to appeal to the liberal activists who had a strong voice in the caucuses. Representative Dave McCurdy of Oklahoma, a fellow member of the DLC, told political scientist Kenneth Baer about a conversation in which Gephardt acknowledged: "I'm going to take some positions in this campaign that you are not going to like because I have to win Iowa."[37]

Gephardt had already been gravitating to the liberal camp. He won his first term in 1976, and for the next eight years, he took moderate to conservative stands, such as support for constitutional amendments to limit abortion and racial-balance busing. At a 1981 dinner, Gephardt said: "I would get rid of government in health care. I would get rid of government in education to a much greater extent than we have. I would discharge those responsibilities either to the private sector or to the states."[38] After he won the chairmanship of the House Democratic Caucus in 1985, staying in the good graces of his party required him to take more liberal positions. As Edmund Burke put it: "In all bodies, those who will lead, must also, in a considerable degree, follow."[39] He switched sides on abortion, and in line with the rising protectionist sentiment among his Rust Belt colleagues, he sponsored tough trade legislation. Though he apparently thought these shifts would help with rank-and-file voters as well as Democratic politicians, they also exposed him to accusations of flip-flopping. Hedrick Hertzberg wrote in the *New Republic* that Gephardt "puts me in mind, unreasonably to be sure, of an earthling whose body has been taken over by space aliens. . . . How else to explain the fact that Gephardt, who until a few months ago was a sort of neoconservative neoliberal, has suddenly begun talking, in his slow, robotic voice, like a devotee of the cult of Populism?"[40]

If Gephardt was eager to tell people what they wanted to hear, then Bruce Babbitt took the opposite approach. His early television appearances were hardly telegenic. During the first Democratic debate in July 1987, viewers noticed his odd gestures and head bobs. At times he seemed to be imitating Dan Aykroyd's imitation of Richard Nixon. More important, Babbitt's policy positions called to mind a dentist recommending root canals. His signature proposal was a "universal needs test," under which any kind of federal benefits—mortgage interest deductions, farm subsidies, Social Security payments—would go only to people who needed them.[41] At a December 1987 debate, he said: "It's time to acknowledge that we must raise taxes. Now, the American people know that. The problem is that Gephardt says it's time to stand up. But the President won't stand up. The Congress won't stand up. These candidates won't stand up." To make his point, he rose from his seat and went on: "And I'm gonna stand up and say it's time to speak the truth about these issues, and say we can balance the budget only by cutting and needs-testing expenditures and entitlements, and by raising taxes."[42] Babbitt's candor was purposeful. Campaign manager Frederick DuVal said: "We tried to present Babbitt as the uncandidate, the antipolitician, the truth-teller; not slick on TV; not racked up with a lot of endorsements; but a man pushing unpopular ideas which we felt most of the public instinctively knew were right."[43]

This high-risk strategy made sense because Babbitt had little going for him except the strength of his ideas. He had little money and came from a relatively small state (seven electoral votes) where his party was not dominant. To moderate Democrats seeking to pick the GOP's purported lock on the Electoral College, young Al Gore of Tennessee seemed like a better bet. Babbitt's long-shot wager was that standing up and talking straight would set him apart—but were voters longing for pain?

Paul Simon was like Babbitt in a couple of ways. Despite sharing a name with a famous singer, he cultivated the image of being genuine and unhip. In a *Saturday Night Live* parody of a Democratic debate, future real-life senator Al Franken portrayed Simon: "With Paul Simon, what you see is what you get. And I'm not about to change my bow tie to please some media advisor. And so . . . I wear the bow tie. And I think that the American people want a president who's not afraid to say I am who I am, bow tie and all."[44] Also like Babbitt, he talked about reducing the deficit. Simon supported a constitutional amendment to require a balanced budget, and he claimed that he could achieve it in three years. But whereas Babbitt was excruciatingly specific about raising taxes and cutting federal benefits, Simon was elusive about how he would sweat $155 billion from the deficit. While preaching balanced budgets, he tried to portray himself as an old-style Truman Democrat.[45] His message was at war with itself. His caginess about budget details clashed with his effort to convey honesty. Liberals wondered how he could square massive deficit reduction with the preservation of the social safety net, which is why Gephardt dismissed the Simon agenda as "Reaganomics with a bow tie."[46]

Simon had something in common with Gephardt: he came from a state bordering Iowa. According to campaign manager Terry Michael, "His rationale was partly based on geographic proximity to Iowa, obviously. But also it was a cultural proximity . . . the small-town guy, nice guy, respected guy, standup guy image." Michael quoted Simon on another reason for an Iowa focus: "Well, I've done well with labor over the years, and labor is a major factor in Iowa."[47]

Al Gore pinned his hopes on Super Tuesday. Campaign manager Fred Martin said: "The strategy was to try to use the new calendar and take advantage of 20 states casting their votes on the same day, on the 8th of March—two-thirds of them in the South—to win a bunch of those states. We thought we had a good chance to do so with the candidate from the South."[48] Gore had roots in Tennessee, which he emphasized whenever he campaigned in the region. During the North Carolina primary campaign, he assured tobacco farmers: "Throughout most of my life I raised tobacco. I want you to know that with my own hands, all of my life, I put it in the plant beds and transferred it, I've hoed it. I've chopped it. I've shredded it, spiked it, put it in the barn and stripped it and sold it."[49] He was the only candidate in the race who had served in the Vietnam War, which potentially gave him credibility among the South's many military veterans. Gore enjoyed the support of party conservatives including Rick Perry, a veteran who was then an obscure Democratic state legislator in Texas.[50]

Gore announced his candidacy in his hometown of Carthage, Tennessee. The state was a comfortable starting point for a Southern Democratic candidate. Democrats held the governorship, both US Senate seats, both houses of the state legislature, and a majority of US House seats. Governor Ned McWherter and Senator Jim Sasser gave brief warm-up speeches before Gore came to the podium. In his remarks, he tried to be many things to many people: "I am not running as a Southern candidate, but as a national candidate from the South and proud of it."[51] He likened himself to Woodrow Wilson, "a son of the South" who united and led the nation. At age thirty-nine, he stood to be the youngest-ever president, which enabled him to draw a Kennedy comparison: "Twenty-seven years ago, the voters of America, looking for the strength and hope of a new generation, replaced the oldest man ever to serve in the office of the presidency with the youngest ever to be elected to that office. I believe they're ready to do so again." He was both a warrior and a peace lover: "I served in Vietnam. I know the importance of protecting our national security and I know there must be better ways to resolve our differences than through war." He pledged to "combat unfair trade practices overseas" while fostering "quality and efficiency" in the domestic economy. In a clumsy attempt at alliteration, he called for "perfectionism, not protectionism." He touched on what would later become his trademark issue, environmentalism. He called for international environmental action without mentioning coal, still a significant industry in Southern and border states.

The speech was of a piece with his congressional career. He played up his small-town roots and pursued wonkish interests such as nuclear arms control, regulation of organ transplants, and the development of high technology. (A favorite GOP urban legend is wrong: he never claimed to have invented the internet.[52]) He combined a reputation for conservatism with a generally liberal voting record. "Sometimes he comes across as a farmboy, sometimes as a yuppie. Truth is, he's both," wrote the executive editor of the *Nashville Tennessean*. "His southern accent comes and goes, depends on which side of the Mason–Dixon he is standing."[53]

For all his rhetorical base-broadening, his path to the nomination still ran through the Southern states of Super Tuesday. He would face an enormous obstacle named Jesse Jackson.

"KEEP HOPE ALIVE"

Jackson's 1988 campaign was more professional than his ramshackle 1984 effort. As his campaign manager, he chose Gerald Austin, who was a veteran of successful gubernatorial campaigns in the key state of Ohio. Austin was also Jewish. He claimed that Jackson was unaware of his faith before hiring him, but it surely did not hurt Jackson's effort to overcome the charges of anti-Semitism that had dogged him since the Hymietown incident. "I told Jesse that I, as a Jew and a New Yorker, was doubly offended at 'Hymietown'—a word I had never even heard before," Austin told Myra McPherson of the *Washington Post*. "He said it was a mistake. So then I said, what about Farrakhan, and he said he hadn't seen him or talked to him in 2½ years. . . . I was very well satisfied that Jesse Jackson is not an anti-Semite."[54] Jackson's campaign chair was Willie Brown, the brilliant speaker of the California state assembly. Brown, like Jackson, had grown up poor and black in the segregated South. He was a fighter for civil rights, and he was also a legendary dealmaker who excelled at multidimensional political chess. His involvement was a signal that Jackson was serious.

Could he win? Many Democrats thought that his presence on the ticket would doom the party. Around the time that he announced, one poll showed that 42 percent of the public thought that he was unqualified to be president, the worst such rating for any Democrat in the survey. (Pat Robertson, another preacher without government experience, got the same negative response on the GOP side.[55]) Even if he did not win the nomination, he could build a movement and push the Democratic Party in his ideological direction.

That direction was leftward. Much more than in the 1984 campaign, he focused on policy specifics, and he drew on progressive think tanks such as the Institute for Policy Studies (IPS). Said Robert Borosage, a former IPS director who advised the Jackson campaign: "We think our position isn't radical, but sensible. What distinguishes this campaign is its direct appeal to working people and Jackson's emphasis on 'economic violence.' That was not a thematic of the 1960s."[56] In his announcement speech, Jackson explained what he meant by the term: "When merger maniacs make windfall profits and top management is given excessive bonuses, golden parachutes to aid a soft landing, while workers are asked to take a wage cut, a benefit cut and a job loss, a crash landing—that's economic violence."[57] He proposed extensive regulation of big business, along with huge spending increases for welfare, housing, education, Medicaid, and drug treatment. To pay for these programs, he called for a freeze in defense spending with no adjustment for inflation, meaning $58 billion less than the projected budget by 1993. He also backed increasing taxes on corporations and affluent individuals.[58]

Jackson's Rainbow Coalition struggled to recruit Hispanics and blue-collar whites, but it did draw progressive activists, one of whom was Bernie Sanders. In 1981, Sanders ran as an independent for mayor of Burlington, Vermont. His narrow victory got national attention because he was a self-described socialist.[59] He had previously run for governor and US senator as a third-party candidate, and in 1986, he would run as an independent against incumbent Democratic governor Madeleine Kunin. In that race, he had support from Democratic activists who had worked in Jackson's 1984 campaign.[60] Sanders endorsed Jackson's 1988 candidacy, and for the first time in his political life, he took part in a formal Democratic function. At a party caucus in Burlington, he gave the nominating speech for Jackson. Resentful that Sanders had always opposed Democratic candidates in the past, some attendees stood up and turned their backs. "And when I returned to my seat," he recalled, "a woman in the audience slapped me across the face. It was an exciting evening."[61]

Sanders's speech was consistent with Jackson's message, and it augured the themes of his own presidential campaign twenty-eight years later:

> Tonight we are here to endorse the candidate who is saying loud and clear that enough is enough, that it's time that this nation was returned to the real people of America, the vast majority of us, and that power no longer should rest solely with a handful of banks and corporations who presently dominate the economic and political life of this nation. It is not acceptable to him, to me, or to most Americans, that 10 percent of the population of this nation is able to own 83 percent of the wealth, and the other 90 percent of us share 17 percent of the wealth.[62]

In his memoir of the 2016 campaign, Sanders reflected, "I have always believed that his campaign was enormously important in breaking down barriers and opening up new political space in our country."[63]

Jackson's core was the black vote, heavily concentrated in the Super Tuesday states. The DLC—which Jackson disparaged as "Democrats for the Leisure Class"—had backed the Super Tuesday concept. "Obviously Super Tuesday had been planned as the Waterloo for a candidate like Jesse Jackson," said former Gary, Indiana, mayor Richard Hatcher, a Jackson adviser. "However, those who devised that strategy obviously were thinking of the Old South and not the New South."[64] African American registration had increased greatly, in part because of Jackson's 1984 campaign. He planned to build on that base to win Super Tuesday states. Accordingly, it was no accident that announced his candidacy in Raleigh, North Carolina. "I'm a son of the South," he said. "I've spent all of my adult life trying to build a New South. As the poor of the South are liberated, the New South will lead the nation—with a commitment to liberal arts and science, peace and prosperity."[65]

PRIMARIES AND CAUCUSES: ROUND ONE

One last surprise announcement filled out the field of Democratic candidates. On December 15, 1987, Gary Hart said that he was running again. A mid-January Gallup poll put him in front with 25 percent support among Democrats, and Jackson in second place, with 19 percent.[66] Dukakis was third at 10 percent. Experienced politicians knew that these numbers reflected name identification as much as anything else, and probably would not foretell the outcome. Rather than a national referendum, the nomination campaign would be state-by-state struggle with its own rules and peculiar logic.

Candidates needed money, which Dukakis had in abundance. Hart's late restart meant that he would not have time to raise enough. Federal law capped individual contributions at $1,000 (about $2,048 in 2016 dollars). It also offered matching funds for individual contributions to presidential nomination campaigns, with the money coming from by a small "check-off" on the individual income tax form. To qualify for the matching funds, candidates had to gather $100,000 from at least twenty states in contributions of $250 or less. Once a campaign met that requirement, the federal government would match up to $250 of each individual contribution. One aspect of the law encouraged early departures. Any candidate who fell short of 10 percent in two back-to-back primaries would no longer get the matching funds.

The law also capped the total amount that candidates could spend during a nomination campaign—about $23 million in 1988. There are also ceilings on spending for individual states. Campaigns hated these limits, which they considered too restrictive, and which led to elaborate work-arounds such as renting vehicles in one state and using them in another

Against that backdrop, the formal campaign started. The Iowa caucuses were a must-win event for both Gephardt and Simon, who had high expectations because they came from neighboring states. Gore was bypassing Iowa and New Hampshire, planting nearly all of his political capital in the South. The others were hoping to do well enough to carry on. Hart was looking for a quantum of solace, and for a moment, it looked as if Iowa could give him more than that. Before his announcement, Simon led the Iowa Poll with 35 percent to 16 percent for Dukakis. Afterward, Hart leapt to the front at 29 percent, with Simon falling to 18 percent.[67] By mid-January, it was clear that the Hart surge was just a momentary reaction to media attention. His poll numbers were dropping, and his first debate appearance was underwhelming. *Rolling Stone*'s David Handelman wrote of his answer to a question about the character issue: "Hart's answer is garbled, even though he clearly prepared his defense. . . . Later he uses the word 'immorality' to describe homelessness, hunger and the lack of health care. In general, his debating style seems out of practice."[68] Perhaps more significant, the Iowa caucuses required a great deal of ground-level organizing, and the eleventh-hour reentry meant that Hart had practically none.

Meanwhile, after some early campaign doldrums, Gephardt started picking up support. One television spot got a good deal of notice from the news media, which amplified its effect. Opening with scenes of American autoworkers on the assembly line, it featured Gephardt speaking first as voice-over and then directly into the camera:

> They work their hearts out every day, trying to turn out a good product at a decent price. Then the Korean government slaps on nine separate taxes and tariffs, and when that government's done, a $10,000 Chrysler K Car costs $48,000 in Korea. It's not their fault we can't sell our cars in a market like that, and I'm tired of hearing American workers blamed for it. I've been criticized for my trade policies, for saying it's time to open up markets and push down trade barriers like those Korean taxes and tariffs. The Gephardt Amendment calls for six months of negotiations. If that doesn't work and I'm president, and we have to walk away from that table, the Koreans will know two things. They'll know that we'll still honor our treaties to defend them, because that's the kind of country we are. But they'll also be left asking themselves, how many Americans are going to pay $48,000 for one of their Hyundais?[69]

Gephardt campaign manager William Carrick said: "We started at 6 percent and in 10 days we were at 28 or 29. So it probably moved numbers faster than any other spot I know of, at least in the primary scene."[70] Dukakis manager Susan Estrich agreed: "In Iowa, I think Gephardt's was the only advertising that really made a difference."[71] Scholars tend to be skeptical of such claims, but there is some evidence that television had an impact. When a poll asked likely Iowa Democratic caucusgoers if a candidate had aired spots that made them more likely to support that candidate, 22 percent said Gephardt, compared with just 7 percent who mentioned Simon.[72] Though it came under criticism for factual inaccuracies, the Hyundai ad was a vivid piece of work that stood out just as voters were focusing their choices. It spoke to the widespread concern about the decline of manufacturing employment and the belief that Asian countries were to blame. (In contrast to 2016, there was little specific emphasis on China in 1988.) Gephardt picked a good place to make this appeal. For a state that is synonymous with farming, Iowa has long had a significant manufacturing sector, and it had lost thousands of factory jobs since the 1970s.[73]

Simon lost ground as Gephardt was gaining it. Trying to put some flesh on his budget plan, Simon floated the idea of a 1 percent surtax on the wealthy. Babbitt scorned the idea: "I'm sorry, soaking the rich and telling 99 out of 100 Americans they can get something for nothing is not a hard choice, It's the same old politics."[74] Terry Michael, Simon's campaign manager, said that the attacks on his credibility added to other problems: "We started losing some of that bonding that had been creating on the basis of biography with a lot of voters in Iowa. And then, Gary Hart reentered and things got jumbled up. Just at that point in time, Gephardt came in with the Hyundai ad."[75]

On February 8, Iowa voters caucused in a process that was more complicated than a primary. Eligible caucusgoers showed up at meeting places in precincts all over the state to form presidential preference groups. If candidate's group did not add up to 15 percent of the attendees, its members could join the group of their second choice or try to sway other people into their group to meet the threshold. Then the caucus allocated delegates to county conventions according to the size of the preference groups. The state party reported these figures as a measure of candidate strength. The News Election Service, a cooperative of news organizations, sought to report results quickly by gathering first-round results from the caucuses. Gephardt edged out Simon, 27.4 to 24.3 percent, with Dukakis running a strong third at 20.5 percent. Critics pointed out that this tally missed results from 30 percent of the caucus sites and did not account for switches among the preference groups. The "state delegate equivalent" percentages put the three in the same order, but with greater shares: 31.3 percent for Gephardt, 26.7 percent for Simon, and 22.2 percent for Dukakis. Jackson and Babbitt were in single digits, and Hart's delegate equivalent share was a humiliating 0.3 percent.[76]

Gephardt was hoping that an Iowa victory would provide him with the ineffable resource of momentum. It did not. His margin was slender, and his delegate equivalent share was less than one third. "Unlike 1976, when Jimmy Carter burst from the pack here, the state produced no Democratic breakthrough and established no one as a frontrunner," wrote R. W. Apple of the *New York Times*. "Mr. Dukakis remains the solid favorite in New Hampshire, where Mr. Simon is considerably better established than Mr. Gephardt."[77] A bigger problem was that Bush's surprise third-place showing on the GOP side was crowding media coverage, leaving little room for the Democratic results.[78]

The New Hampshire primary came eight days later—much sooner than in 1984. Dukakis was the presumptive leader, so Gephardt and Simon fought for second place. During a debate, Babbitt took a sharp dig at Gephardt, saying that he had downplayed his vote for Reagan's 1981 tax cut in Iowa and then called himself a tax cutter in New Hampshire. "That's not a flip-flop," Babbitt said. "That's a triple back somersault with a half twist."[79] As Babbitt was talking, Jesse Jackson used his hands to mime a somersault.

(Jackson had special contempt for Gephardt. At another debate, when Gephardt compared hard political choices to castor oil, Gore leaned over and asked Jackson if he had ever had to take castor oil. "No," he replied behind his hand, "But I was never that full of shit either."[80])

Dukakis won his expected victory in New Hampshire, and the size of his margin was impressive: 35.9 percent to 19.9 percent for Gephardt. Simon came in third, at 17.2 percent, which effectively ended his chances at the nomination. Babbitt got just 4.6 percent, a showing that was all the more dismal in light of the state's reputation for flinty fiscal conservatism. If he could not sell his palette of pain there, it was hard to see where else he could take it, so he withdrew a couple of days later. Hart did even worse, at 4.0 percent—a heartbreaking comedown from his surprise victory there four years earlier. He hung on a little longer, but after failing to clear 10 percent in any primary, he pulled out in March.

Gephardt's ad makers scored another coup in South Dakota. Consultants Robert Shrum and David Doak wanted to make Dukakis sound clueless about the heartland. They wrote a spot claiming that Dukakis had once advised farmers to grow "blueberries, flowers, and Belgian endive," and the narrator drove home the point by ending with, "Belgian endive?"[81] The spot helped Gephardt, who won a double-digit victory in the February 23 primary. Unfortunately for him, this victory was a second-tier media story at most. The Belgian endive attack angered Dukakis, who said that he was merely referring to something that Massachusetts farmers had done. Dukakis, who had expressed public reluctance about airing negative spots, suggested that his tactics would change. "People in glass houses shouldn't start throwing stones, and they shouldn't be surprised if they get it back," he said during a Florida forum on health care. On stage with Gephardt, Dukakis answered a question on changes of position by pointing to his opponent and saying: "Here's the flip-flopper over here. I'm not the flip-flopper"[82]

Vermont held a nonbinding primary a week after South Dakota, and as in New Hampshire, proximity helped Dukakis win by a wide margin. The second-place finisher provided a minor jolt to the political community. With the help of Bernie Sanders and other progressives, Jesse Jackson more than a quarter of the vote—notable in a state with only a tiny African American population.

SUPER TUESDAY

After South Dakota, a *Newsweek* article proclaimed Gephardt "the smart money pick for the Democratic nomination."[83] The smart money was wrong. He had burned his resources in Iowa for what turned out to be only a mild boost. He later admitted that he had erred by spending a hundred days in Iowa instead of using that time to raise campaign funds.[84] Even if his South Dakota victory had been a bigger story, he would have had little chance to exploit it. In the front-loaded 1988 schedule, Super Tuesday came only fourteen days later. In those days before online donation enabled campaigns to collect money almost instantly, it could take weeks between the drafting of a direct-mail fundraising appeal and the arrival of whatever checks it would generate. Without enough money coming in, Gephardt had to stretch his television budget thinly over the vast Southern landscape. Gore campaign manager Fred Martin said that Gephardt's message might have worked in the South if he had been able to buy more air time.[85]

What is more, Gephardt was now paying a price for changing his issue positions. Dukakis made good on his threat to respond in kind to Gephardt's attacks, airing a memorable ad in Super Tuesday states. The screen showed a red-haired acrobat in a suit and tie doing cartwheels and flips, and jumping through hoops. The voice-over said: "Congressman Dick Gephardt has flip-flopped on a lot of issues. He's been both for and against Reaganomics. For and against raising the minimum wage. For and against freezing Social Security benefits. Congressman Dick Gephardt acts tough toward big corporations but takes their PAC money." Then came images of Dukakis as the narration continued: "Mike Dukakis refuses PAC money, opposes Reaganomics and supports a strong minimum wage and Social Security. You know where Mike Dukakis stands." Then back to the acrobat and a midair freeze-frame: "But Congressman Gephardt? He's still up in the air."[86]

Gore and Gephardt went after each other. At a debate in Dallas, Gephardt likened Gore to a former general had who been Nixon's chief of staff and a recent GOP presidential candidate: "You've been sounding more like Al Haig than Al Gore." Gore had an effective comeback: "That line sounds more like Richard Nixon than Richard Gephardt."[87] The two had an intense rivalry because they were competing for the same constituency: moderate and conservative whites. Gore ran as the defense hawk and Gephardt as the trade hawk; otherwise, their differences were nominal. Gore aide Roy M. Neel noted, "This was really a campaign between Gore and Gephardt, at the tier below Dukakis. Jackson was just out there doing his thing and getting support as well. But Gore and Gephardt just ripped at each other and Gore got very tough on Gephardt. It was more of a style issue than substance."[88]

Gore had more money and had been focusing on the South, while Gephardt was slogging through Iowa. When Super Tuesday arrived on March 8, Gephardt only won his home state of Missouri, while Gore took Arkansas, Kentucky, North Carolina, Oklahoma, and Tennessee, along with the Nevada caucuses. That result was far short of the Super Tuesday sweep that Gore had needed.[89]

The big winner was Jesse Jackson. He had less money than the other candidates, but he did not need as much because he enjoyed high name identification and was a natural draw for free media. In the 1984 primaries, he had lost part of the black vote to Mondale. This time, he was running a more professional and substantive campaign, and his African American support was around 90 percent. With Gephardt, Gore, and Dukakis splitting most of the white vote, Jackson won five states in which African Americans made up at least a third of the Democratic primary electorate: Alabama, Georgia, Louisiana, Mississippi, and Virginia. Jackson did so well because the black share of the Democratic primary electorate had grown, partially from his 1984 registration efforts. Another demographic change contributed a smaller portion of Jackson's vote, albeit one with implications for the future. Even as Jackson lost Arkansas and North Carolina to Gore, he narrowly won voters with postgraduate degrees. In Florida, Dukakis won every education category, but his margin was smaller among voters with more schooling. He carried voters with less than a high school education with 43 percent to 18 percent for Jackson, whereas his margin among postgraduate degree holders was 37–26 percent.[90] In the years to come, the ranks of the highly educated would continue to grow within the Democratic Party, and these voters would lean toward progressive candidates.

Going into Super Tuesday, Dukakis had assets. The first, of course, was the biggest treasury of any Democratic candidate. Although Gore spent nearly as much on the Southern Super Tuesday states as Dukakis did ($2.9 million to $3 million), good polling led Dukakis to allocate his resources more effectively. Whereas Gore spent across the map, Dukakis put most of his money into the two states where he had the best chance: Florida and Texas.[91] John Sasso, who drew up Dukakis's campaign strategy before the Biden affair forced his ouster, later told scholar Elaine Kamarck: "We watched the southern Super Tuesday and realized that because of Florida and Texas it was pretty good for us. Florida had a lot of northern Jews and Texas had Hispanics, and Mike spoke Spanish. So we agreed not to say anything to anyone about this in order to keep expectations low."[92] Dukakis won 78 percent of Jewish voters in the Florida primary and 60 percent of Hispanics in Texas.[93] In addition to these states, he won primaries in

Maryland, Rhode Island, and his home state of Massachusetts, along with caucuses in Hawaii, Idaho, Washington, and American Samoa.

Super Tuesday had produced a result that its creators had not intended: the top two Democratic candidates were Michael Dukakis and Jesse Jackson.

A DIFFERENT KIND OF VOTE

On March 15, Simon won the Illinois beauty contest primary, with 42 percent to 32 percent for Jackson. The result was hardly a shock. Simon was the home state favorite and had the backing of Chicago's "regular" Democratic leaders, who could still turn out votes. Jackson had lived in Chicago and enjoyed support in its African American community. (Mayor Harold Washington had endorsed Jackson in fall 1987, only to die of a heart attack a couple of months later.) In the separate election for convention delegates, Simon had a wider lead because Jackson's support was so densely packed in African American districts.[94] The victory did nothing to change the contours of the race because Simon had won no other contests, and political leaders had taken it for granted that he would win his own state.

The most surprising outcome came on Saturday, March 26, when Jesse Jackson won 53 percent of the vote in Michigan's precinct caucuses. Dukakis was second with 29 percent and Gephardt a distant third with 13 percent. This result shook up the Dukakis campaign and finally ended the candidacy of Gephardt, who had hoped that his trade message would work in the center of auto manufacturing. Two days later, he announced that he was ending his presidential campaign and seeking reelection to the House.

Caucuses require a deeper time commitment from participants than primaries, so turnout is lower and tends to favor candidates with good organization and energized supporters. Michigan does not register voters by party, so we cannot measure turnout as a share of registered Democrats. The presidential vote offers a rough proxy. The 213,000 Michiganders who took part in the Democratic caucuses equaled just 13 percent of the number who voted Democratic in the fall. Jackson had intense support in Detroit's African American community, and adviser Richard Hatcher noted another source of strength: "I believe that we won Michigan simply because Michigan had same-day, on-site voter registration. College students came out, registered, and voted for Jesse Jackson in large numbers."[95] Jackson's victory made the cover of *Time*, where Walter Shapiro wrote: "At last the Democrats have a heavyweight contender, a candidate who can win a major Northern industrial state away from his native turf. . . . With his stunning upset victory in last Saturday's Michigan caucuses, Jesse Jackson has staked his claim to be taken seriously as the party's front runner."[96] On CBS, Dan Rather also bestowed front-runner status on Jackson.[97] Even after Dukakis won the Connecticut primary a few days later, the New York Times estimated that Jackson led him 638–637 in convention delegates. [98]

In the pre-internet era, these news sources influenced ordinary voters and political elites. Their proclamations of front-runner status came at a high cost to Jackson. Campaign manager Gerald Austin said: "Because we won in Michigan, people were saying, 'This guy could be president. This guy could win this nomination. I don't know that I want to vote for him. When I was voting for him as sort of a protest because I liked what he had to say, that was one thing. But now I've got to look at it in a different way. It's a different kind of vote.'"[99] Newsweek reporters Peter Goldman and Tom Mathews wrote: "A voter for Jackson was no longer just a protest vote for a movement preacher after Michigan; in one stroke, his victory certified him as a serious candidate for President and made it all but impossible for him to win."[100]

Voters who cared about qualifications noted Jackson's lack of government experience and the questions surrounding his self-help organization, Operation PUSH.[101] Those who cared about electability would have gotten sobering news from a March 1988 New York Times survey showing that 51 percent of registered voters would not support him under any circumstances, while just 32 percent said so about Dukakis.[102] Part of the opposition stemmed from his inexperience, his positions, and his purported anti-Semitism. Some stemmed from prejudice. In 1987, 79 percent of respondents told Gallup that they would vote for a well-qualified presidential candidate of their own party who happened to be black. Though this figure was higher than the 37 percent who answered in the affirmative in the summer of 1958, it was well below than the 93 percent that Gallup recorded late in 2007, a year before Barack Obama's victory.

After Michigan, the next major contest was the Wisconsin primary. Simon was still trying to hang on, hoping that he might have an outside chance in a Midwestern state with a progressive tradition. Jackson wanted to show that he could take a primary in a non-Southern state. He was so eager to win Wisconsin that he resorted to some old-fashioned pandering. "The fact is farmers deserve fair prices and workers deserve fair wages and the rich must pay fair taxes,'" he said at a dairy farm in a small Wisconsin town. "The reality is if urban people are working, they can pay a few more pennies for a glass of milk or for a cone of ice cream or for a loaf of bread."[103] (A quarter century later, Twitter would have lit up with charges of hypocrisy—that he was saying one thing to hungry poor people in cities and another to farmers in a state with a large dairy sector.) Both Jackson and Simon fell short. Dukakis took Wisconsin by 47 percent, 19 points ahead of Jackson. Simon got just 5 percent, and dropped out two days later.

Gore's third-place finish in Wisconsin was not enough to put him into the top tier, so he needed to do well in the next big contest, New York. A few days before the April 19 primary, he got the endorsement of New York City mayor Ed Koch. Gore hoped that such a high-profile backer could rescue him from single-digit purgatory, where the polls had been placing him. Instead, Koch probably did him more harm than good. Over his long political career, Koch had evolved from a young reformer to an aging curmudgeon whose administration was oozing with scandal.[104] New Yorkers thought that the city's race relations were getting worse, and Koch was no help.[105] Before the Gore endorsement, he said that Jews would have to be "crazy" to vote for Jackson, and he accused Jackson of lying about cradling Martin Luther King as he lay dying.[106] The comments angered African Americans without shifting any white votes. More broadly, Koch was presiding over the crime-ridden dystopia that Tom Wolfe had recently described in his novel, *The Bonfire of the Vanities.* Just before Christmas, the shooting of a nineteen-year-old man in Staten Island would become the city's 1,842nd killing of the year—an all-time record.[107]

Gore tried to make crime an issue in the New York campaign. Journalist Robert Shogan reported on a debate exchange in which Gore got to put a question directly to Dukakis:

[Gore] brought up a prison reform program that Dukakis had sponsored in Massachusetts, which granted weekend passes to prisoners, including some serving life sentences for murder. As Gore noted, 11 of these convicts failed to return, and two committed murders.

"If you were elected President, would you advocate a similar program for federal penitentiaries?" Gore asked to hoots and laughter from the audience.

"Al, the difference between you and me is that I have run a criminal justice system and you never have," Dukakis replied heatedly. "Let me tell you that I'm very proud of my record when it comes to fighting crime."

But Gore insisted that Dukakis answer the question directly, and the governor said: "Obviously not."[108]

Most New Yorkers did not notice that exchange. A Bush opposition researcher did. As the next two chapters will explain, the GOP's handling of the furlough program would become the most controversial aspect of the fall campaign.

Dukakis won the New York primary decisively, 51 percent to 37 percent for Jackson. Gore's meager 10 percent earned him an exit from the race two days later. Now that it was a two-man contest, moderate-to-conservative white Democrats coalesced around Dukakis, putting him on a glide path to victory. Of the remaining primaries, Jackson won only in the District of Columbia. Dukakis won all the rest by margins ranging from 19 points in Oregon to 70 points in North Dakota. By early June, he clinched the Democratic nomination.

For a defeated candidate, Jackson still made an impressive showing. On the night that Dukakis won the New York primary, Jackson edged him out the Vermont caucuses. Though Dukakis had earlier come out ahead in the nonbinding primary, the caucuses determined the delegate count. Jackson's energized base and good organization earned him a victory. "In Vermont, more than in any other state, white people did not hesitate to vote for Jesse Jackson," said Jackson state coordinator Liz Blum, who added that Jackson fared better in the caucuses because "it takes more of an effort to go to a caucus."[109] A *New York Times* analysis of primary exit polls estimated that Jackson won about 2.1 million white votes in 1988, compared with 650,000 four years earlier. His share of the white vote more than doubled, from 5 percent to 12 percent.[110] In the June 7 California primary, the last big-state contest, Jackson got 35 percent of whites with a graduate degree and 42 percent of white liberals.[111] These signs of support for a progressive candidate offered a hint of where the Democratic Party would eventually be heading.

IDEOLOGY AND COMPETENCE

Jackson did not have the nomination, but he did have leverage. His 1,219 delegates (out of 4,162) were enough to cause headaches for Dukakis on the Democratic convention floor. Dukakis needed a robust African American turnout in November, which he might not get if Jackson were to withhold his endorsement.

What did Jesse Jackson want? Shortly after the California primary, he suggested that he was the best choice for the vice presidential nomination. "Any combination of criteria used historically—I match those criteria," he said. "No one else at this point that's active in politics has shown the breadth of support I have shown at the voting polls. No one else has shown the ability to impact upon the country's tone and the party's priorities as I have shown."[112] No one else had the depth of opposition either. In a survey of Democratic convention delegates, a majority said that putting Jackson on the ticket would hurt the party's chances in their own states.[113] Dukakis never seriously considered Jackson, but he also never explicitly said in public that Jackson was out of the running.[114] Jackson was disappointed that he did not get the vice presidency, and he resented Dukakis's failure to give him advance notice of his eventual choice. He did get other things, however.

Dukakis insisted on a brief thematic party platform instead of a litany of positions. He agreed to themes that pleased Jackson. Issue adviser Robert Borosage said: "The reason we didn't have a real fight over the platform is that the Dukakis people gave us so much of what we wanted—as long as we were willing to accept language so broad and generalized that the ideas sound innocuous. Seventy percent of the platform is actually from Jackson's agenda, but you'd never be able to figure that out unless you were an expert."[115] Among other things, it borrowed one of Jackson's signature phrases when it blamed the Reagan administration for "economic violence against poor and working people." It also alluded to Jackson's proposals for tax increases and a defense freeze by saying that "reducing the deficit requires that the wealthy and corporations pay their fair share and that we restrain Pentagon spending."[116]

Dukakis also sought to make peace with Jackson over party rules. Although superdelegates did not decide the nomination in 1988, most of them supported Dukakis. Jackson argued that superdelegates stifled the people's voice, and he sought to reduce their ranks. Dukakis yielded to him on the point, though the Democratic National Committee reversed the agreement in 1989. Another deal would last. Jackson noted that his delegate count did not correspond to his share of the aggregate vote in primaries and caucuses, and he blamed practices such as the direct election of delegates. With Dukakis's blessing, the convention passed a resolution requiring that delegate allocation be proportional to the expressed preferences of primary voters or caucus participants.[117] As we shall discuss in the final chapter, proportional allocation would shape every subsequent Democratic nomination race; it would be especially significant in Barack Obama's 2008 victory.

For vice president, Dukakis picked the un-Jackson. As David Rosenbaum of the *New York Times* pointed out, Senator Lloyd Bentsen of Texas bore a passing resemblance to Bush: "Bentsen is a lanky Texan from a wealthy family, a bomber pilot in World War II who earned a fortune in business and served briefly in the House of Representatives before moving into bigger political pastures."[118] Bentsen looked like a shrewd choice. No Democrat had ever won the White House without Texas. As recently as 1976, Carter had carried the state, which was still strongly Democratic at the grassroots level. Democrats controlled both chambers of the state's legislature and most of its US House seats. Bush may have been a Texan, but he had never won a statewide general election, and he had lost the 1970 Senate race to none other than Lloyd Bentsen. In 1976 and 1982, Bentsen had easily won reelection, and in 1988, he remained popular among Texas voters. The Democratic primary had suggested that Dukakis appealed to the state's Hispanic voters, so it was plausible to think that the ticket might have an outside chance of winning the state—or at least a chance of forcing the Republicans to divert valuable resources into defending it. Aside from geography and the Electoral College, Bentsen passed the gravitas test. His experience in government and business, along with his obvious intelligence and dignified manner, made it easy to picture him as a potential president. Dukakis could be confident that Bentsen would not generate costly distractions, as the party's vice presidential nominees had done in 1972 and 1984.

Furthermore, Bentsen was acceptable to a broad spectrum of Democrats. "He sees himself as a moderate Democrat," his legislative director told political scientist Nicol Rae. "Conservatives see him as conservative. Moderates see him as moderate, and liberals see him as moderate. He's conservative on some issues and liberal on others."[119] Political timing had helped him achieve this balance. He had won election to the House in 1948 but declined to run for a fourth term in 1954 in order to make his fortune in the insurance business. He did not serve in office again until his 1970 victory over Bush. This sabbatical from politics not only allowed him to become wealthier but also kept him from casting roll-call votes on the civil rights bills of the 1950s and 1960s. As a conservative Texan, he would have faced intense local pressure to vote no, as his immediate successor did on the 1957 Civil Rights Act. Such a voting record might have made him unacceptable for the 1988 Democratic ticket. But he reentered office just as Southern Democratic politicians were adapting to the changes wrought by the civil rights era. Though he was critical of racial-balance busing, Bentsen ended up supporting most civil rights measures that came to the Senate floor.[120]

The Democratic convention was a hit. Texas treasurer Ann Richards delivered a rousing keynote that scalded the GOP candidate's verbal clumsiness: "Poor George, he can't help it. He was born with a silver foot in his mouth."[121] Jim Hightower, the state's agriculture commissioner and a Jesse Jackson supporter, waged class warfare. He said that Bush belonged to "an upper-class world in which wealth is yours at birth," adding, "He is a man who was born on third base and thinks he hit a triple."[122] House majority whip Tony Coelho asked: "When the titans of Wall Street were looting the small investors on Main Street, where was George Bush?"[123] (The following year, Coelho resigned amid questions about his financial dealings and ties to the savings-and-loan industry.) Jesse Jackson's convention speech struck a tone of unity but with a touch of backhanded praise for the nominee. "I've watched his perspective grow as his environment has expanded," he said, alluding to Dukakis's platform concessions. "Mike Dukakis's parents were a doctor and a teacher; my parents a maid, a beautician and a janitor. There's a great gap between Brookline, Massachusetts, and Haney Street in the Fieldcrest Village housing project in Greenville, South Carolina."[124]

One rare low point was the speech placing Dukakis's name in nomination. Arkansas governor Bill Clinton, making his first appearance before a national audience, badly misjudged the length of his remarks and went far over his time limit. After his tedious discourse, he got an enthusiastic response by uttering the words "In conclusion." The reviews were scathing, and there was some talk that Clinton might have scarred his political future. His instinct for self-preservation was intact, however, and he soon redeemed himself with a self-deprecating appearance on *The Tonight Show.*

When it came time to accept the nomination, Dukakis entered the hall to the strains of Neil Diamond's "Coming to America," a song that evoked patriotism and emphasized Dukakis's immigrant heritage. His delivery was strong and confident, and he brushed aside GOP attacks on his liberalism: "This election isn't about ideology; it's about competence. It's not about meaningless labels; it's about American values—old-fashioned values like accountability and responsibility and respect for the truth."[125] At the end, the delegates cheered long and hard, and Jesse Jackson embraced his former rival.

The party was unified and energized. In the aftermath of the convention, one poll showed Dukakis with a 17-point lead over Bush.[126]

6

THE GENERAL ELECTION

THE TRIUMPH OF THE FUNDAMENTALS

Like Mondale's postconvention bump in 1984, Dukakis's surge did not last. A survey after the Republican convention found that Bush had leapt ahead of Dukakis, 46 to 40 percent, despite widespread misgivings about Quayle.[1] Bush's "read my lips" speech had gotten a good reception from Republicans, but it was hardly enough to produce a big shift in public opinion. There were other reasons for the campaign's reversal of fortunes.

Ronald Reagan posed a question to the audience at the end of his single debate with Jimmy Carter in 1980: "Are you better off than you were four years ago?" Those ten words sum up what most presidential elections are about. In 1976, Jimmy Carter won because America had suffered an oil embargo, a deep recession, Watergate, and a humiliating defeat in Vietnam. Four years later, Reagan's question carried weight because we had endured another oil shock, another recession, and another foreign humiliation, this time with the hostages in Iran. George Bush was not as charismatic as Reagan, but if he had been the GOP nominee in 1980, he probably would have won too.

Eight years later, he was his party's standard-bearer at last. His fate would now depend mostly on things outside of his control.

A YEAR OF PEACE AND PROSPERITY

"The stock market has often portended economic declines," the *New York Times* reported after the crash of October 1987. "What a decline such as has occurred may mean is hard to imagine. . . . Large firms may have to cut back, and it is not inconceivable that the ripples may spread to the banking community, which has been edging into the securities business. That could lead to layoffs, and further economic dislocations. 'One word is operative out there now,' said one very shaken trader. 'Fright.'"[2] Republicans worried. If the stock market drop had been the leading edge of a recession, any credible Democrat would beat any Republican in the 1988 election, end of story.

For the GOP, the shadows soon vanished. Unlike the crash of 2008, the Wall Street turmoil of 1987 turned out not to be part of a broader economic panic. Instead, it grew out of specific features of the stock market, such as program trading. The market soon recovered, and the national economy kept growing during every quarter of 1988. Joblessness had been falling throughout Reagan's second term, and the trend continued throughout the election year. Inflation, which had been a major worry when it reached double-digit levels in the late 1970s and early 1980s, was now under control and off the public's radar. The favorable economic conditions showed up in surveys of economic well-being and right track–wrong track numbers.[3] This setting would have given just about any Republican candidate an edge over any Democrat.[4] As out-party candidates must when the economy is flourishing, Lloyd Bentsen gamely tried to argue that the good times were not really real. "My fellow Democrats, it is easy enough to create an illusion of prosperity," he said at the Democratic convention. "All you have to do is write hot checks for $200 billion a year. That's what the Reagan–Bush Administration has done. That's how they doubled our national debt in just seven years."[5] And as usual when the public is happy with the economy, the argument did not take.

One true economic dark spot was the savings-and-loan industry. As it happened, 1988 was the peak year for failures of federally insured thrift institutions, though more would collapse in the years to come.[6] For several reasons, the issue seldom came up in the presidential campaign. First, many of the thrift failures took place in Texas. Notwithstanding Lloyd Bentsen's presence on the Democratic ticket, Texas was not a swing state, and so it got little media attention from journalists on the campaign trail. Second, to the extent that the press did cover the crisis that year, the stories appeared on the financial pages, not the political pages.[7] Third, and most important, politicians in both parties had good reason to keep mum about savings and loans. A 1980 law, which gained bipartisan support and President Carter's signature, had the unintended consequence of encouraging thrifts to make risky investments. Two years later, President Reagan signed another bipartisan bill that further eased regulations, and arguably made matters worse. Democratic and Republican lawmakers alike had close ties to the industry. As mentioned in the previous chapter, one was House Democratic whip Tony Coelho. The Speaker of the House, Jim Wright, along with other Texas lawmakers, had taken campaign contributions and other favors from savings-and-loan operators. When Dukakis tried to raise the issue, both Bentsen and Wright privately urged him to drop it, which he did.[8]

The Republicans could run on peace as well as prosperity. During the 1980 campaign and for much of his first term, Democrats tried to raise fears that Reagan would start a nuclear war. Over time, it became evident that the skies were free of mushroom clouds. US–Soviet relations improved when Mikhail Gorbachev came to power, and in May 1988, the Senate approved Reagan's INF treaty, marking the first agreement to cut back on offensive nuclear weapons. Reagan then visited Moscow, where he said that the Soviet Union had ceased to be an evil empire.[9] The Cold War was not quite over yet, but Democrats had lost the apocalypse card.

Similarly, the specter of conventional war was no longer as scary. In 1985, Reagan's advisers pondered military options for toppling the Marxist regime in Nicaragua, including an invasion.[10] The idea was hardly far-fetched: in 1983, Reagan had made such a move on Grenada. Congressional Democrats pushed back hard against war in Nicaragua, and talk of invasion died down. The administration continued to supply the rebels, both lawfully and through the zany Iran–Contra scheme. But because of the Democratic wall of resistance, Reagan could go no further. In the twenty-first century, we can see something that the thwarted hawks of the time failed to grasp: Democrats had unintentionally done the GOP a huge political favor. America's limited involvement in Nicaragua was unpopular, but a full-scale commitment could have become a political disaster. Even if an American invasion had succeeded at first, a bloody insurgency might well have followed, as would happen years later in Iraq. A Nicaraguan quagmire would have damaged the GOP as badly in the late 1980s as the Iraqi hurt locker would in 2006 and 2008.

One fundamental aspect of the 1988 campaign gave hope to the Democrats. Not since Roosevelt and Truman had either party held the White House for more than two consecutive terms. After eight years, Democrats reasoned, voters would think that it was time for a change. Bush seemed to be at a special disadvantage because no incumbent vice president had won the presidency since Martin Van Buren. Although the "time for a change" impulse is real, it does not work in isolation.[11] The desire for change does handicap the in-party, but it dooms it only if other burdens are weighing down the incumbent side. In every one of the post–World War II eight-year-itch elections, something else was in play: the Korean War (1952), a recession (1960), the Vietnam War (1968), and the lingering effects of Watergate (1976). Throughout much of 1987, Iran–Contra potentially loomed as Watergate redux, but as we have seen, it had faded by the end of the year. Amid peace and prosperity, 1988 Gallup surveys consistently showed approval of Reagan's job performance running ahead of disapproval by double digits.[12]

Despite the burden of being standard-bearer for a two-term in-party, Bush still had the other fundamentals on his side. During the summer of 1988, some politicians took their eye off the basics. Instead, they followed early polls and media speculation suggesting that Dukakis was the stronger candidate.[13] Memories of the previous election should have given them pause about staring at these shiny objects. In both 1984 and 1988, media attention gave a temporary and misleading survey lift to the Democratic candidate. The Bush campaign, like the Reagan campaign before it, would now use some muscle to push the contest back into its natural shape.

THE CAMPAIGNS

In one way, the Bush and Dukakis campaigns were competing on even terms. In 1988, both sides were still working within the post-Watergate presidential campaign finance system, which would break down during the early twenty-first century. In return for forgoing direct contributions, a campaign would receive public funds coming from an income-tax checkoff. Bush and Dukakis each got $46.1 million in federal money. Each national party committee could also spend up to $8.3 million to supplement the federal money. There was some outside spending as well, but nothing on the scale that would become common after the 2010 *Citizens United* decision. Organized labor spent $25 million for Dukakis and $5 million for Bush. Independent expenditures—spending by groups that could not directly coordinate with campaigns or parties—amounted to $6.8 million for Bush and only $600,000 for Dukakis.[14]

Both campaigns underwent a change in leadership for the general election. On this score, Bush came out ahead. During the summer, when his poll numbers were sagging and backbiting was plaguing his headquarters, Bush asked James Baker to step down as secretary of the treasury and take over as campaign chairman. In bureaucracy speak, Bush was layering Atwater, keeping him in the job of campaign manager but making clear that he would answer to Baker. Whatever resentment Atwater and other campaign aides may have harbored, they knew that they had to accept the new

Baker order.[15] Bush regarded the wealthy, Princeton-educated Baker as a social peer and close friend; he had even served as Baker's daughter's godfather. As a cold-eyed ex-marine, Baker knew how to give orders and make them stick. As a former White House chief of staff and Cabinet member, Baker was media savvy as well as fluent in foreign and domestic policy. Atwater, whose knowledge of the issues was minimal at best, would have to admit that Baker would be a far more effective spokesperson.

Bush's postconvention surge had an effect on the Dukakis campaign. Fearing that he was losing the initiative, he brought back John Sasso, whom he had fired the previous year because of the Biden attack video. With the official title of vice chairman, Sasso expected to be the de facto head of the campaign. Estrich had other ideas, and their infighting would hamper the campaign through November.

Having spent his entire career in a liberal state, Dukakis suffered from a special kind of parochialism. In 1978, he had lost his first reelection bid to Ed King in part because economic conditions had forced him to break an imprudent pledge not to raise taxes. He spent the next few years retooling at Harvard's Kennedy School, then beat King over the issue of mismanagement. This experience reinforced his tendency to think of politics through the lens of economic policy and public administration. The key to politics, he thought, was to run government smoothly and explain yourself logically. It was natural for him to say that the 1988 election was about competence, not ideology.

There was a problem with this attitude. Though he had campaigned in Democratic primaries and caucuses across the nation, he had little first-hand experience with what political observers would later call red-state America. In places such as Texas and Florida, the kinds of voters who took part in Democratic nomination politics were not typical of the broader electorate. In the America of NASCAR, Waffle House, and small-group Bible study, there were plenty of people who had conservative views of social and cultural issues. Dukakis failed to grasp that these voters might see him as something other than a practical problem solver. Dukakis, wrote Sidney Blumenthal, "did not even understand his own liberalism as liberalism, but as rationalism."[16] His staff was ill-equipped to make up for this blind spot. Sasso was a seasoned operative, but only within the confines of Massachusetts politics. Estrich was on leave from her regular job as a tenured professor at Harvard Law School.

The Dukakis campaign lacked strategic focus. One problem was that the fundamentals favored Bush. "If the issues on voters' minds are America's place in the world and the family squeeze, we win," Sasso reportedly said at the time. "If it's peace and prosperity, we lose."[17] Because peace and prosperity usually dominate appraisals of the in-party, Dukakis automatically had a weak hand. Another problem was Dukakis's preference for talking about competence. One aide told the New York Times: "We want this campaign to be 'steady and dependable' versus 'Dan Rather and tension city.'"[18] This approach did not make much sense. In the specific case of the Dan Rather interview, Bush's posture was aggressive but hardly unhinged. More generally, the "steady and dependable" image did not set up a good contrast with Bush. If anything, the most potent criticism of his long record in high office was that he had been overly cautious. That was the very quality for which comedian Dana Carvey lampooned him in a Saturday Night Live sketch: "What am I going to do? Can't say. Wouldn't be prudent. Got to watch out for the vision thing. Wouldn't be prudent."[19]

Despite Bush's easily parodied Eastern mannerisms, he and his team knew red-state America. Bush, Baker, and Atwater had come up through the South, and the campaign had recently fought off Pat Robertson. They also had years of experience in Washington politics and national campaigns, so they could anticipate Democratic attacks. Ever the student of Sun Tzu, Atwater believed that Bush should not stay on the defensive about the Reagan record but instead should go on the offensive about the Dukakis record. Though Bush gave many policy speeches, his strategists knew that the media would ignore them. Roger Ailes put it memorably:

> Let's face it, there are three things that the media are interested in: pictures, mistakes and attacks. That's the one sure way of getting coverage. You try to avoid as many mistakes as you can. You try to give them as many pictures as you can. And if you need coverage, you attack, and you will get coverage. It's my orchestra pit theory of politics. You have two guys on stage and one guy says, "I have a solution to the Middle East problem," and the other guy falls in the orchestra pit, who do you think is going to be on the evening news?[20]

As soon as the nomination campaign was over, Atwater assigned James P. Pinkerton to identify points of attack. Atwater said: "Actually, I gave him a three-by-five card and I said, 'You come back with this three-by-five card, but you can use both sides, and bring me the issues that we need in this campaign.'"[21] Pinkerton later recalled: "So I actually typed on a little 3 × 5 card, here's everything that's wrong with Dukakis, furloughs, whatever, oppose every defense program known to man, I managed to get it all into one card and know that became something of a useful document in terms, as they reproduced it various ways."[22] Focus groups confirmed that social issues such as the furlough program might be particularly effective. Baker had no qualms about greenlighting the use of these issues.

FURLOUGHS

It is no mystery why crime was an issue in the campaign. The rate of violent offenses had nearly quadrupled since 1960. In 1988 alone, homicide took 20,675 lives—more than would die in all of America's wars during the next quarter century.[23] The bloodshed led to calls for tough action, and 79 percent of Americans now favored the death penalty.[24] Dukakis nevertheless opposed capital punishment, saying that imprisonment was enough of a deterrent. From a political standpoint, his support for furloughs for first-degree murderers undercut his position. One case would cause him trouble.

On the night of October 26, 1974, seventeen-year-old Joseph Fournier was working at a gasoline station in Lawrence, Massachusetts, when William R. Horton and two other men robbed him. His dead body, with nineteen stab wounds, later turned up in a trash barrel. The authorities caught Fournier's attackers and charged them with murder. In some states, these circumstances might have led to the death penalty, but Dukakis had vetoed a bill to restore capital punishment in the state. A court gave the three the most severe sentence possible under the law: life imprisonment without parole. Massachusetts, however, allowed brief furloughs for prisoners serving such sentences. Dukakis had pocket-vetoed a 1976 bill that would have ended this program, so it continued. Horton eventually had nine furloughs without incident. On June 6, 1986, he left prison for his tenth and never came back. On April 3, 1987, in Oxon Hill, Maryland, he broke into the home of Cliff Barnes, binding and torturing him. When Barnes's fiancée arrived, Horton raped her twice. Barnes escaped and called the police. Horton tried to get away in a stolen car, and after a violent chase, police arrested him. A Maryland court sentenced him to life in prison. The judge told him: "You should never breathe a breath of fresh air again. You should be locked up until you die."[25]

The incident got publicity in Massachusetts. The *Lawrence Eagle-Tribune* ran 175 articles on the incident and related problems in the furlough program. In 1988, this reporting won the Pulitzer Prize.[26] The story of Horton's crimes in Maryland stunned the family of murder victim Joseph Fournier. "We really were kind of confused," said his sister. "We thought he was sentenced to life without parole. How could he be out on furlough?"[27] She started a campaign for a ballot measure to end furloughs for first-degree murderers. Dukakis balked, but after the state legislature passed such a measure, he reluctantly signed it. In the meantime, he and his administration had given plenty of ammunition to Republicans eager to portray him as clueless about crime and cold to victims. "Don't forget that Mr. Horton had nine previous successful furloughs," said Dukakis's secretary of human services after the Maryland arrest.[28] When Barnes and his wife (who had married him after the ordeal) sought to speak with Dukakis about the furlough program, he brushed them off. "I don't see any particular value in meeting with people," he said. "I'm satisfied we have the kind of furlough policy we should have."[29]

Even in those pre-Web days, any research on Dukakis would have quickly turned up the furlough story. As a previous chapter explained, however, the Bush campaign did not have the luxury of focusing on its likely general-election opponent until it had vanquished Bob Dole. And so on a spring day when Pinkerton was reading a transcript of the New York primary debate in which Gore had raised the issue against Dukakis, he was surprised. He called Andrew Card, a Bush campaign official who had served in the Massachusetts legislature. "We had no great insight into this, but Card said, 'Yes, this has been a huge thing up here, this whole prison furlough thing.'" Despite the *Lawrence Eagle-Tribune*'s Pulitzer Prize, said Pinkerton, "nobody else had heard of it, it was just sort of totally hiding in plain sight. . . . *The Lawrence Eagle-Tribune* had done all our work for us, it was just like discovering gold."[30] A campaign focus group in Paramus, New Jersey, suggested that the issue might move votes, so Bush started talking about it. "What did the Democratic governor of Massachusetts think he was doing when he let convicted first-degree murderers out on weekend passes?" Bush asked in a mid-June speech. "Even after one of the criminals brutally raped a woman and stabbed her fiancé, why didn't he admit his mistake?"[31] *Reader's Digest* gave a boost to the issue in July, when it published a story about Horton with the provocative title "Getting Away with Murder."

The furlough issue frustrated Dukakis. Although Massachusetts was the only state to furlough prisoners serving life without parole, nearly every state had some furlough program, and many granted furloughs to killers serving life with the possibility of parole. "A distinction without a difference," Dukakis told the *New York Times,* adding that that "premeditated murder is premeditated murder."[32] From a legal perspective, Dukakis had a point. Politically, he had an albatross. An electorate that so strongly favored the death penalty for murderers would surely have seen all such programs as a scandal. To such voters, Dukakis did not deserve a pass just because other states had programs that were nearly as lenient.

Did this issue cause Bush's late-summer surge in the polls? The *Reader's Digest* article did not immediately drive coverage in the mainstream media. One analysis of the national press found only twenty-five stories about Horton between June 13 and October 2.[33] Bush's acceptance speech made only a fleeting reference to the furlough program. Although the issue may have helped Bush at the margins, it seems unlikely that summer media coverage was heavy enough to shift voter sentiment all by itself.

The furlough issue gathered momentum when it appeared on television ads. The first came from an independent-expenditure group called the National Security Political Action Committee (NSPAC), which had been raising money for a project titled "Americans for Bush." In May, the Bush campaign's counsel had written the group, saying that it disapproved of its activities and demanding that it stop using Bush's name.[34] In June, the campaign filed a complaint with the Federal Election Commission.[35] The complaint did not discuss the content of any ads but instead accused the group of tricking donors into thinking that it was part of the Bush campaign. NSPAC kept scooping up checks, and in early September made a small cable television ad buy for a spot about crime. The spot mentioned Horton without showing him. After two weeks, it ran a new version of the ad showing ugly black-and-white photos of Horton.

> Bush and Dukakis on crime. Bush supports the death penalty for first degree murderers. Dukakis not only opposes the death penalty, he allowed first degree murderers to have weekend passes from prison. One was Willie Horton, who murdered a boy in a robbery, stabbing him 19 times. Despite a life sentence, Horton received 10 weekend passes from prison. Horton fled, kidnapped a young couple, stabbing the man and repeatedly raping his girlfriend. Weekend prison passes. Dukakis on crime.[36]

Critics questioned the factual assertions in the ad, pointing out that the furlough program had started under Republican governor Francis Sargent and that the trial court never determined which of Joseph Fournier's three attackers had stabbed him. But the far bigger issue was that it showed Horton's face—that of a violent black man who had raped a white woman. For decades to come, many commentators would call the ad a case of overt racism. In 2013, one Democratic strategist said that "it made white Americans—especially white southerners—raise an eyebrow and think, 'We can't have a man from Massachusetts releasing quote black criminals all across the country and letting them rape our white women and children.' That was the point of that ad."[37]

Atwater and Baker both wrote NSPAC to complain about the use of Bush's name, but neither asked the group to stop the Horton ads.[38] A Bush campaign lawyer explained that such a request would be legally problematic, "as it might raise a presumption that NSPAC's activities were coordinated with the campaign, if NSPAC complied with the request."[39] To the end of his life, Atwater insisted that he had nothing to do with the NSPAC ad, and no hard evidence ever directly linked him to it. Roger Stone, who had recently been Atwater's business partner and who would later go on to greater notoriety, claimed many years later that Atwater was indeed responsible. "Atwater came in with this version that had Willie Horton's picture— and he said they were going to have an independent group put it on the air. . . . I told Atwater that it was a mistake, that we were winning the issue without having to resort to this racist crap."[40] There is no corroboration for Stone's story, and his purported complaint about "racist crap" seems wildly inconsistent with his rough approach to campaign politics.[41]

Even if there was no overt collaboration, it is likely that NSPAC picked up some pointers from the Bush campaign. The law forbids campaigns and outside groups from working together, but they have developed signal mechanisms to get around this ban. GOP guru Karl Rove said of his super PAC: "And you can't talk to the campaigns directly. You can't coordinate with them. But you can play bridge."[42] For instance, they can give press interviews laying out campaign themes and tactics, in hopes that the intended recipient will get the hint. Atwater might have been playing some bridge in 1988. At a July meeting in Atlanta, he noted Dukakis with his arm around Reverend Jesse Jackson and joked, "Willie Horton, for all I know, may turn out to be his [Dukakis's] running mate."[43] At a postelection conference, Atwater tried to walk it back: "I said it once. I said I was sorry I said it and apologize for it. That's the only time I mentioned it."[44] Still, once the ads aired, NSPAC sensed that it was getting a wink and a nod from the Bush campaign. "Officially," said the group's founder, "the campaign has to disavow themselves from me. Unofficially, I hear that they're thrilled about what we're doing."[45]

NSPAC had probably gotten an additional hint from the Bush forces, this one involving Horton's first name. Atwater kept referring to him as "Willie." The name stuck, even though it did not appear on official records.

Many years later, Horton told an interviewer: "My name is William. No one has ever called me 'Willie.'"[46] Was Atwater trying to send a racial signal with this nickname? He never said.

Personnel choices are another form of indirect coordination. People staffing campaigns and outside groups have often worked together in the past, so they know each other's moves as intimately as members of a repertory company know each other's lines. In 2012 and 2016, former aides to presidential contenders went to work for super PACs supporting them. In 1988, the man who made the Horton ad for NSPAC was Larry McCarthy, who had spent years working for Bush's media strategist, Roger Ailes. Another former Ailes employee who worked on the spot had simultaneously received compensation from NSPAC and the Bush campaign.[47] Did Ailes send his alumni any signals? Just before the NSPAC ads aired, he told *Time* magazine: "The only question is whether we depict Willie Horton with a knife in his hand or without it."[48]

In 1990, Ohio Democrats complained to the Federal Election Commission, charging illegal coordination between NSPAC and the Bush campaign. During FEC's brief investigation, Ailes gave a deposition. Just as Atwater had downplayed the Horton-as-running-mate line, Ailes said that he had not been talking seriously. "Yes, I did say something to a reporter for *Time* magazine in a joke. It was meant as a joke, and unfortunately, when you—it got a big laugh at the time—but when you read it in the press it isn't quite as funny."[49] When FEC's lawyers asked the NSPAC founder about her "I hear they're thrilled" comment, she answered: "Specifically, I don't know. It could be out context. I'm not sure. My premise—well, I shouldn't suppose what I was thinking. Because I really don't recall."[50] In the end, FEC decided that the evidence was inconclusive and dismissed the complaint.

After the Horton ad ended its run, the Bush campaign aired its own spot about the furlough program. The grainy black-and-white visual showed a group of criminals going into and out of a prison revolving door. The voice-over was ominous:

> As Governor Michael Dukakis vetoed mandatory sentences for drug dealers he vetoed the death penalty. His revolving door prison policy gave weekend furloughs to first degree murderers not eligible for parole. [Onscreen text: 268 Escaped] While out, many committed other crimes like kidnapping and rape, and many are still at large. Now Michael Dukakis says he wants to do for America what he's done for Massachusetts. America can't afford that risk.[51]

Ailes took care to cast a mostly white group of actors to play the prisoners. Nevertheless, the ad drew criticism for misleading viewers into thinking that Massachusetts was crawling with killers who had escaped while on furlough. Of the 268 escapees over the previous decade, four were murderers. At least seventy-two were on the books as escapees because they had come back from furlough more than two hours late. Only three were still at large, and none was a murderer.[52]

The NSPAC ad and the Bush "revolving door" ad both got coverage in the mainstream media. Many voters who did not see these spots in their original airings could learn about them in news stories. For most of the campaign, there was surprisingly little media discussion of the racial angle, though it is likely that voters knew that Horton was black. Later in October, Democrats raised the salience of the racial dimension by accusing the Bush campaign of playing to prejudice. "There have been a number of rather ugly race-conscious signals sent from that campaign," said Jesse Jackson.[53] Then the issue took an odd turn. Before the Democratic counterattack, one analysis found, racial resentment seemed to predict attitudes toward the candidates, to Bush's benefit. Afterward, the effect diminished.[54] To the extent that the furlough issue had an impact—and remember that Bush had pulled ahead of Dukakis before any of these ads were on the air—it worked only when the racial aspect was mostly below the line. As soon as race entered center stage, it stopped helping Bush.

OPPO YEAR

Other issues went down in political lore as Dukakis weaknesses. One involved the American Civil Liberties Union. On May 26, 1988, the *Los Angeles Times* ran the text of a Dukakis interview by Robert Scheer, the writer who had elicited Jimmy Carter's "lust in my heart" comment in a 1976 issue of *Playboy*. Scheer raised the question of pornography, mentioning a controversial report on the subject commissioned by conservative Attorney General Edwin Meese.

Q: How do you draw the line? Henry Miller? "Lady Chatterley's Lover"? D. H. Lawrence?

A: That's a good question and great people have been trying to make that distinction for years. I can't define it, but I know it when I see it, you know? All I'm saying is that, constitutionally, I make a distinction between those two things.

Q: When you say this thing about pornography are you endorsing the work of the Meese Commission?

A: No, no, no, no. Look, I'm a card-carrying member of the American Civil Liberties Union and I think you have to be very restrained, but I'm not somebody who takes the position that under no circumstances can society impose restrictions on material that, by any standard, is clearly pornographic.[55]

Dukakis was trying to stake out a moderate position, opposing certain kinds of pornography while affirming his support for civil liberties. The "card-carrying member of the American Civil Liberties Union" line was no mere figure of speech, because he had belonged since college. As an attorney and civil libertarian, he undoubtedly thought that his self-description made sense. And because it came up during an abstract discussion of the First Amendment, Dukakis probably was not thinking of other issues when he uttered those words. That oversight invited trouble. At a time of high crime rates and deep worry about the safety of the streets, the ACLU defended the rights of heinous criminals—a mission that was both deeply principled and widely unpopular. By proudly acknowledging his membership in the group, Dukakis had unwittingly given Bush a freebie—a term that opposition researchers use for a damaging on-the-record statement that requires no work to find. Bush pounced, often using the "card-carrying" line to suggest that Dukakis would privilege crooks over victims. Democrats called foul, saying that the phrase carried a whiff of McCarthyism and the hunt for "card-carrying communists."[56] The Bush camp countered that it was a verbatim quotation and that Dukakis literally was a card-carrying member of a group that defended criminals. Liberals leapt to Dukakis's defense, making sound arguments about the ACLU's good works and the constitutional right to counsel, but they did him no favors by keeping attention on crime, an issue that belonged to the GOP.

In early July, Bush had only had a slight advantage in a national poll asking whether each candidate would be "tough enough in dealing with crime and criminals." Just 23 percent said that description fit Bush, and Dukakis was close behind at 20 percent. By late October, 62 percent said Bush would be tough, compared with 37 percent for Dukakis.[57]

The "flag issue" also achieved great notoriety, much to the sardonic amusement of the press corps. Two postelection books were titled *Pledging Allegiance: The Last Campaign of the Cold War* and *Whose Broad Stripes and*

Bright Stars? The Trivial Pursuit of the Presidency, 1988. The whole matter had started more than a decade earlier, during Dukakis's ill-starred first term as governor, when he vetoed a 1977 bill imposing $5 fines on public-school teachers if they failed to lead their classes in saying the Pledge of Allegiance. Before acting, he got an advisory opinion from the state's Supreme Judicial Court. By a 5-to-2 vote, the court agreed with Dukakis that it was unconstitutional. The state justices cited *West Virginia v. Barnette,* a 1943 Supreme Court decision that government could not make students recite the pledge.[58] They concluded that "the rationale of the *Barnette* opinion applies as well to teachers as it does to students."[59] Both chambers of the legislature overrode the veto, and members of the House sang "God Bless America" as they did so.[60]

One of those legislators was Andrew Card. Eleven years later, when he answered Jim Pinkerton's questions about the furlough program, he also mentioned the pledge veto. Focus groups indicated that the issue could hurt Dukakis, so Bush started talking about it during the summer of 1988. At the end of his acceptance speech, he led the entire convention in reciting the pledge. As with furloughs and the ACLU, Dukakis's lawyerly instincts kicked in. "The flag-salute cases are studied by every first-year law student," he said.[61] When a media adviser complained to campaign manager Susan Estrich that the issue could hurt Dukakis, she showed her background as a Harvard law professor. "They're not going to get anywhere with that," she said. "Because we've got the Supreme Court answer."[62]

First-year law students may know *West Virginia v. Barnette.* Average voters do not. Legal merits aside, the 1977 veto override should have taught Dukakis that the pledge issue might matter to the public. A September survey by the *Los Angeles Times* asked: "How do you usually feel when someone doesn't pledge allegiance to the flag? Do you think of that person as being somewhat less patriotic or doesn't it concern you very much one way or the other?" Among those who took a side, 62 percent said that such people were less patriotic and only 33 percent said they were unconcerned.[63] In later September, Bush may have pushed the pledge a step too far with a much-mocked campaign stop at a flag factory. In any event, though, once he had exhausted this issue, he had others to use.

One was Boston Harbor. Bush repeatedly blamed Dukakis for the gross pollution of the harbor, running an ad that made it look like a radioactive hellscape.[64] Dukakis shared in the blame for grungy conditions in those waters, but so did the Reagan administration. "Nobody's hands are clean, including the EPA's," said the head of the Environmental Protection Agency's

Boston office.[65] No matter. The attack kept Dukakis on the defensive, and in a way that he had not anticipated. Democrats had long owned the issue of the environment, and Dukakis was running on his problem-solving ability. Now a Republican was poaching on the issue in a way that made Dukakis look negligent. It is not clear that the Boston Harbor issue moved many votes, but every hour that Dukakis spent defending his environmental record was an hour that he could not spend slamming Reagan–Bush policies.

If Democrats owned the environment, Republicans owned national security. In his acceptance speech, Bush had taken note of the recent thaw in the Cold War, and he credited Reagan's policy of peace through strength: "It happened when we acted on the ancient knowledge that strength and clarity lead to peace; weakness and ambivalence lead to war. You see, weakness tempts aggressors. Strength stops them. I will not allow this country to be made weak again, never."[66] Such rhetoric appealed to voters who were optimistic yet cautious about the Soviet Union. It especially resonated with people whose livelihoods depended on Cold War spending. In the late 1980s, national defense accounted for about seven million jobs. [67] Concentrations of military families and defense workers helped keep California and Washington State within reach for the GOP. Accordingly, Dukakis thought he needed to show his strength on national security. So it came to pass that his campaign arranged a photo opportunity at a General Dynamics facility in Sterling Heights, Michigan, where he would ride a sixty-eight-ton M1A1 Abrams main battle tank. Company officials insisted that he wear a helmet for safety reasons, and he complied.[68] The oversized headgear made him look like Snoopy from the *Peanuts* comic strip. Hilarity ensued. Roger Ailes quickly made an ad showing footage of the tank ride, with text and voiceover suggesting that Dukakis was weak on defense:

> He opposed new aircraft carriers. He opposed anti-satellite weapons. He opposed four missile systems, including the Pershing II missile deployment. Dukakis opposed the stealth bomber, a ground emergency warning system against nuclear testing. He even criticized our rescue mission to Grenada and our strike on Libya. And now he wants to be our commander in chief. America can't afford that risk.[69]

Like the Boston Harbor spot, "Tank Ride" took flak for its factual assertions. Among other things, Dukakis insisted that he supported the stealth bomber.[70] Ironically, Bush would end up presiding over a sharp decline in military spending. In fiscal year 1988, with the Cold War waning but still in effect, national defense accounted for 27.3 percent of the federal budget.

By 1992, after the fall of the Berlin Wall and the dissolution of the Soviet Union, that figure had fallen to 21.6 percent—a huge drop for a four-year period.[71]

In the fall of 1988, however, nobody knew how quickly the Cold War would end. The Soviet Union was still around, and Americans wanted a president who could stand up to it. Bush started with an edge on this score, and the "Tank Ride" attacks on Dukakis might have widened it slightly. In early September, poll respondents thought Bush was stronger on defense by a 55–32 percent margin. By late October, that advantage had ticked up to 58–33 percent.[72]

It is tough to measure the extent to which any ad affected the outcome of the election, especially one in which the fundamentals so strongly favored Bush. It is plausible, however, that the ads shored up Bush's margin and made it harder for Dukakis to overperform. The Democratic candidate had issues that potentially appealed to large swaths of the public—educational opportunity and the economic squeeze on many working families—but first he had to keep people from laughing at his Snoopy helmet. Whatever their impact on the 1988 race, as we shall see, these ads did have significant and unforeseen consequences in the years to come.

DUKAKIS: NEGATIVES AND NEGATIVITY

The 1988 campaign involved a remarkable role reversal. The incumbent party candidate had a clear and aggressive attack strategy, whereas the challenger did not. Although Dukakis ran more negative television ads than Bush did, they did not add up to a coherent message.[73] Much of his problem was situational. When the unemployment lines are growing, it is no trick to convince voters that it is time for a change. At a time of peace and prosperity, the out-party must dig up other issues. Deficits had been mounting since the early 1980s, and the Dukakis campaign argued that the Republicans were "mortgaging our children's future."[74] Although the criticism of deficit spending was rational on the merits, it did not stir the public. In isolation, the deficit and the debt are abstract issues that seem remote from everyday life. The deficit had been rising four years earlier, when Reagan won forty-nine states. Fiscal shortfalls would get much more attention four years later, but only because a recession raised broader worries about the state of the economy.

As a longtime reformer, Dukakis was appalled by what he saw as the rampant corruption of the Reagan–Bush administration. Exhibit A was the Iran–Contra scandal, which might have been a mighty issue a year earlier.

Unfortunately for Dukakis, the intricate arms-for-hostages scheme was old news by the fall of 1988, and Bush had used the Dan Rather interview to reframe it as a case study in media bias. Early in September, Dukakis tried to raise another ethics issue. A Democratic House member from Ohio had given the *New York Times* a memorandum from Black, Manafort, and Stone, a Republican consulting firm whose partners were advising the Bush campaign. (Atwater had worked with the trio in a separate campaign firm.) The 1984 document solicited business from the government of the Bahamas, saying that "personal relationships between the Department of State officials and Black, Manafort, and Stone can be utilized to upgrade a back-channel relationship in the economic and foreign policy spheres."[75] Roger Stone said that he had visited the Bahamas to discuss drug interdiction. He added that Paul Manafort had primary responsibility for dealings with the Bahamas.[76] Throughout the fall campaign, Manafort took part in morning meetings with Baker, Atwater, and other members of the Bush high command.[77]

Democrats raised questions not only because of the firm's blatant influence marketing but also because the Bahamian prime minister allegedly had ties to the very drug traffickers he claimed to be fighting. Dukakis said: "The American people have a right to know that the back door of the White House will not be the front door for paid agents of a foreign government." Trying to turn around the flag issue, he proclaimed: "My staff will not have divided loyalties. In a Dukakis White House, the staff will pledge allegiance to only one flag—Old Glory."[78]

Although the lobbying memo looked sleazy, it contained no proof of criminal behavior, and the attack fizzled. For years to come, Manafort would continue to make mounds of money in international political consulting. Many of his clients, like the Bahamian government of the mid-1980s, were not entirely reputable. In 2018, amid the investigation of Russian meddling in the 2016 election, a jury would convict Manafort for crimes relating to his lobbying for Ukraine, its political parties, and its leaders.

Dukakis resented Bush's attacks, so tried to make an issue of negativity itself. His campaign made a spot that started with a few seconds of "Tank Ride" playing on a television. It showed Dukakis switching it off, saying, "I'm fed up with it. Haven't seen anything like it in 25 years of public life. George Bush's negative TV ads, distorting my record, full of lies and he knows it. I'm on the record for the very weapons systems his ads say I'm against."[79] The message was weak because the GOP held an advantage on national defense issues, and he displayed an image that had embarrassed him. He would have been better off ignoring the tank ad instead of reminding people about it.

Dukakis responded to the furlough issue by finding a horror story from the federal prison system.[80] In late October, the campaign ran an ad saying that Dukakis had stopped the Massachusetts furlough program. It continued: "And Bush won't talk about the thousands of drug kingpins furloughed from federal prisons while he led the war on drugs. Bush won't talk about this drug pusher, one of his furloughed heroin dealers, who raped and murdered Patsy Pedrin, pregnant mother of two."[81] In Dukakis's lawyerly mind, it was wise to rebut Bush's attacks by pointing out that other prison programs had gone wrong too. As with the tank ad, however, the spot merely drew attention to a topic on which Dukakis was vulnerable. What was even worse from a political viewpoint was that the ad briefly showed a picture of the killer, a Hispanic man named Angel M. Medrano. (His name did not appear in the ad.) By running a spot featuring a villain of color, the Dukakis campaign undercut its own argument about the racial overtones of Bush's furlough ad. And it surely did not help Dukakis with the Hispanic voters he needed in California and other key states. The ad did not run for long, and if it had, Dukakis would have had another problem. After a jury convicted Medrano for the murder, a judge sentenced him to death. Because Dukakis opposed the death penalty, he would have faced questions about why he would spare the life of the very criminal that he had featured in his ad.

Dukakis had to fight nasty rumors. Senator Steven Symms (R-ID) said in a home-state radio interview: "I haven't seen this but I've heard that there are pictures around that will surface before the election is over of Mrs. Dukakis burning the American flag when she was an anti-war demonstrator during the '60s."[82] No such photo existed. Kitty Dukakis angrily denied the charge, then tried to use it against Bush. "Senator Symms did this as part of an orchestrated campaign," she said. "George Bush has used it himself—describing Dan Quayle—when he said that Dan Quayle didn't burn the flag."[83] There were rumors about Dukakis himself. Supporters of fringe candidate Lyndon LaRouche spread a bogus story that Dukakis had once undergone treatment for depression. At a presidential press conference, a writer for a LaRouche publication asked President Reagan if Dukakis should release his medical records. "Look, I'm not going to pick on an invalid," Reagan answered.[84] Reagan soon expressed regret for the remark, saying that he had been joking. His quip, however, got the matter into the national conversation and prompted Dukakis to release medical records showing that he was in good health. The Dukakis campaign never found hard evidence that the Bush camp was behind either rumor, but critics smelled a whiff of Atwater. Whoever was responsible, the cycle of rumor and rebuttal did not work to Dukakis's advantage. Estrich said that the Reagan quip "had every local television show in American news saying, 'Dukakis not crazy. More at 11.' What do you do with that?"[85]

A Dukakis aide made news with a low blow. In response to an odd rumor that newspapers would soon expose a Bush extramarital affair, the stock market briefly dipped. Deputy field director Donna Brazile told reporters: "I think that George Bush owes it to the American people to 'fess up. The American people have every right to know if Barbara Bush will share that bed with him in the White House."[86] The rumor was unsubstantiated. Dukakis promptly apologized to Bush, and Brazile resigned. This incident, like the attack video during the primary season, undercut Dukakis's claim to the high ground. It probably did not hurt Bush. Tales of scandal tend to catch fire when they confirm some preexisting belief about a candidate. Gary Hart already had a reputation as a womanizer, so there was plenty of fuel to ignite his tryst into a campaign-ending conflagration. Bush's case was different. Supporters admired him as a family man while detractors regarded him as a prissy wimp. Neither image suggested adultery.

DEBATES AND THE ENDGAME

In 1988, debates between presidential nominees were just starting to become an institution. There had been none between 1960 and 1976, and Reagan had only one debate with Carter in 1980. Until the Reagan and Mondale camps reached an agreement in September 1984, it was not a sure thing that the nominees would debate at all. Because of this uncertainty, the chairs of the two major party committees worked to form a private, nonpartisan organization to host debates and ensure that they would continue. In 1988, the Bush and Dukakis campaigns agreed that the new group, the Commission on Presidential Debates, would sponsor the first presidential and vice presidential debates, while the League of Women Voters would sponsor the second presidential debate.

The first debate on September 25 not go especially well for Bush. Dukakis had the stronger, more confident delivery, and Bush botched a question about a sensitive issue. If abortion were again illegal, asked Ann Groer of the *Orlando Sentinel*, would Bush favor jail for women who have abortions, and the doctors who perform them? "I haven't sorted out the penalties," he answered. "But I do know, I do know that I oppose abortion. And I favor adoption. . . . I'm for the sanctity of life, and once that illegality is established, then we can come to grips with the penalty side." Dukakis replied: "Well, I think what the vice president is saying is that he's prepared to brand a woman a criminal for making this decision. It's as simple as that. I don't think it's enough to come before the American people who are watching us tonight and say, well, I haven't sorted it out."[87]

At a press conference he next day, James Baker tried to clarify Bush's position. Baker said: "I have discussed the issue with the Vice President and I can tell you that it is his view that he would not wish to see a woman labeled as a criminal, notwithstanding his view in favor of right to life."[88] Baker declared the question "closed" and sought to move on. Dukakis did not pursue the issue aggressively. Putting the issue at the center of his campaign messaging would have cracked party unity. Although he and a majority of his party had long favored preserving the legality of abortion, a substantial minority of Democratic voters and politicians still supported abortion restrictions. Just a couple of weeks before the debate, the House voted to forbid the use of Medicaid funds for abortion except when the woman's life was in danger. Ninety Democrats joined 126 Republicans in voting for the motion.[89]

On October 5, things appeared to get worse for the GOP ticket. Trying to establish his credibility as a vice presidential candidate, Dan Quayle had been comparing himself to John F. Kennedy. There was some superficial similarity: like Kennedy in 1960, Quayle had served eight years in the Senate, and his legislative record was arguably just as good (though Kennedy never really had a reputation as a master lawmaker). The comparison was politically fraught because voters remembered Kennedy not as the journeyman senator of 1960 but as the martyred president of 1963. Worried about blowback, Bush aides warned Quayle against seeming to equate himself with Kennedy. He should have taken their advice. Representative Dennis Eckart (D-OH), who was to portray Quayle in mock debates with Lloyd Bentsen, was studying the senator's rhetoric and he noticed the Kennedy comparison.[90] Eckart raised the point in his sessions with Bentsen, who recalled that he had served with Kennedy in the House. Bentsen prepared a response in case Quayle should bring it up on stage. He did.

> QUAYLE: I have as much experience in the Congress as Jack Kennedy did when he sought the presidency. I will be prepared to deal with the people in the Bush administration, if that unfortunate event would ever occur.
>
> BENTSEN: Senator, I served with Jack Kennedy, I knew Jack Kennedy,

Jack Kennedy was a friend of mine. Senator, you are no Jack Kennedy. [*Prolonged shouts and applause.*][91]

Bentsen was stretching the truth: though he may have had a passing acquaintance with Kennedy, the two were not close. That inaccuracy did not keep the exchange from going down in debate history as a victory for Bentsen and a humiliation for Quayle. The Dukakis campaign tried to exploit it. A Democratic television ad showed actors as Bush handlers bemoaning Quayle's poor performance and wondering whether they could replace him with Bob Dole.[92] The ad makers thought that they were being clever, which was the problem. The only people who would have understood the ad were political sophisticates who had followed the debate—and such people already knew which side they were voting for.

On October 13, the second presidential debate contained another "defining moment," and this one purportedly worked against Dukakis. CNN reporter Bernard Shaw opened with a shocking question: "Governor, if Kitty Dukakis were raped and murdered, would you favor an irrevocable death penalty for the killer?" Dukakis answered: "No, I don't, Bernard. And I think you know that I've opposed the death penalty during all of my life. I don't see any evidence that it's a deterrent, and I think there are better and more effective ways to deal with violent crime."[93] The answer would have worked if the question had come up during a Harvard seminar or an episode of his old public-TV program *The Advocates*. But once again, his lawyerly mind was blind to the politics of the moment. His matter-of-fact demeanor made it sound as if he were talking about Swedish land-use planning instead of the hypothetical rape and murder of his wife. For decades, commentators would refer to Dukakis's oddly passionless answer as the moment that doomed his candidacy.

Was it? "No, I don't, Bernard" was an embarrassment and maybe a missed opportunity for Dukakis to show a flash of Greek passion. But at this late stage in the campaign, it was no game changer. Dukakis had run behind in the polls since August, and in the Hotline/KRC National Tracking poll, Bush's margin went from 6 percent in the last batch of survey interviews before the debate to 7 percent in the first batch conducted afterward.[94] In other words, it was statistically unchanged. Bush's lead did temporarily widen later in the month, but it is implausible to explain that shift as a delayed reaction to Dukakis's robotic response. (Nobody woke up on the morning of October 20 and thought, "Wow, that answer Dukakis gave last week was really weird!") Similarly, the poll numbers twitched a little after the first presidential debate and the vice presidential debate, but there is no evidence of anything more than a short-lived effect.

From the perspective of seven subsequent presidential races, one can see that debates do not change the course of a general election campaign for the White House. By the autumn of an election year, the contenders are familiar and the background conditions (notably, the state of the economy) have already made their mark. And the people who tune into the debates are knowledgeable and motivated—that is, hard to persuade. Viewers watch debates to root for their favorites, not to make up their minds. In 2004, John Kerry outpointed George W. Bush on the debate stage, and then Bush won in the voting booth. In 2012, Mitt Romney overwhelmed Barack Obama in their first encounter, to no effect whatsoever. In 2016, pundits thought that Donald Trump's coarse and ill-informed performances would contribute to his doom. They kept thinking so, right until election night. Still, political activists believe that debates matter, and this belief shapes the lessons they draw from an election. The next chapter will discuss how these lessons affect future campaigns.

In 1988, Bush's late-October spike in the polls led to talk that he might win a landslide. The fundamentals did not support such speculation. Economic growth was good enough to push him across the finish line, but not nearly as strong as it was during the Reagan landslide of 1984. Because his party had already been in power for two terms, the "time for a change" sentiment cut into his lead. Reagan's approval rating varied around 50 percent—good, but not great. A few weeks before the election, political scientist Alan Abramowitz used the latest available data about economic growth and presidential approval to forecast the popular vote. He reckoned that Bush would win the two-party vote by the modest margin of 51–49 percent.[95]

As the elections drew closer, the polls started to tighten, and talk shifted from a Bush landslide to the outside chance of a Dukakis squeaker. The Democrat grew more animated in his campaign appearances and claimed to be gaining on Bush: "He's slipping and sliding. We're rocking and rolling."[96] Dukakis was not the first nominee to say such things. Lagging candidates often pick up some points in the last days of the campaign, and enthusiastic rallies give them hope that they are heading for an upset. Sometimes it happens. This time it did not.

THE POPULAR TALLY

Bush got 53.37 percent of the national popular vote to Dukakis's 45.65 percent. Bush did better than the Abramowitz forecast, though it is hard to say whether the difference stemmed from the strength of his campaign or was mere statistical noise. By historical standards, Bush made a good showing—just about the same as Franklin Roosevelt in 1944. But coming after the 1984 Reagan landslide, it seemed like a second-rate success. A *Washington Post* headline summed up the media reaction: "REAGAN'S 1984 VOTER COALITION IS WEAKENED IN BUSH VICTORY."[97] What no one could have known at the time was that Bush's share of the popular vote would top that of any presidential candidate through at least 2016.

With most demographic groups, exit polls showed, Bush ran several points behind Reagan. There were exceptions. Among African Americans, Jews, and white evangelicals, Bush ran 3 points ahead.[98] Reagan was unpopular with the first two groups, so it was no surprise that Bush did better. (Stock traders would call it a "dead cat bounce.") But he also managed to outdo Reagan's 78 percent among evangelicals. Doug Wead, Lee Atwater, and George W. Bush could take some credit here: this performance reflected the campaign's dogged courtship of a group that had been outside the candidate's religious comfort zone. More broadly, it confirmed the deepening alliance of Republicans and conservative Christians.

Dukakis, the bookish candidate from the Route 128 high-tech corridor, did slightly better among voters with postgraduate degrees than among the broader public. In 1980, according to the ABC exit poll, this group split for Reagan by 12 points, about the same as his overall national margin. In 1988, these voters went 50 percent for Dukakis, 49 percent for Bush.[99] Similarly, professionals trended toward Democrats during the 1980s, while managers stuck with the GOP.[100] This trend might have been even more pronounced in 1988, except that the Yale-educated Bush had a certain appeal to many professionals, and his campaign statements suggested that he would strike a moderate tone on education and the environment, two issues that mattered to such voters. Accordingly, Bush did well in the suburbs, though some hints of GOP erosion were evident.

Hispanics broke for Dukakis by a 2-to-1 margin, better than Democrats had done in the previous two elections. But the Hispanic vote did not help the party as much as it would in the future. According to census data, Hispanics accounted for just 3.6 percent of the electorate in 1988, compared with 9.2 percent in 2016.[101] One reason for the increase was the immigration reform legislation that President Reagan signed in 1986. During the 1990s, immigration would become an increasingly contentious issue and would remain so through the 2016 election. In 1988, however, it hardly registered because politicians believed that the 1986 legislation had drained the issue of much of its potency. Neither party platform gave more than a few words to immigration, and during the presidential debates, the only mention of the issue came when Dukakis mentioned his immigrant roots. Asian Americans cast just a sliver of the 1988 vote, and exit polls did not report their preferences. By 2016, thanks in part to liberalized immigration laws, they made up about 4 percent of the electorate, and they voted as heavily Democratic as Hispanics.

In 1988, voters paid attention to the crime issue. In the CBS/*New York Times* exit poll, one respondent in five listed punishment of criminals among the most important issues, and these voters backed Bush by 2 to 1.[102] In the ABC exit poll, 27 percent mentioned the death penalty as a "very important" issue, and they voted for Bush by 3 to 1.[103] Yet for all the attention to crime and other social concerns, voters were more likely to mention economic issues. Not surprisingly, the state of the economy seemed to help Bush. Forty-three percent of voters said that they were better off than when Reagan took office, and they went for Bush by nearly 4 to 1. Of the 38 percent who said that they were faring about the same, Dukakis ran ahead, but by a narrower margin, 54–45 percent. He got 84 percent from those who said that they were worse off, but they accounted for only 19 percent of the vote.[104] National security also worked to the GOP's advantage. Reagan and Bush had argued that their policy of "peace through strength" had succeeded in easing Cold War tensions, and the voters agreed. Of those who picked defense or foreign policy as their top issue, 88 percent chose Bush.[105]

The country's good times help explain why third-party voting was at low levels. People are most likely to reach outside the two-party system when times are bad, as would be the case with the Perot candidacy four years later.[106] Not so in 1988. Dr. Ron Paul, who had previously served as a Republican House member from Texas, got less than one half of one percent as the Libertarian Party candidate. Decades later, after returning to the House, he would gain greater prominence as a two-time contender for the Republican presidential nomination.

THE MAP

As the 2000 and 2016 elections have reminded us, the popular vote does not determine the winner. Only the electoral vote counts. In this light, picture someone who knows about politics in the early twenty-first century but is unfamiliar with elections before the millennium. That person would find some surprises in the 1988 electoral map.

One would be Dukakis's victory in West Virginia. In 2016, Trump carried the state by 42 points, and Republicans dominated most other elections as well. In 2017, its Democratic governor switched to the GOP. In 1988, however, West Virginia had been a Democratic stronghold since the New Deal. The United Mine Workers had labored hard for the party, and West Virginia had voted for Republican presidential candidates only in the landslide years of 1956, 1972, and 1984.[107] Even though coal mining had long been on the decline and union membership was ebbing, the state still maintained its Democratic loyalty through the 1990s. In 2000, however, George W. Bush's campaign strategist Karl Rove reckoned that Republicans had an opportunity because Democratic environmental and social policies were unpopular in West Virginia.[108] The Bush campaign pushed hard and won the state, whose five electoral votes provided a bare margin of national victory. In the early years of the new century, West Virginia galloped into the GOP base.

During the 1988 nomination contest, Dukakis lost the Iowa caucuses to Richard Gephardt, but he carried the state in the general election. This result was less than shocking. Iowa was not as reliably Republican as nearby Kansas or Nebraska. In 1976, it nearly went for Jimmy Carter, and in 1984, it gave Reagan only a modest margin while electing liberal Democrat Tom Harkin to the Senate. In 1988, the farm woes that cost Bush the state's GOP caucuses also hurt him in the general election. A preelection poll showed Iowa farmers supporting Dukakis 52–42 percent. And although Reagan was popular nationwide, his approval rating in the state was a mediocre 47 percent.[109] For most of the next three decades, Iowa would be in play.[110]

For several other states, the 1988 campaign marked the end point either of GOP dominance or competitiveness in presidential elections. Bush carried these states, which then voted Democratic in every race through 2016. Their political realignment stemmed from demographic, economic, and cultural evolution.

In his 1936 landslide, Franklin Roosevelt carried every state except Maine and Vermont. Both were full of old-stock whites whose families had been voting Republican since the Civil War. Vermont changed colors in the 1960s and 1970s with an influx of newcomers who liked the state's natural beauty and strong environmental policies. The university city of Burlington attracted educated professionals along with a fair number of bohemians, which is how Brooklyn-born Bernie Sanders got to win elections as an avowed socialist. In 1988, however, just enough of the old Vermont had lingered so that Bush could scrape by with 51 percent. The new Vermont then became dominant, and through 2016, no GOP candidate got more than 41 percent. Political and economic shifts also took place in Maine, albeit less dramatically. The 1954 gubernatorial election went to Democrat Edmund Muskie, the son of Polish immigrants and a symbol of an Ellis Island generation that was partially supplanting the state's Yankees. By the mid-1970s, Democrats tended to have the upper hand in state elections. Still, the state voted for GOP presidential candidates throughout the 1970s and 1980s. Bush not only benefited from this residue of Republicanism but also had something of a favorite-son advantage stemming from the family's summer home in Kennebunkport. After his victory in 1988, Democratic presidential candidates carried Maine regularly, though by smaller margins than in Vermont.

Bush had another home base in Connecticut. He grew up in Greenwich, and after returning from military service, he earned his undergraduate degree at Yale. Democrats had been gaining strength in the state, but in the 1950s, Republicans could still elect people such as Prescott Bush. And twenty-six years after the elder Bush concluded his service in the Senate, George Bush carried the state. The Connecticut GOP then grew weaker, in part because of demographics. The state was becoming more ethnically diverse, with a large increase in the Hispanic population: by 2010, 7.1 percent of the state's residents had roots in Puerto Rico, the largest share of any of the fifty states. Another reason was the broader shift of educated professionals and suburbanites from the GOP. Howard Reiter and Jeffrey Stonecash found that that the share of Northeastern affluent white Protestants who identified with the GOP plunged from more than 70 percent in the 1950s and 1960s to less than 45 percent in the first decade of the twenty-first century.[111] Fairfield County, the locale of Greenwich and other New York City bedroom communities, went for Bush by a margin of 59–40 percent. By 2016, the numbers had flipped almost precisely: George H. W. Bush's boyhood county voted for Hillary Clinton over Trump, 58–38 percent.

New Jersey and Illinois followed Connecticut's path in presidential politics, moving from purple to deep blue. After Bush carried them in 1988, the Hispanic population grew in both states, and the Asian population soared in New Jersey. By 2016, about 11 percent of the state's people had Asian roots, the third highest share in the country after Hawaii and California.[112] And as in Connecticut, affluent suburbs trended Democratic. New Jersey's Bergen County voted 58 percent for Bush in 1988, 55 percent for Clinton in 2016. The Collar Counties of Illinois, five suburban counties near Chicago, gained African American and Hispanic voters, and saw educated professionals adopt more liberal attitudes.[113] DuPage, the largest of the five, voted 69 percent for Bush, 53 percent for Clinton.

The Democratic trend in the suburbs helped tip the border states of Delaware and Maryland. Delaware's New Castle County went from 53 percent for Bush to 62 percent for Clinton. Maryland's Baltimore County, a suburb of the city of Baltimore and launching pad for the career of Spiro Agnew, went from 57 percent Bush to 56 percent Clinton. Montgomery County, the home of many of federal executives and lobbyists, gave 48 percent of its vote to Bush. Clinton carried it with 75 percent.

And then there was California. Contrary to many media accounts, it had not been a solidly Republican state for a long time. Since 1958, Democrats had usually held majorities in the state legislature and the US House delegation. For most of this period, at least one California Democrat served in the US Senate. The state's "red" reputation stemmed from a string of presidential elections. Except for the Johnson landslide of 1964, California had voted Republican in every race between 1952 and 1984. But in seven of these eight state victories, a Californian was on the GOP ticket: Nixon five times and Reagan twice.[114] Only in 1976 did the party win the state without a Californian, and then just barely.

In 1988, both campaigns thought that California would be tight. In contrast to the elections of the Obama and Trump years—when party nominees assumed that the state would automatically go Democratic and so put their resources elsewhere—Bush and Dukakis spent a good deal of time and money in California. On election eve, Dukakis held big rallies in San Francisco and Los Angeles.[115] He fell short. Bush won a modest victory in the state, 51 to 48 percent. As was the case in other states, Bush owed much to the Southern California suburbs, racking up 60 percent in San Diego County and 68 percent in Orange County. Though Dukakis carried the city of Los Angeles, nearby communities went to Bush, so Dukakis carried Los Angeles County only by about 5 percentage points. In 2016, Clinton won all three counties. In Los Angeles County, her margin was 50 points.

A LONELY VICTORY

As Bush was triumphing in the presidential context, his party was struggling down the ballot. Republicans finished the election with 175 House seats, three fewer than they had won two years before. The Senate balance remained the same as it had been after the 1986 midterm, fifty-five Democrats to forty-five Republicans, but that outcome obscured a small setback for the GOP. After the death of Nebraska's Democratic senator, Edward

Zorinsky, the state's Republican governor had appointed a member of her party to the vacancy, shifting the balance to fifty-four to forty-six. Democrat Bob Kerrey, who had won the Medal of Honor in the Vietnam War and had served a term as governor, beat the appointed senator and thus restored the Senate's previous party ratio.[116] Democrats went into 1988 in control of a majority of governorships and state legislatures, and they came out with slightly larger majorities.

And so Bush made history in two ways. On the one hand, he beat the so-called Van Buren curse, becoming the first sitting vice president to win the White House in more than a century and a half. On the other hand, he was the first person ever to win a presidential election while the opposing party gained ground in the House, the Senate, the governorships, and the state legislatures.[117]

Ticket splitting, which would decline during the next century, was very much alive in 1988. About a third of House districts voted for a presidential candidate of one party and a congressional candidate of the other. Incumbency insulated many House members from national tides.[118] Few lost, and most won with more than 60 percent of the vote. Senate elections also went their own way, bearing only a weak statistical relationship to statewide presidential results.[119] The disconnect between presidential and congressional elections was particularly striking in the South. In spite of Bush's Southern sweep, Democrats retained most of the region's House seats. The same was true in the Senate. Republicans did win contests in Florida and Mississippi, but Virginia and Tennessee gave landslides to Democrats Chuck Robb and Jim Sasser. Both were prominent members of the Democratic Leadership Council, and they personified the DLC approach of being acceptable to the national party while being conservative enough for Southern electorates. One victory in the South provided some consolation to the Democrats. Thanks to a 1959 Texas law, Lloyd Bentsen could simultaneously run for reelection while appearing on the national ticket. (State lawmakers had passed it to accommodate Lyndon Johnson's ambitions for 1960.) In the presidential race, Bush won Texas with about 56 percent of the vote. In the Senate race, however, Bentsen got nearly 60 percent.

The 1988 congressional results provided the new president with little leverage over his partisans on Capitol Hill. Republicans liked and respected Bush, but they did not fear him. On the House side, most had run ahead of Bush in their districts, and he lacked a base of zealous followers who would vote in primaries against GOP lawmakers who crossed him. He had not brought them out of permanent minority status, and there was scant reason to hope that he would do so in the future. Political scientist Thomas E. Mann had written in a prescient 1987 essay: "It is virtually impossible for a party to strengthen its position in the House at the same time that it occupies the White House. If the initial election that wins the presidency for a party does not produce a House majority, the window is effectively closed for the duration of that administration."[120] No in-party had won House seats in a midterm since the Great Depression year of 1934. And though Eisenhower, Nixon, and Reagan had all won massive reelection victories, the 1956, 1972, and 1984 House races did not produce GOP majorities. As long as George H. W. Bush was president, House Republicans knew that their plight would continue.

The combination of GOP presidential victory and down-ballot frustration helped put Newt Gingrich into congressional leadership. Since 1983, he had been the voice of the Conservative Opportunity Society, a group of House Republicans seeking a more aggressive strategy to break out of their permanent-minority rut. Although Republican leader Bob Michel (R-IL) had been remarkably successful in passing much of the Reagan agenda while in the minority, the Young Turks were gaining adherents, and the 1988 results added to their momentum. Michel, among the last of the World War II veterans in Congress, was nearing the end of his tenure as GOP leader. Most lawmakers assumed that his successor would be Dick Cheney (R-WY), who had been rising in the GOP leadership structure since 1980, and who won the number-two job of party whip after the 1988 election. Things took an unexpected turn early in Bush's tenure. Former senator John Tower, his nominee for secretary of defense, lost a confirmation vote in the Senate after stories of drinking and womanizing broke into the public. (At a Senate hearing, Paul Weyrich broached the topic, which had long been the subject of rumors on Capitol Hill.) Bush then tapped Cheney, who had been President Ford's chief of staff and enjoyed widespread respect on Capitol Hill. By a 2-vote margin, House Republicans elected Gingrich as whip. Events would put him at odds with Bush, but this course of events was not foreseeable as the new president prepared to take office.

"A NEW BREEZE"

On January 20, 1989, Bush said in his inaugural address: "A new breeze is blowing, and a nation refreshed by freedom stands ready to push on. There is new ground to be broken and new action to be taken. There are times when the future seems thick as a fog; you sit and wait, hoping the mists will lift and reveal the right path. But this is a time when the future seems a door you can walk right through into a room called tomorrow."[121] The talk of new beginnings was old hat. Every administration takes office with high hopes for a fresh start. Disappointments always follow. Legal, political, and economic constraints inevitably limit the extent to which the incoming president can change foreign and domestic policy. The forty-first president would be no exception.

As he took the oath on the Capitol steps, Bush could easily see one major source of constraint: Democratic control of the House and Senate. In his inaugural address, Bush rhetorically offered his hand to the Democratic leaders of the House and Senate. On some issues, they would cooperate. On others, the Democrats would be tough adversaries eager to bring him down with hard bargains.

One of those issues was the deficit. Since the tax cuts of 1981, the federal government had been running deficits of at least $100 billion a year. Concern had been mounting about the debt burden on future generations. A couple of weeks before taking office, he wrote author Willie Morris: "I am now getting excited about moving down the hall and getting to work. If it weren't for the damned deficit I'd be kicking up my heels and feeling like a Spring colt."[122] During the campaign, he had spoken optimistically about cutting spending through gimmicks such as a balanced-budget amendment and the line-item veto. His inaugural approached the issue more soberly: "We have more will than wallet, but will is what we need. We will make the hard choices, looking at what we have and perhaps allocating it differently, making our decisions based on honest need and prudent safety." He did not specify what the "hard choices" would look like.

Foreign policy was the bright spot. In December of 1988, Mikhail Gorbachev visited the United States, and a photo opportunity with Reagan and Bush symbolized the enthusiasm of the moment. As Reagan put it: "Since 1985, extraordinary things have happened, and nothing more extraordinary than the sight yesterday of a President of the United States and a future President of the United States and a President of the Soviet Union standing together in New York Harbor under the protective gaze of the Statue of Liberty."[123] In the following year, developments in the Eastern Bloc would be more rapid and dramatic than Americans could have anticipated. In November, however, columnist David Broder offered a word of caution about the end of the Cold War: "Republican euphoria at the prospect of a huge diplomatic victory for President Bush when he meets with Mikhail Gorbachev, the beleaguered master of the crumbling Communist empire, is tempered by one historical fact. When wars end, governments change."[124]

7

CAMPAIGNS HAVE CONSEQUENCES

It bears repeating that the fundamentals of an election—bread and butter, war and peace—have more impact on the outcome than speeches, debates, or television ads. Still, campaigns matter at the margins, and the margins matter. In 1988, Bush's efforts shored up his popular and electoral tallies, providing insurance against last-minute disasters such as another stock market crash. In 2016, Hillary Clinton probably would have won the presidency if she had put spent more time and money into Wisconsin, Michigan, and Pennsylvania.

The consequences of a presidential campaign go beyond its direct effects on vote counts. The winning candidate's policies and personnel choices reflect explicit promises, implicit commitments, and political debts. Candidates and political operatives draw lessons from each campaign, and even if those lessons rest on myths, they guide the strategy and tactics of future races. Political reputations may rise or fall, shaping the cast of characters for the next presidential drama. Campaigns can inspire activism for years to come. Despite landslide losses, the crusades of George McGovern and Barry Goldwater each recruited new political troops and launched the national political careers of leaders such as Gary Hart and Ronald Reagan. Presidential races can also leave a residue of resentment. Those who lost in the primaries or general election may nurse grudges, believing that that the winners relied on underhanded tactics or ugly campaign messages. So 1988 was important not just because it put George H. W. Bush in the White House but also because it left lasting marks on public policy and electoral politics.

"THIS EMPTY BOX"

Even before Election Day, journalists were lamenting that Bush had run a negative, issueless campaign that would deprive him of a mandate.[1] In December, the Republican National Committee tried to rebut such claims by collating Bush's policy speeches and position papers into a 347-page book entitled *Leadership on the Issues*. At first glance, it looked like a comprehensive catalog of specific proposals that would guide the incoming administration. On second glance, it was a mishmash of standard GOP stands (the balanced-budget amendment), dubious innovations (a "flexible freeze" on spending, which Dukakis had derided as an "economic Slurpee"), and silly ideas that the campaign probably hoped that no one would notice. "George Bush will challenge every student government of every high school in this country to work to stop drug use at their schools." That line, complete with the underlining, really appeared on page 210 of the document.[2]

Both in the campaign and the White House, Bush dutifully read his briefing books and could competently answer questions on diverse topics. Nevertheless, he had little interest in domestic policy.[3] The hundreds of bullet points did not add up to a coherent agenda, and voters did not associate him with a big initiative such as the tax cut that Reagan had championed eight years earlier. His 1988 acceptance speech movingly described voluntary organizations as "a thousand points of light," and his administration did encourage community service, but these efforts were a minor part of federal policy, His one big pledge—"no new taxes"—was a promise *not* to change course. Despite his skillful response to Iraq's invasion of Kuwait, his general approach to governing remained more reactive than revolutionary. Pundits summed up his tenure up as an "in-box presidency."[4] It was not a bad way to govern because many of the items that passed through his in-box—the 1990 Americans with Disabilities Act, for one—were good for the country. But in such cases, he left the impression of a president who was letting good things happen rather than making them happen.

Bush was only the second elected president since the 1840s to enter office with opposition majorities both chambers of Congress. Nixon was the first, but with a significant difference: Nixon could count on large numbers of conservative Southern Democrats who would vote with Republicans are certain issues. By time Bush took the oath of office, the old conservative coalition had weakened. Accordingly, liberal Democrats got to pick the bills that reached Bush's desk. He disliked many of them, and he cast forty-four vetoes during his four years. As White House aide Charles Kolb said, there was a catch: he wanted to kill bills to show political strength, so he usually set aside his veto pen when he thought that Congress would override him. "The issue was counting heads, not standing on principle. If Fred McClure or Nick Calio, his two assistants who headed his legislative shop, told him he was shy on votes, Bush rarely applied the veto. Simple as that."[5] And when he did apply the veto, he did not necessarily win the political battle. Democrats sometimes passed popular measures in hopes of making him and the congressional GOP look bad. In 1992, they voted for campaign finance reform because they wanted Bush to take the blame for blocking it. He obliged them, and congressional Republicans upheld his veto.[6]

Kolb said the Bush White House was a whirl of meetings, briefings, and fact sheets. "What was lacking, however, was a sense of purpose and direction. There was no focus."[7] James P. Pinkerton, who had moved from the campaign to the White House policy office, likened the administration to the 1946 film classic *The Big Sleep*, whose talented cast and crew could not figure out the movie's plot. "But we weren't bad people; we were more like scriptwriters with no sense of the story line. And we had no Raymond Chandler to explain it all to us."[8] Bob Teeter, Bush's 1992 campaign chairman, assembled an elaborate chart to guide speechwriters on the issues. One box was empty: "Theme/Slogan/Name." Teeter told the speechwriters, "What I want from you, is to help fill this empty box."[9]

"READ MY LIPS": TRUTH, CONSEQUENCES, AND CONTEXT

Not all election promises are created equal. American voters understand that many pledges represent hopes rather than hard commitments, the pretty poetry of campaigning instead of the pragmatic prose of governing. But when a candidate speaks clearly about something that matters to them, they apply a higher standard. On October 21, 1964, Lyndon Johnson said, "We are not about to send American boys 9 or 10,000 miles away from home to do what Asian boys ought to be doing for themselves."[10] As he uttered those words, his policy in Vietnam was quietly ratcheting toward that very situation. After Johnson sent so many young Americans so far for so little result, the country lost faith in his leadership.

Taxes were not a life-or-death issue like Vietnam, but they did affect people in a direct way. When Bush repeatedly promised no new taxes—period—voters noticed. As he reiterated the pledge in his acceptance speech, his delivery was strong and his prose memorable. That speech helped give him a bump in the polls, and it also tattooed "Read My Lips: No New Taxes" on his political persona. Pinkerton later said, "If you make one big promise in your campaign, keep it. I said Bush could have surrendered to the Soviets, had mandatory quotas for AIDS victims going into convents, whatever it could have been, anything you could dream up, as long as he kept the tax pledge."[11]

He broke it.

In 1990, a weakening economy caused revenues to fall short. Because of the Gramm–Rudman law that Congress had passed during the second Reagan term, the resulting increase in projected deficits would automatically trigger deep across-the-board cuts. To avert reductions in popular programs, Bush bargained with congressional Democrats. On their insistence, he issued a May 26 statement that a budget package would require several elements including "tax revenue increases."[12] The reaction was fast and furious. Most House Republicans quickly signed a letter to Bush: "We were stunned by your announcement that you would be willing to accept tax revenue increases as a part of a budget summit package. A tax increase is unacceptable."[13] Michael Dukakis said: "I told the truth, and I paid the price. Mr. Bush did not tell the truth, and now we must all pay the price." The most memorable comment was a headline in the New York Post: "READ MY LIPS . . . I LIED!" (By coincidence, this front page also had a smaller headline for an unrelated story on a future president: "DONALD DOES IT.")

The immediate public reaction was not as harsh as legend would have it. Bush's approval rating dropped from 69 percent in mid-June to 60 percent in mid-July—a noteworthy change, but less than a political calamity.[14] In autumn 1990, Bush haggled with lawmakers to reach a budget agreement, and the approval number fell to 51 percent by November. It is unlikely, however, that looming tax increases were the main reason for this sharp decline. The economy was continuing to worsen, and the November seasonally adjusted unemployment rate was 6.2 percent—a full point increase since March, and the first time in three years that it had topped 6 percent.[15]

His relationship with his own party was fraying. Despite his post as House GOP whip, Gingrich openly opposed Bush's position. The president felt a sense of betrayal. "You are killing us; you are just killing us," he told Gingrich at a GOP fundraiser. Gingrich said that he regretted "that this is happening," but did not change his position.[16] At the National Republican Congressional Committee, co-chair Ed Rollins wrote a memo to GOP candidates urging them to stay consistent on the tax issue: "Do not hesitate to distance yourself from the President." He later wrote: "I was unrepentant. My job was electing Republicans to the House. George Bush and his tax deal made that impossible. Now my job was seeing how many we could save."[17] Compared with 1988, the party suffered a net loss of eight House seats and one Senate seat. By midterm standards, the loss was not huge, but the party was starting from a low baseline.

War with Iraq soon overshadowed the tax hike and other economic issues. In August, Saddam Hussein had invaded Kuwait. Bush responded by sending troops to Saudi Arabia and building an international coalition to reverse the Iraqi aggression. After Congress approved the use of force in January 1991, coalition forces soon unleashed a massive air campaign. In February, a ground campaign was a spectacular success, pushing Saddam's forces back to Iraq in just 100 hours. Bush's approval rating soared, hitting a high of 89 percent in early March, ebbing to a still-impressive 77 percent in mid-May.[18] After a few months, bad economic news began to erode Bush's standing. The recession had started in the summer of 1990, and though it was technically over by the following spring, recovery was sluggish and the unemployment rate kept rising, hitting a seasonally adjusted peak of 7.8 percent in June 1992. And because the tax increase had not yet fully kicked in, the federal deficit remained high. Just as a good economy had helped Bush in 1988, a bad one was bringing him down four years later.

In a December 1991 internal memo, Bush pollster Fred Steeper warned that the dual victories in the Cold War and the Gulf War would not be enough to overcome an economic slump. In May 1945, Winston Churchill's Conservative Party lost its parliamentary majority. "Historians concluded that Churchill was needed for war time, but he was not appropriate to rebuild Britain's economy during peace time," Steeper wrote. "Leaders are not necessarily reelected for their foreign policy and wartime successes, even when monumental."[19]

In the fall of 1992, Democratic nominee Bill Clinton attacked the Bush record. One of his ads featured a clip of the "read my lips" promise. "Then he gave us the second biggest tax increase in American history. Bush increased the gas tax by 56 percent. Can we afford four more years? Bill Clinton—a different kind of Democrat. As governor, Arkansas has the second lowest tax burden in the country. Balanced twelve budgets. You don't have to read his lips. Read his record."[20] Independent candidate Ross Perot linked the issue to broader economic distress, as well as a famous Bush line from the past: "It is called 'Trickle-Down Economics.' It assumes lower taxes on the rich create prosperity that trickles down to all the American people. Instead of a sound economic principle, it turned out to be political voodoo. 'Trickle-Down' simply didn't trickle."[21]

A town hall debate made things worse for Bush. A woman asked the candidates how the "national debt" had affected them personally. Bush fumbled with the question, talking about the debt's impact on his grand-children. When the moderator explained that questioner seemed to be ask-ing about the overall economy, Bush was awkwardly defensive: "But I don't think it's fair to say, you haven't had cancer. Therefore, you don't know what's it like. I don't think it's fair to say, you know, whatever it is, that if you haven't been hit by it personally." Clinton's answer was firm and crisp: "I have seen what's happened in this last 4 years when—in my state, when people lose their jobs there's a good chance I'll know them by their names. When a factory closes, I know the people who ran it. When the businesses go bankrupt, I know them."[22]

The recession hurt Bush even more than the tax issue did. Regardless of other policies, any incumbent president seeking reelection amid such a weak economy would have lost. An exit poll asked voters which issues had influenced them, and candidate positions on the economy ranked first among Clinton and Perot voters. Bush's "read my lips" reversal ranked a distant third.[23] Nevertheless, Republicans soon forgot the broad circum-stances of 1992 and focused instead on the tax issue. George W. Bush de-fended the budget deal on the merits but concluded that it was a political disaster. "Dad's decision to break his 'no new taxes' pledge fractured the Republican Party."[24] In 1995, House Speaker Newt Gingrich said: "All I can say is that I was there when people told President Bush it was OK to raise taxes. It destroyed his presidency."[25]

That belief became GOP doctrine. Whereas Reagan had acceded to several tax increases—albeit in rhetorical disguise—Republicans now as-sumed that they could never do any such thing. Each Republican nominee between 1996 and 2016 pledged not to raise taxes, and both George W. Bush and Donald Trump won passage of tax cuts that greatly increased the federal deficit. During a GOP primary debate in 2011, Bret Baier of Fox News posed this question: "Say you had a deal, a real spending cuts deal, 10 to one . . . spending cuts to tax increases. Speaker [Gingrich], you're already shaking your head. But who on this stage would walk away from that deal? Can you raise your hand if you feel so strongly about not raising taxes, you'd walk away on the 10 to one deal?"[26] Every Republican presidential candidate raised a hand.

RELIGION AND PARTY EVOLUTION

Bush went from "voodoo economic policy" in 1980 to "read my lips" in 1988. His shift on social issues was more gradual but just as striking. He criticized a papal encyclical on contraception in 1968 and then embraced a strict pro-life platform twenty years later. After his clumsy "haven't sorted out the penalties" answer to a 1988 debate question, he added: "And you see, yes, my position has evolved. And it's continuing to evolve, and it's evolving in favor of life. And I have had a couple of exceptions that I support—rape, incest and the life of the mother. Sometimes people feel a little uncomfortable talking about this, but it's much clearer for me now. As I've seen abortions sometimes used as a birth control device, for heavens sakes."[27] One political reason for the change was the growing influence of the religious right. As we saw earlier, he made an early decision to court this constituency, even to the point of adopting God-talk that did not come naturally to a mainline Episcopalian. During the nomination campaign, this strategy succeeded in heading off Pat Robertson. In public, he welcomed Christian conservatives to his side, but he privately expressed misgivings. In his diary, he wrote of one Robertson supporter who refused to shake his hand:

> Still, this staring, glaring ugly—there's something terrible about those who carry it to extremes. They're scary. They're there for spooky, extraordinary right-wing reasons. They don't care about Party. They don't care about anything. They're the excesses. They could be Nazis, they could be Communists, they could be whatever. In this case, they are religious fanatics, and they're spooky. They will destroy this party if they're permitted to take over.[28]

Unsuccessful campaigns can sometimes advance political movements. Barry Goldwater suffered a crushing defeat in the 1964 general election, but his campaign helped move conservatism from a set of ideas on the pages of small-circulation magazines into a force that would dominate the GOP for decades. Eight years later, George McGovern's presidential campaign did something similar for the liberal wing of the Democratic Party. In the case of Robertson, a one-shot presidential candidacy strengthened the long-term position of religious conservatives within the Republican Party.

As with Jesse Jackson, poisonous poll numbers ruled Robertson out as a plausible presidential nominee after 1988. He instead chose to influence GOP politics in other ways. In the early days of the Bush administration, there was a power vacuum in the religious right. Scandals had discredited some major figures, and Jerry Falwell's Moral Majority was moribund. (From the mid-1980s until his death in 2007, Falwell's most significant political role was as a bogeyman in fundraising letters for progressive organizations.) Robertson filled the vacuum by using remnants of his campaign to found a new organization, the Christian Coalition. The group's day-to-day operations were under the command of Ralph Reed, a Republican operative who was finishing his PhD in history at Emory University. Learning from the failure of the Moral Majority, Reed focused on organizing Christian conservatives at the grass roots.[29]

The organization grew rapidly, and its clout was evident in the 1992 campaign. In April 1992, Robertson sent the Bush campaign a ten-page list of "persons I would like to see as Bush campaign co-chairmen," and most of them got jobs.[30] Pat Robertson scored a prominent speaking role at the Republican convention, where he attacked Bill Clinton: "He wants to repeal the ban on homosexuals in the military and appoint homosexuals to his administration. He is running on a platform that calls for saving the Spotted Owl, but never once mentions the name of God."[31] In September, Bush spoke to the Christian Coalition Road to Victory conference.[32]

By the end of the decade, the organization was in decline, but it had accomplished its mission: the GOP firmly stood with Christian conservatives. Aside from some blue-state governors such as Arnold Schwarzenegger of California, party officials adopted language and positions in line with the Christian right's agenda. George W. Bush confirmed this trend with his 2000 presidential campaign. During a debate in Iowa, a reporter asked him to name a philosopher with whom he identified, and he answered: "Christ, because he changed my heart. . . . When you turn your heart and your life over to Christ, when you accept Christ as the savior, it changes your heart, it changes your life, and that's what happened to me."[33] Sixteen years later, Donald Trump skipped the personal testimonials and went to the heart of the deal. Despite his louche lifestyle and comical ignorance of the Bible, he offered the religious conservatives the policies and personnel choices that they wanted. "And if it's my judges, you know how they're going to decide."[34] White evangelicals disregarded his character and voted for him by a 5-to-1 margin.[35]

The rising power of the religious right came at a cost. Particularly after the 1989 formation of the Christian Coalition, Jewish voters came to see evangelical political activity as a threat to their religious and cultural identity.[36] After Bush got 35 percent of the Jewish vote in 1988, later GOP candidates through 2016 averaged only 21 percent. (Orthodox Jews were an exception to the trend.[37]) Only Mitt Romney, himself a member of a religious minority distrusted by evangelicals, scored as high as 30 percent. Trump got just 24 percent.[38]

MEMORIES OF HORTON

If any aspect of the 1988 campaign was even more memorable than "read my lips," it was Willie Horton and the Massachusetts furlough program. The furlough issue probably did not have a major direct impact on the election results, and the link between the Bush campaign and the Willie Horton ad was unclear. Nevertheless, it soon became conventional wisdom that Lee Atwater had reversed a double-digit poll deficit by pushing Horton's face onto the nation's television screens.

After the election, Bush installed Atwater as chair of the Republican National Committee. Seeking to change course from the racially fraught furlough issue, Atwater declared: "Making black voters welcome in the Republican Party is my pre-eminent goal."[39] By doubling the GOP share of the black vote from 10 to 20 percent, his thinking went, the party could strengthen its base in the Electoral College and increase its numbers in Congress.[40] With that approach in mind, Atwater created an outreach division at RNC. It would focus on recruiting African American candidates and getting the GOP message into media with large black audiences.

To put it mildly, outreach was a challenge. In February 1989, former Ku Klux Klan leader David Duke won election to the Louisiana legislature as a registered Republican. Atwater got the RNC executive committee to censure Duke, who responded that he was "just as Republican as Lee Atwater."[41] Two years later, Duke made the runoff for governor. Although President Bush and the RNC denounced him and took the extraordinary step of opposing a Republican in a statewide general election, Democrats cited the Duke candidacy as a natural outgrowth of the 1988 campaign. Former senator Paul Tsongas pictured Duke standing outside the White House calling to Bush, "Father, father. . . . You made me, father."[42]

Another gesture of outreach blew up badly. After Atwater joined the board of historically black Howard University, students mounted an intense protest. "He masterminded use of the Willie Horton issue to contribute to the rising anti-black sentiment of the American people," said one of the protest organizers.[43] Fearing that the protest could lead to violent confrontations with riot police, Atwater quit the board. Shortly after the incident, RNC gauged African American opinion by commissioning focus groups of African Americans in Cleveland, Ohio, and Jackson, Mississippi. An internal memo to Atwater summed up the results:

> When your name was recognized, which was rarely, you were recalled as the instigator of the Willie Horton ad. (That ad is seen as an affront

to black men generally.) If I were to draw a grand conclusion I'd say you were persona non grata in the black community, but with a positive twist. For the moment, you, not Bush, have replaced Ronald Reagan as the Republican devil which allows Bush to make his own record with blacks. Your intention to bring blacks into the Republican Party and the Howard University incident have not reached Cleveland and Jackson.[44]

Although Bush initially enjoyed respectable approval ratings among African Americans, the bad economy brought his numbers down. So did his 1990 veto of a civil rights bill, which gave Democrats another chance to revive memories of the furlough issue. In a floor speech, Senator Edward Kennedy (D-MA) said: "Many of us hoped that the Willie Horton strategy adopted by President Bush as a candidate in the 1988 Presidential campaign was an aberration that would never be repeated. But it does not appear to be. When the chips are down, President Bush, like candidate Bush, is willing to divide the Nation for narrow or partisan advantage."[45]

The RNC outreach effort did recruit some African American candidates for the 1990 midterm, most notably Gary Franks of Connecticut, who became the first black Republican House member since the 1930s.[46] The effort failed to impress rank-and-file African Americans, who continued to shun the GOP. The following spring, RNC shuttered the outreach division. In 1992, Bush got roughly the same dismal share of the black vote that he had received in 1988. The Horton issue, of course, was hardly the only reason; rather, it was one more brick in a barrier that had been in place since Goldwater cast his fateful vote against the 1964 Civil Rights Act. African Americans distrusted the GOP, and not only because of civil rights. As the memo on the 1989 focus groups explained: "Blacks perceive the Republican Party as the party of the rich. To them, our main policy goal is to preserve the economic status quo, which leaves them out. In no way do they see us as the party of economic opportunity and advancement for everyone."[47]

Through the early decades of the next century, Republicans regularly proclaimed their commitment to minority outreach. Just as regularly, Democrats replied by invoking Willie Horton. In 2017, Joseph Biden—by now an elder statesman and former vice president—attacked a Republican candidate for governor of New Jersey by calling one of her television spots "the return of Willie Horton."[48] This issue was just one of many problems for the GOP, whose share of the African American vote never exceeded 12 percent in the decades after the 1988 election.

WHO TELLS YOUR STORY?

Atwater did not live to see the long-term impact of the furlough issue. In March 1990, he learned that he had an aggressive and inoperable brain tumor. Though he retained the chairmanship for several more months, his condition deteriorated quickly, and staffers took over his duties. After the midterm, Bush directed the RNC to pick a new leader, leaving Atwater with the honorary title of general chairman. In his last months, he embarked on his last campaign: personal redemption. Seeking to get right with God, he nominally converted to Catholicism and dabbled in other religions too. And he selectively expressed remorse. "In 1988," he said, "fighting Dukakis, I said that I 'would strip the bark off the little bastard' and 'make Willie Horton his running mate.' I am sorry for both statements: the first for its naked cruelty, the second because it makes me sound racist, which I am not."[49] On the whole, however, he continued to defend his tough approach to campaigning, including the Pledge of Allegiance and furlough issues.[50] He died on March, 29, 1991, at the age of forty.

Much of the political community bought into the notion of Atwater's supernatural effectiveness. Noting that the 1988 campaign marked an abrupt increase in press coverage of negative ads, political scientist John Geer wrote: "When I asked journalists and consultants what happened in 1988 to produce this change, each of these individuals raised the name of the mercurial operative from South Carolina, without prompting on my part. My question was open ended, but Atwater was at the top of their list."[51] Of course, there were other reasons both for the increase in negative spots and the heightened media attention that they attracted. But to many, Atwater was the prime mover.

Some remembered him for something much worse than political negativity. In the years after his death, a 1981 interview about Southern politics came to light, and to his detractors, it validated a belief that bigotry was the beating heart of his political messages. "You start out in 1954 by saying, 'N——, n——, n——.' By 1968 you can't say 'n——'—that hurts you, backfires. So you say stuff like, uh, forced busing, states' rights, and all that stuff, and you're getting so abstract."[52] Atwater defenders say that he was acknowledging that America was making racial progress. But his critics say that the interview is a smoking gun for the accusation that he was trafficking in coded racism.[53]

The 1988 campaign left other reputational casualties. Dan Quayle learned the bitter wisdom of the old saying that one never gets a second chance to make a first impression. Between his botched rollout and his embarrassing debate moment with Lloyd Bentsen, he acquired an unshakable image as a buffoon. Quayle jokes became common, and news stories sometimes treated them as if they were true. To this day, many people still think that he said: "I was recently on a tour of Latin America, and the only regret I have was that I didn't study Latin harder in school so I could converse with those people."[54] In 1992, when he gave a thoughtful speech that described the social costs of out-of-wedlock births, commentators mocked him because he briefly mentioned a television character.[55] (Two years later, there was no such derision when Bill Clinton made a similar point about nonmarital childbearing.[56]) After the reelection defeat of the Bush–Quayle ticket, there was no call for a Quayle comeback. In the early stages of the 2000 campaign, he flirted with a presidential race, then dropped out because his Republican support lingered in single digits—a sad showing for the party's most recent vice president.[57] Ironically, had he not been on the 1988 ticket, he might have matured into a significant GOP leader. But he was unready for the test of a national campaign and would not get a do-over.

Two of Bush's rivals for the nomination fared better. Bob Dole went back to what he did best: leading the Republicans in the Senate. Setting aside their history of personal conflict, he worked hard for Bush's policies. In a diary entry following his 1992 defeat, Bush recounted a dinner with Republican senators: "He [Dole] was so generous in his comments and so thoughtful, and I thought to myself, 'Here we are, a guy who I fought bitterly in the New Hampshire primary, and now I salute him as a true leader, a wonderful leader, a guy who bent over backwards to do what the President wanted.'"[58] In 1996, Dole was the party's presidential nominee. As his running mate, he picked Jack Kemp. Though the two men had been trading insults for years, Dole reasoned that Kemp's presence on the ticket would help make peace with antitax Republicans. Kemp had given honest service as Bush's housing secretary, and Dole hoped that he might restore GOP's lines of communication with the African American community. In the end, Kemp had no discernible effect. Economic conservatives still distrusted Dole, and black voters still distrusted the Republican Party. This time, peace and prosperity were on the side of a Democratic administration, and Bill Clinton won reelection by a healthy margin.

On the Democratic side of the 1988 roster, a future vice president benefited by flaming out early. Joseph Biden left the 1988 race before most voters were paying attention. He focused on his work in the Senate, and before long, only political junkies remembered the awkward circumstances of his withdrawal. He eventually became chairman of the Senate Foreign

Relations Committee, where he gained the political community's respect for being knowledgeable and fair-minded. He ran again for president in 2008, but the esteem of the Washington establishment was not much of an asset in an outsider's year. He did impress Barack Obama, who chose him as his running mate. Republicans tried to bring up the problems that had brought him down in 1988, to no avail. The passage of twenty years had taken away their sting.

Gary Hart, another early 1988 dropout, had a steeper path to political rehabilitation. Whereas Biden could use his Senate work to repair his reputation as a statesman, Hart had no natural platform because he had given up his seat to run for president. The gregarious Biden could count on a reservoir of affection from colleagues and journalists. The cold and cerebral Hart could not. He did write a series of books, which got a middling reception. His most memorable accomplishment after 1988 consisted of a warning that went unheeded. He co-chaired a commission on national security, which offered this blunt assessment: "States, terrorists, and other disaffected groups will acquire weapons of mass destruction and mass disruption, and some will use them. Americans will likely die on American soil, possibly in large numbers."[59] The report containing that prediction came out on September 15, 1999, and it got practically no media coverage at the time. Only after the attacks of September 11, 2001, did it get some attention, too late to do any good.

And then there was Dukakis. Despite the fundamentals that favored Bush, Dukakis got the blame for losing a purportedly winnable race. The putative negatives piled up: too liberal, too Northern, too passive in the face of the Bush–Atwater assault. Popular culture reflected and reinforced the notion that he was a hapless loser. A 1991 slapstick comedy featured a scene in a blues bar festooned with pictures of great disasters: the *Hindenburg*, the *Titanic* . . . and Michael Dukakis.[60] A few years later, in *The American President*, screenwriter Aaron Sorkin imagined how a politician should have disposed of the issue of the American Civil Liberties Union: "For the record, yes, I am a card-carrying member of the ACLU. . . . Now this is an organization whose sole purpose is to defend the Bill of Rights, so it naturally begs the question, why would a senator, his party's most powerful spokesman and a candidate for President, choose to reject upholding the constitution?"[61] It is unlikely that such lines—or any other sound bite, for that matter—could have changed the course of the 1988 race. But the conventional wisdom set in, and Democrats decided that they did not want another Dukakis.

CLINTON AND 1992

The judgment against Dukakis was bad news for former senator Paul Tsongas, another technocratic Greek American from Massachusetts. He did fairly well in the 1992 Democratic primaries, but unfortunately for him, he was running against a candidate who offered the party a clean break from Dukakis: the man who had given the 1988 nominating speech, Governor Bill Clinton.

Where Dukakis was short (5'8"), Clinton was tall (6'2"). Where Dukakis was from the Northeast, Clinton was from the South. Where Dukakis opposed the death penalty, Clinton supported it—and had even let executions go forward in Arkansas. Clinton aide George Stephanopoulos wrote that liberals "understood that Clinton wasn't really one of us. But it felt good to get lost in the partisan reverie, to be carried back to . . . a time long before McGovern, Carter, Mondale, and Dukakis were caricatured into a sadly comic Mount Rushmore, symbols of a party out of touch and doomed to defeat. It felt good, again, to think about winning."[62] Soon after the 1992 Democratic convention, a TV spot drove the point home:

> They are a new generation of Democrats, Bill Clinton and Al Gore, and they don't think the way the old Democratic Party did. They've called for an end to welfare as we know it, so welfare can be a second chance, not a way of life. They've sent a strong signal to criminals by supporting the death penalty. And they've rejected the old tax and spend politics. Clinton's balanced 12 budgets and they've proposed a new plan investing in people, detailing $140 billion in spending cuts they'd make right now.[63]

Though Clinton wanted to appeal to voters who had disliked Dukakis's liberalism, he also needed the support of progressive Democrats, so he framed his positions with language that liberals could accept—or at least rationalize. An "end to welfare as we know it" could mean many things, including an expansion of day care programs for poor working families. The spending cuts could mean lower defense spending, and "investing in people" could translate into expanded social services.

Jesse Jackson's showing in the 1988 campaign had highlighted the growing importance of the African American vote in Democratic nomination contests. Clinton strategist James Carville said: "That is the first thing I said in the campaign when I went to work. I said, you can cut this thing any way you want to cut it but unless you have Southern blacks in there, you can't figure this thing. There is no way we can get the nomination without a substantial black vote in the South."[64] Clinton caught a huge break when Jackson decided not to run again. He got another when Virginia governor Douglas Wilder—the first African American to hold such a post since Reconstruction—also opted out of the race. He carefully courted black Democratic leaders and voters, who indeed proved crucial in securing the Democratic nomination. Clinton also understood that Jackson had high disapproval ratings and that many voters worried that Democrats pandered to interest groups. In June, he addressed this vulnerability by seizing the "Sister Souljah moment." After the deadly Los Angeles riots in May, rap singer Sister Souljah had told the *Washington Post:* "If black people kill black people every day, why not have a week and kill white people?"[65] In mid-June remarks to Jackson's Rainbow Coalition, Clinton condemned her. The attack annoyed Jackson and prompted Sister Souljah to accuse Clinton of using her as a vehicle, "like Willie Horton and various other black victims of racism."[66] But her "kill white people" comment had been so extreme that she found few supporters, and African American leaders generally sided with Clinton.[67] By this time, he had already locked up the nomination, managing the neat trick of demonstrating courage without actually risking his political neck.

Clinton assailed the Bush record and set up a war room to respond rapidly to GOP attacks. Carville had little use for those who criticized the approach: "Well, your opponent, who's trying to eviscerate you, has a charge up. Do you let the charge go? Is that their idea of brilliant politics? That's exactly what they all attacked Dukakis for doing. Said he was inept."[68]

Clinton benefited from a radical shift in the political setting. For decades, the Cold War had been at the heart of presidential politics. The possibility of direct combat with the Soviet Union was never far from the public mind, and candidates with military experience tended to have an advantage: every president of this era had served in uniform. Clinton, by contrast, was not a veteran. During the Vietnam War, in fact, he had used questionable tactics to avoid the military draft. And during his time as a Rhodes scholar, he had briefly visited Moscow—a trip that would have raised a flotilla of red flags during the height of American anticommunism. The Bush campaign hoped that these facets of Clinton's biography—together with his lack of experience in national security issues—would cause voters to reject him in favor of the foreign policy hand and war hero who was already in the White House. But things had changed since the "Dukakis in the tank" ad, and Bush failed to get traction with these issues. Now that the Soviet Union was gone and the United States seemed to be making friends with Russia, a long-ago student trip did not move votes. The president's apparent cluelessness about economic distress mattered more than his challenger's lack of a foreign policy résumé.

SCANDAL

In May 1988, Bush wrote his son, George, asking him not to contact federal officials. "A call from a 'Bush' will get returned, but there is a great likelihood that it will be leaked; maybe deliberately misrepresented. If there is a legitimate inquiry, call my office. It is certainly appropriate to contact your own government, but let's do it through my office so no one can accuse any of the family of trying to use influence."[69] As president, he strove to prevent conflicts of interests. He was largely successful in this effort, but there were some embarrassments.

During the Reagan administration, the Department of Housing and Urban Development had issued dubious contracts. The scandal came to light early in the Bush administration, leading one Bush campaign adviser to make a memorable admission during Senate testimony. Paul Manafort, whose lobbying for foreign interests had briefly been the target of Democratic attacks, acknowledged that his firm had also lobbied HUD: "I would stipulate that for the purposes of today, you could characterize this as influence peddling."[70] Although a HUD official was eventually convicted of felonies, Manafort avoided prosecution.

Another problem involved John Sununu, Bush's chief of staff. Bush named him to the job in gratitude for his help in winning the New Hampshire primary. Despite his high intelligence (a PhD from MIT) and tenure as the state's governor, Sununu was an odd choice. He had never worked in Washington and had little connection to the national political community. His inexperience was exceeded only by his confidence in himself and his contempt for nearly everyone else. His brusque manner made enemies within the GOP, as did his political misjudgments. He thought that the "no new taxes" reversal would be an easy sell, and he assured Bush that his fellow New Hampshirite, David Souter, would be a solid conservative vote on the Supreme Court.[71] When the news media reported on that he had used a government car and military aircraft for personal travel, calls for his ouster spread more quickly than such minor missteps would have otherwise warranted. Bush dispatched his son George to inform Sununu that he had to step aside.

A much more serious matter—the Iran–Contra scandal—lingered from the Reagan years and continued to bedevil Bush. The independent counsel's investigation continued throughout his term, and in the fall of 1992, it revealed documents contradicting his claims that he had been "out of the loop." A Gallup poll for *Newsweek* asked respondents: "Are you satisfied with Bush's explanation of his involvement in the Iran–Contra arms deal when he was vice president?" By a margin of 54–36 percent, Americans said no.[72] On the Friday before the election, the independent counsel got a grand jury to indict Reagan's defense secretary, Caspar Weinberger, for the second time that year. The media reported that Weinberger's notes on a 1986 meeting provided even more evidence that Bush had been very much in the Iran–Contra loop.[73] Some Republicans later blamed the story for Bush's defeat, but it is more likely that the economic fundamentals had already doomed him. On Christmas Day, after his 1992 defeat had liberated him from worries about public reactions and charges of cover-up, Bush issued a full pardon to Weinberger and five other figures in Iran–Contra.

ELECTRONIC POLITICS

The one time that the Iran–Contra issue worked in Bush's favor was when pushed back against Dan Rather in their famous live interview. Bush and his media adviser, Roger Ailes, knew that Republicans had long distrusted the mainstream media. In 1964, Dwight Eisenhower—hardly a fringe figure—got cheers at the Republican National Convention when he said: "So let us particularly scorn the divisive efforts of those outside our family, including sensation-seeking columnists and commentators, because, my friends, I assure you that these are people who couldn't care less about the good of our party."[74] Five years later, Vice President Spiro Agnew briefly became a GOP folk hero when he delivered a speech (written by Pat Buchanan) attacking the "small and unelected elite" running the television networks. And after the 1988 campaign, Republican politicians took the Bush–Rather exchange as a model for prevailing in a difficult media situation.

Press bashing had its limits, and Bush understood that he needed the mainstream media. So like his predecessors, he held press conferences, did one-on-one interviews, and maintained friendly (or at least civil) relationships with reporters covering the White House. A few days before he left office, he had his last presidential press conference, together with the prime minister of Canada. He said that he looked forward to becoming a private citizen again. "I'm not looking to have press conferences. I love you guys, especially the photo dogs."[75]

The media world would soon undergo upheaval, in part because of Roger

Ailes. Talk radio had turned into a national political force, and Rush Limbaugh would soon become a major figure in Republican and conservative politics. Ailes served as executive producer of Limbaugh's short-lived television program. The show never found a large audience, but together with Limbaugh's far more successful radio program, it offered an early glimpse of what conservative media would look like without the "mainstream" filter.

For decades, conservatives had yearned for a television network of their own, but economic and technological barriers kept them from founding a rival to the Big Three of ABC, CBS, and NBC. In the 1970s, Ailes briefly worked at a company that provided conservative-leaning news content to local stations, but it was nothing close to a true network, and it soon collapsed.[76] Two decades later, the spread of cable television opened many opportunities, and Ailes was ready. In 1996, Rupert Murdoch hired him to launch Fox News, which would provide a "fair and balanced" alternative to the existing networks. Even at this early stage, there was synergy between cable and the other burgeoning medium of the 1990s, the internet. Ailes gave a show to Matt Drudge, whose website had broken the story of President Clinton's affair with a White House intern. Though the program did not last long, the relationship continued, with Drudge prominently featuring Fox programs and personalities. When Ailes died in 2017, his widow let Drudge break the news.

On social media, many of the reactions to Ailes's death emphasized the sexual harassment scandal that had recently led to ouster from Fox. One Twitter post, however, was more positive. "He wasn't perfect, but Roger Ailes was my friend & I loved him," said George H. W. Bush. "Not sure I would have been President w/o his great talent, loyal help. RIP."[77] As usual, Bush was being gracious: he probably would have won the fall election with or without Ailes's ads. But there was also some truth to the tweet. Bush's 1988 nomination was not a sure thing, and Ailes played a key supporting role in two episodes that had helped Bush keep his edge over Dole: the confrontation with Dan Rather on CBS, and the "Straddle" ad in the New Hampshire primary.

By this time of his death, ironically, Ailes had prepared the way for the anti-Bush. For years, Fox had provided Trump with positive coverage, establishing him as a political leader in the minds of its Republican-leaning audience. Despite a brief estrangement over Trump's attack on Fox anchor Megyn Kelly, Ailes spent the months after his departure from Fox as a media adviser to the campaign. And the network that he had founded set aside the "fair and balanced" mantra to become an overt cheerleader for Trump.

Bush was unhappy about Trump's rise. "I don't like him," he told author Mark Updegrove. "I don't know much about him, but I know he's a blowhard. And I'm not too excited about him being a leader."[78] Trump had crushed Jeb Bush's presidential hopes and had attacked George W. Bush over the Iraq War (although he had vaguely supported the invasion when it was under way). The elder Bush's opposition was more than a matter of family loyalty, however. He had spent most of his public life working for international cooperation, and now Trump was proclaiming "America First." Bush grew up learning that a gentleman should be courteous, generous, and humble. Trump's character represented the opposite of those qualities. Bush focused on substance and disdained self-promotion, much to the frustration of his staff. Speechwriter Mark Davis recalled that Bush "often complained that the 'I-factor' was too high in his speeches, meaning they were too full of braggadocio."[79] Trump's speeches were little more than braggadocio, often untethered to reality. Bush launched his presidency by calling for more civility. "To my friends, and, yes, I do mean friends—in the loyal opposition and, yes, I mean loyal—I put out my hand. . . . The American people await action. They didn't send us here to bicker."[80] Davis wrote: "Bush sensed that America's Augustan era had already passed, but seemed unready to accept that fact as a challenge."[81]

ENDINGS

According to political scientist Hugh Heclo, "Bush was the last president to govern without the 'permanent campaign' mindset that has become mandatory in American politics."[82] Like any high-level politician, Bush was alert to polls and upcoming elections, but he saw a distinction between campaigning and governing. The latter sometimes required decisions that hampered the former. If he had to break a campaign pledge for what he saw as the country's long-term economic interest, so be it.

Other leaders of his generation also separated campaign politics and public policy. During the Reagan and Bush administrations Bob Michel and Bob Dole both supported unpopular tax increases and spending cuts because they thought it was their responsibility Like Bush, both of them maintained civil relations with the opposite party, and were ready to work together even at the expense of campaign issues. In 1985, after a controversial House vote on a disputed election triggered a walkout by Republican members, Michel enraged his younger, more confrontational GOP colleagues by shaking hands with the Democratic winner.[83]

Bush had something else in common with Michel and Dole: all had seen combat in World War II. That conflict shaped their lives and the way that they viewed the world. When the House debated a 1991 resolution to approve the use of force against Iraq, Michel said: "I, like so many other members of my generation, am haunted by the ghosts of Munich and the ghosts that Munich produced, and that is why I am so opposed to a policy of delay against aggression threatening our vital national interests."[84] In the 1990s, Bush, Michel, and Dole all left power. Bush lost the 1992 election to Clinton. In 1994, Michel retired from Congress, and the leadership of the House GOP passed to Newt Gingrich. In 1996, finding it difficult to balance his leadership duties with the demands of a presidential campaign, Dole resigned from the Senate. After his defeat that November, no member of his generation would ever again win a nomination for national office. The last remaining World War II veterans in Congress retired at the end of 2014.

Of sixteen million Americans who served in the war, only half a million were still alive in 2018. Their ranks shrank each day. Michel had passed in 2017, and Bush died the next year. Like many other veterans of the conflict, he respected rank and protocol. Though he disliked Trump, he had made clear that he wanted the forty-fifth president at his funeral. As he lay in state in the Capitol Rotunda, another veteran came to pay his respects: Bob Dole, now ninety-five years old. He had spent the last seventy-three years without the use of his right arm, and now he had to use a wheelchair. He and Bush had long been rivals and had never been friends, but he saw a duty to honor a deceased president. A young aide lifted Dole from behind, standing him up before Bush's casket. He raised his left arm and saluted.

APPENDIX A 1988 DEMOCRATIC PRIMARY RESULTS

State	Turnout	Dukakis (%)	Jackson (%)	Gore (%)	Gephardt (%)	Simon (%	Hart (%)	Other (%)	Uncommitted (%)
NH (2/16)	123,512	35.7*	7.8	6.8	19.8	17.1	4.0	8.8	x
SD (2/23)	71,606	31.2	5.4	8.4	43.5*	5.6	5.4	0.5	x
VT (3/1)	50,791	55.8*	25.7	x	7.7	5.2	4.0	1.6	x
AL (3/8)	405,642	7.7	43.6*	37.4	7.4	0.8	1.9	0.8	0.4
AK (3/8)	497,544	18.9	17.1	37.3*	12.0	1.8	3.7	2.0	7.1
FL (3/8)	1,273,298	40.9*	20.0	12.7	14.4	2.2	2.9	0.8	6.2
GA (3/8)	622,752	15.6	39.8*	32.4	6.7	1.3	2.5	0.5	1.2
KY (3/8)	318,721	18.6	15.6	45.8*	9.1	2.9	3.7	0.9	3.3
LA (3/8)	624,450	15.3	35.5*	28.0	10.6	0.8	4.2	5.5	x
MD (3/8)	531,335	45.6*	28.7	8.7	7.9	3.1	1.8	1.3	2.8
MA (3/8)	713,447	58.6*	18.7	4.4	10.2	3.7	1.5	1.2	1.7
MS (3/8)	359,417	8.3	44.7*	33.5	5.5	0.6	3.9	0.9	2.6
MO (3/8)	527,805	11.6	20.2	2.8	57.8*	4.1	1.4	0.9	1.3
NC (3/8)	679,958	20.3	33.0	34.7*	5.5	1.2	2.4	0.6	2.4
OK (3/8)	392,727	16.9	13.3	41.4*	21.0	1.8	3.7	1.9	x
RI (3/8)	49,029	69.8*	15.2	4.0	4.1	2.8	1.5	1.0	1.7
TN (3/8)	576,314	3.4	20.7	72.3*	1.5	0.5	0.8	0.3	0.5
TX (3/8)	1,767,045	32.8*	24.5	20.2	13.6	2.0	4.7	2.2	x
VA (3/8)	364,899	22.0	45.1*	22.3	4.4	1.9	1.7	0.9	1.7
IL (3/15)	1,500,930	16.3	32.3	5.1	2.3	42.3*	0.9	0.7	x
PR (3/20)	356,178	22.9	29.0	14.4	3.0	18.2	7.5	5.0	x

(continued on the next page)

APPENDIX A Continued

State	Turnout	Dukakis (%)	Jackson (%)	Gore (%)	Gephardt (%)	Simon (%)	Hart (%)	Other (%)	Uncommitted (%)
CT (3/29)	241,395	58.1*	28.3	7.7	0.4	1.3	2.4	1.0	0.8
WI (4/5)	1,014,782	47.6*	28.2	17.4	0.8	4.8	0.7	0.	0.3
NY (4/19)	1,575,186	50.9*	37.1	10.0	0.2	1.1	x	0.1	0.7
PA (4/26)	1,507,690	66.5*	27.3	3.0	0.5	0.6	1.4	0.8	x
DC (5/3)	86,052	17.9	80.0*	0.8	0.3	0.9	x	0.1	x
IN (5/3)	645,708	69.6*	22.5	3.4	2.6	1.9	x	x	x
OH (5/3)	1,383,572	62.9*	27.4	2.2	x	1.1	2.1	4.4	x
NE (5/10)	169,008	62.9*	25.7	1.5	2.9	1.2	2.5	0.4	2.8
WV (5/10)	340,097	74.8*	13.5	3.4	1.8	0.7	2.7	3.2	x
OR (5/17)	388,932	56.8*	38.1	1.4	1.7	1.2	x	0.7	x
ID (5/24)	51,370	73.4*	15.7	3.7	x	2.7	x	x	4.5
CA (6/7)	3,138,748	60.9*	35.1	1.8	x	1.4	x	0.8	x
MT (6/7)	121,871	68.7*	22.1	1.9	2.8	1.3	x	x	3.4
NJ (6/7)	654,302	63.4*	32.7	2.8	x	x	x	1.1	x
NM (6/7)	188,610	61.0*	28.1	2.5	x	1.5	3.7	1.5	1.7
ND (6/14)	3,405	84.9	15.1	x	x	x	x	x	x
National total	23,318,128	42.5	29.1	13.7	6.0	4.6	1.8	1.3	1.0

Source: Rhodes Cook, "The 1988 Nominations: Process and Patterns," in *The Elections of 1988,* ed. Michael Nelson (Washington, DC: CQ Press, 1989). Values in parentheses indicate primary dates. An "x" indicates that the candidate or uncommitted line was not on the ballot. The April 19 New York primary was for election of delegates only. An asterisk indicates the winner.

APPENDIX B

1988 REPUBLICAN PRIMARY RESULTS

State	Turnout	Bush (%)	Dole (%)	Robertson (%)	Kemp (%)	Other (%)	Uncommitted (%)
NH (2/16)	157,644	37.6*	28.4	9.4	12.8	11.8	x
SD (2/23)	93,405	18.6	55.2*	19.6	4.6	0.6	1.3
VT (3/1)	47,832	49.3*	39.0	5.1	3.9	2.7	x
SC (3/5)	195,292	48.5*	20.6	19.1	11.5	0.3	x
AL (3/8)	213,561	64.5*	16.3	13.9	4.9	0.3	x
AR (3/8)	68,305	47.0*	25.9	18.9	5.1	1.0	2.1
FL (3/8)	901,222	62.1*	21.2	10.6	4.6	1.4	x
GA (3/8)	400,928	53.8*	23.6	16.3	5.8	0.5	x
KY (3/8)	121,402	59.3*	23.0	11.1	3.3	1.4	1.8
LA (3/8)	144,781	57.8*	17.7	18.2	5.3	1.0	x
MD (3/8)	200,754	53.3*	32.4	6.4	5.9	2.0	x
MA (3/8)	241,181	58.5*	26.3	4.5	7.0	2.3	1.4
MS (3/8)	158,526	66.1*	16.9	13.5	3.5	x	x
MO (3/8)	400,300	42.2*	41.1	11.2	3.5	0.7	1.4
NC (3/8)	273,801	45.4*	39.1	9.8	4.1	0.5	1.0
OK (3/8)	208,938	37.4*	34.9	21.1	5.5	1.0	x
RI (3/8)	16,035	64.9*	22.6	5.7	4.9	0.8	1.1
TN (3/8)	254,252	60.0*	21.6	12.6	4.3	0.6	0.9
TX (3/8)	1,014,956	63.9*	13.9	15.3	5.0	0.7	1.2
VA (3/8)	234,142	53.3*	26.0	13.7	4.6	0.8	1.6
IL (3/15)	858,637	54.6*	36.0	6.8	1.5	1.0	x
PR (3/20)	3,973	97.1*	2.7	0.1	x	0.1	x
CT (3/29)	104,171	70.6*	20.2	3.1	3.1	x	3.1
WI (4/5)	359,294	82.2*	7.9	6.9	1.4	1.0	0.7
PA (4/26)	870,549	79.0*	11.9	9.1	x	x	x
DC (5/3)	6,720	87.6*	7.0	4.0	x	1.4	x
IN (5/3)	437,655	80.4*	9.8	6.6	3.3	x	x
OH (5/3)	794,904	81.0*	11.9	7.1	x	x	x
NE (5/10)	204,049	68.0*	22.3	5.1	4.1	0.5	x
WV (5/10)	143,140	77.3*	10.9	7.3[9]	2.7	1.8	x

(continued on the next page)

State	Turnout	Bush (%)	Dole (%)	Robertson (%)	Kemp (%)	Other (%)	Uncommitted (%)
OR (5/17)	274,486	72.8*	17.9	7.7	x	1.5	x
ID (5/24)	68,275	81.2*	x	8.6	x	x	10.2
CA (6/7)	2,240,387	82.9*	12.9	4.2	x	x	x
MT (6/7)	86,380	73.0*	19.4	x	x	x	7.5
NJ (6/7)	241,033	100.0*	x	x	x	x	x
NM (6/7)	88,744	78.2*	10.5	6.0	x	2.4	2.9
ND (6/14)	39,434	94.0*	x	x	x	6.0	x
National total	12,169,088	67.9*	19.2	9.0	2.7	0.7	0.5

Source: Rhodes Cook, "The 1988 Nominations: Process and Patterns," in *The Elections of 1988*, ed. Michael Nelson (Washington, DC: CQ Press, 1989). Values in parentheses indicate primary dates. An "x" indicates that the candidate or uncommitted line was not on the ballot. An asterisk indicates the winner.

APPENDIX C 1988 PRESIDENTIAL GENERAL ELECTION RESULTS

State	No. of Electoral Votes		Bush Vote		Dukakis Vote		Other Vote	
	R	D	N	%	N	%	N	%
Alabama	9	0	1,378,476	59.17	815,576	39.86	13,394	0.97
Alaska	3	0	200,116	59.59	119,251	36.27	8,281	4.14
Arizona	7	0	1,171,873	59.95	702,541	38.74	15,303	1.31
Arkansas	6	0	827,738	56.37	466,578	42.19	11,923	1.44
California	47	0	9,887,065	51.13	5,054,917	47.56	129,915	1.31
Colorado	8	0	1,372,394	53.06	728,177	45.28	22,764	1.66
Connecticut	8	0	1,443,394	51.98	750,241	46.87	16,569	1.15
Delaware	3	0	249,891	55.88	139,639	43.48	1,605	0.64
DC	0	3	192,877	14.30	27,590	82.65	5,880	3.05
Florida	21	0	4,302,313	60.87	2,618,885	38.51	26,727	0.62
Georgia	12	0	1,812,672	59.65	1,081,331	39.60	13,549	0.75
Hawaii	0	4	354,461	44.75	158,625	54.27	3,472	0.98
Idaho	4	0	408,968	62.08	253,881	36.01	7,815	1.91
Illinois	24	0	4,559,120	50.69	2,310,939	48.60	32,241	0.71
Indiana	12	0	2,168,621	59.84	1,297,763	39.69	10,215	0.47
Iowa	0	8	1,225,614	44.50	545,355	54.71	9,702	0.79
Kansas	7	0	993,044	55.79	554,049	42.56	16,359	1.65
Kentucky	9	0	1,322,517	55.52	734,281	43.88	7,868	0.59
Louisiana	10	0	1,628,202	54.27	883,702	44.06	27,040	1.66
Maine	4	0	555,035	55.34	307,131	43.88	4,335	0.78

(continued on the next page)

State	No. of Electoral Votes		Bush Vote		Dukakis Vote		Other Vote	
	R	D	N	%	N	%	N	%
Maryland	10	0	1,714,358	51.11	876,167	48.20	11,887	0.69
Massachusetts	0	13	2,632,805	45.37	1,194,635	53.23	36,755	1.40
Michigan	20	0	3,669,163	53.57	1,965,486	45.67	27,894	0.76
Minnesota	0	10	2,096,790	45.90	962,337	52.91	24,982	1.19
Mississippi	7	0	931,527	59.89	557,890	39.07	9,716	1.04
Missouri	11	0	2,093,713	51.82	1,084,953	47.84	7,141	0.34
Montana	4	0	365,674	52.07	190,412	46.20	6,326	1.73
Nebraska	5	0	661,465	60.16	397,956	39.19	4,274	0.65
Nevada	4	0	350,067	58.86	206,040	37.92	11,289	3.22
New Hampshire	4	0	451,074	62.41	281,537	36.29	5,841	1.29
New Jersey	16	0	3,099,553	56.24	1,743,192	42.60	36,009	1.16
New Mexico	5	0	521,287	51.86	270,341	46.90	6,449	1.24
New York	0	36	6,485,683	47.52	3,081,871	51.62	55,930	0.86
North Carolina	13	0	2,134,370	57.97	1,237,258	41.71	6,945	0.33
North Dakota	3	0	297,261	56.03	166,559	42.97	2,963	1.00
Ohio	23	0	4,393,699	55.00	2,416,549	44.15	37,521	0.85
Oklahoma	8	0	1,171,036	57.93	678,367	41.28	9,246	0.79
Oregon	0	7	1,201,694	46.61	560,126	51.28	25,362	2.11
Pennsylvania	25	0	4,536,251	50.70	2,300,087	48.39	41,220	0.91
Rhode Island	0	4	404,620	43.93	177,761	55.64	1,736	0.43
South Carolina	8	0	986,009	61.50	606,443	37.58	9,012	0.91

State								
South Dakota	3	0	312,991	52.85	165,415	46.51	2,016	0.64
Tennessee	11	0	1,636,250	57.89	947,233	41.55	9,223	0.56
Texas	29	0	5,427,410	55.95	3,036,829	43.35	37,833	0.70
Utah	5	0	647,008	66.22	428,442	32.05	11,223	1.73
Vermont	3	0	243,328	51.10	124,331	47.58	3,221	1.32
Virginia	12	0	2,191,609	59.74	1,309,162	39.23	22,648	1.03
Washington	0	10	1,865,253	48.46	903,835	50.05	27,902	1.50
West Virginia	0	5	653,311	47.46	310,065	52.20	2,230	0.34
Wisconsin	0	11	2,191,608	47.80	1,047,499	51.41	17,315	0.79
Wyoming	3	0	176,551	60.53	106,867	38.01	2,571	1.46
Total	426	111	91,597,809	53.37	48,886,097	45.65	899,637	0.98

Source: CQ Press, "Voting and Elections Collection, Presidential General Election, All States, 1988 Summary."

HOW STATES VOTED IN 1988 AND 2016

BUSH AND TRUMP

Alabama

Alaska

Arizona

Arkansas

Florida

Georgia

Idaho

Indiana

Kansas

Kentucky

Louisiana

Michigan

Mississippi

Missouri

Montana

Nebraska

North Carolina

North Dakota

Ohio

Oklahoma

Pennsylvania

South Carolina

South Dakota

Tennessee

Texas

Utah

Wyoming

BUSH AND CLINTON

California

Colorado

Connecticut

Delaware

Illinois

Maine

Maryland

Nevada

New Hampshire

New Jersey

New Mexico

Vermont

Virginia

DUKAKIS AND TRUMP

Iowa

West Virginia

Wisconsin

DUKAKIS AND CLINTON

DC

Hawaii

Massachusetts

Minnesota

New York

Oregon

Washington

NOTES

INTRODUCTION

1. Transcript of Jon Meacham's eulogy for former President George H. W. Bush, *CBS News*, December 6, 2018, https://www.cbsnews.com/.
2. Brett Samuels, "Six Touching Moments during George H. W. Bush's State Funeral," *The Hill*, December 5, 2018, https://thehill.com/.
3. Alex S. Jones, "For News Magazines, Growing Identity Crisis," *New York Times*, June 29, 1988, https://www.nytimes.com/.
4. Jonathan Martin, "Richard Ben Cramer's Masterpiece," *Politico*, January 8, 2013, https://www.politico.com/.
5. Michael Grunwald, "Barack Obama Elected President with Mandate for Change," *Time*, November 4, 2008, http://content.time.com/.
6. "How Groups Voted in 1988," Roper Center for Public Opinion Research, https://ropercenter.cornell.edu/.
7. Exit poll data at CNN Politics Election Center (http://www.cnn.com/election/2012/results/race/president/) and CNN Politics Exit Polls (https://edition.cnn.com/election/2016/results/exit-polls/national/president).
8. US Department of Commerce, Bureau of the Census, "Characteristics of Voters in the Presidential Election of 2016," https://www.census.gov/content/dam/Census/library/publications/2018/demo/P20-582.pdf. For additional 1988 data, see Carolyn Smith, ed., *The '88 Vote* (New York: Capital Cities/ABC, 1989), 18.
9. Norman J. Ornstein, Thomas E. Mann, and Michael J. Malbin, *Vital Statistics on Congress* (Washington, DC: Brookings Institution, 2017).
10. David Hawkings, "The Incredible Shrinking Split Tickets," *Roll Call*, February 1, 2017, https://www.rollcall.com/.
11. John T. Pothier, "The Partisan Bias in Senate Elections," *American Politics Quarterly* 12 (1984): 89–100.
12. Gary C. Jacobson, *The Electoral Origins of Divided Government* (Boulder, CO: Westview Press, 1990), 112–120.
13. Debate transcript, George H. W. Bush v. Michael Dukakis, Commission on Presidential Debates, October 13, 1988, http://debates.org/.
14. Hindelang Criminal Justice Research Center, University at Albany, Sourcebook of Criminal Justice Statistics Online, https://www.albany.edu/sourcebook/pdf/t31062012.pdf.
15. As early as 1963, John F. Kennedy warned that it was "easy for some to assume

that the cold war is over, that all outstanding issues between the Soviets and ourselves can be quickly and satisfactorily settled." John F. Kennedy, "Address at the University of Maine," October 19, 1963, American Presidency Project, University of California–Santa Barbara, https://www.presidency.ucsb.edu/.

16. Richard Nixon, "Remarks at the Lighting of the Nation's Christmas Tree," December 14, 1973, American Presidency Project, University of California–Santa Barbara, https://www.presidency.ucsb.edu/.

17. A month before the fall of the Berlin Wall, only 22 percent of respondents told a CNN poll that the United States could now trust the Soviets more, while 72 percent said that the nation should "wait longer to see if these changes stay in place." "Assessing Change in the USSR," *American Enterprise,* January/February 1990, https://web.archive.org/web/20180214055954/https://ropercenter.cornell.edu/public-perspective/ppscan/12/12014.pdf, 93.

18. John F. Kennedy, "Inaugural Address," January 20, 1961, American Presidency Project, University of California–Santa Barbara, https://www.presidency.ucsb.edu/.

19. Kennedy, Johnson, Nixon, Ford, and Bush were naval officers, though Johnson's service was brief. Jimmy Carter was a naval cadet, and Reagan made training films for the army air force.

20. George Bush, "Remarks to Officers and Troops at Hickam Air Force Base in Pearl Harbor, Hawaii," October 28, 1990, American Presidency Project, University of California–Santa Barbara, https://www.presidency.ucsb.edu/.

21. Richard L. Berke, "Still Running; Is Age-Bashing Any Way to Beat Bob Dole?," *New York Times,* May 5, 1996, https://www.nytimes.com/.

22. A common term is WASP (white Anglo-Saxon Protestant), but it is not strictly accurate because many people in the social category had roots in countries other than England. The Roosevelts, for instance, were Dutch.

23. Charles Kenney and Robert L. Turner, *Dukakis: An American Odyssey* (Boston: Houghton Mifflin, 1988), 6.

24. Michael S. Dukakis, oral history interview conducted by Janet Heininger, Edward M. Kennedy Institute for the United States Senate, November 2, 2009, https://www.emkinstitute.org/.

25. Lily Geismer, *Don't Blame Us: Suburban Liberals and the Transformation of the Democratic Party* (Princeton, NJ: Princeton University Press, 2015), 1.

26. Smith, *'88 Vote,* 18.

27. Linda Chavez, "Is Spanish Wrong Signal to Latinos?," *Los Angeles Times,* August 8, 1988.

28. Michael J. Hicks and Srikant Devaraj, "The Myth and Reality of Manufacturing in America," Center for Business and Economic Research, Ball State University, 2015, https://projects.cberdata.org/reports/MfgReality.pdf.

29. Virginia Postrel, Facebook post, August 4, 2018, https://www.facebook.com/vpostrel/posts/10156187295721348.

30. Josh Clinton and Carrie Roush, "Poll: Persistent Partisan Divide over 'Birther' Question," NBC News, August 10, 2016, https://www.nbcnews.com/.

31. Ruth Shalit, "What I Saw at the Devolution," *Reason,* March 1993.

32. Luck plays a big role across an array of political phenomena, including the detection of military and diplomatic surprises. Robert Jervis, *Perception and Misperception in International Politics* (Princeton, NJ: Princeton University Press, 1976), 180.

33. David R. Runkel, *Campaign for President: The Managers Look at '88* (Dover, MA: Auburn House, 1989), 250.

34. John Sides and Lynn Vavreck, *The Gamble: Choice and Chance in the 2012 Presidential Election* (Princeton, NJ: Princeton University Press, 2013), 140.

35. Kyle Mattes and David P. Redlawsk, *The Positive Case for Negative Campaigning* (Chicago: University of Chicago Press, 2014), 27.

36. Louis Bolce, Gerald De Maio and Douglas Muzzio, "The 1992 Republican 'Tent': No Blacks Walked In," *Political Science Quarterly* 8 (1993): 255–270.

37. Jeffrey Schmalz, "Words on Bush's Lips in '88 Now Stick in Voters' Craw," *New York Times,* June 14, 1992, https://www.nytimes.com/.

38. Glenn Kessler, "Grover Norquist's History Lesson: George H. W. Bush, 'No New Taxes,' and the 1992 Election," *Washington Post,* November 27, 1992, https://www.washingtonpost.com/.

CHAPTER 1. RETROSPECT: 1950–1980

1. Calculation from US Department of Commerce, Bureau of the Census, *Historical Statistics of the United States, Colonial Times to 1970* (Washington, DC: Government Printing Office, 1975), 796.

2. US Department of Commerce, Bureau of the Census, *Historical Statistics of the United States,* 84.

3. Theodore H. White, *The Making of the President, 1960* (New York: Signet, 1967), 248, 250.

4. George H. W. Bush and Victor Gold, *Looking Forward* (New York: Doubleday, 1987), 253.

5. United States Bureau of the Census, "Percent of People 25 Years and Over Who Have Completed High School or College, by Race, Hispanic Origin and Sex: Selected Years 1940 to 2016," https://www2.census.gov/programs-surveys/demo/tables/educational-attainment/time-series/cps-historical-time-series/taba-2.xlsx.

6. National Defense Education Act (NDEA) (PL 85-864), September 2, 1958, https://www.gpo.gov/fdsys/pkg/STATUTE-72/pdf/STATUTE-72-Pg1580.pdf.

7. James MacGregor Burns, *The Deadlock of Democracy: Four-Party Politics in America* (Englewood Cliffs, NJ: Prentice-Hall, 1963), 200.

8. John A. Farrell, *Richard Nixon: The Life* (New York: Vintage, 2018), 167–174.

9. Jon Meacham, *Destiny and Power: The American Odyssey of George Herbert Walker Bush,* large print ed. (New York: Random House, 2015), 131–132.

10. Theo Lippman Jr., "Said to George Bush, 'When Joe McCarthy Went,'" *Baltimore Sun,* October 19, 1992.

11. *Congressional Record,* December 1, 1954, 16268.

12. Meacham, *Destiny and Power,* 161.

13. Bush and Gold, *Looking Forward,* 25.

14. An invaluable resource on the partisan composition of statehouses is Michael J. Dubin, *Party Affiliations in State Legislatures: A Year by Year Summary, 1796–2006* (Jefferson, NC: McFarland, 2007).

15. Michael Barone, *Our Country: The Shaping of America from Roosevelt to Reagan* (New York: Free Press, 1990), 286.

16. Adlai Stevenson, "Address Accepting the Presidential Nomination at the Democratic National Convention in Chicago," July 26, 1952, American Presidency Project, University of California–Santa Barbara, https://www.presidency.ucsb.edu/.

17. James L. Sundquist, *Dynamics of the Party System*, rev. ed. (Washington, DC: Brookings Institution, 1983), 262–268.

18. Barone, *Our Country*, 307.

19. Joe McGinniss, *The Selling of the President, 1968* (New York: Pocket Books, 1970), 39.

20. McGinniss, *Selling of the President*, 62–63.

21 Mark R. Levy and Michael S. Kramer, *The Ethnic Factor: How America's Minorities Decide Elections* (New York: Touchstone, 1973), 42-43.

22. Levy and Kramer, *Ethnic Factor*, 44-45.

23. "Why the South Must Prevail," *National Review*, August 24, 1957, https://adamgomez.files.wordpress.com/2012/03/whythesouthmustprevail-1957.pdf.

24. A. James Reichley, *The Life of the Parties: A History of American Political Parties* (Lanham, MD: Rowman & Littlefield, 2000), 265.

25. Patrick J. Buchanan, *The Greatest Comeback: How Richard Nixon Rose from Defeat to Create the New Majority* (New York: Crown Forum, 2014), 36–40.

26. Michael Nelson, *Resilient America: Electing Nixon in 1968, Channeling Dissent, and Dividing Government* (Lawrence: University Press of Kansas, 2014), 145.

27. Nelson, *Resilient America*, 224.

28. Robert A. Dallek, *Flawed Giant: Lyndon Johnson and His Times, 1961–1973* (Oxford: Oxford University Press, 1998), 120.

29. Joan Hoff, *Nixon Reconsidered* (New York: Basic Books, 1994), ch. 3.

30. "Text of Stevenson's Address to the Nation on Major Issues of the Campaign," *New York Times*, September 30, 1952, 26, https://www.nytimes.com/.

31. Geismer, *Don't Blame Us*, 134.

32. Theodore H. White, *The Making of the President, 1968* (New York: Pocket Books, 1970), 497.

33. Hugh Heclo, "George Bush and American Conservatism," in *41: Inside the Presidency of George H. W. Bush*, ed. Michael Nelson and Barbara A. Perry (Ithaca, NY: Cornell University Press, 2014), 54.

34. Geismer, *Don't Blame Us*, 171.

35. Don Gonyea, "McGovern Legacy Offers More than a Lost Presidency," National Public Radio, October 21, 2012, https://www.npr.org/.

36. Sam Rosenfeld, *The Polarizers: Postwar Architects of Our Partisan Era* (Chicago: University of Chicago Press, 2018), 277.

37. Julian E. Zelizer, *Governing America: The Revival of Political History* (Princeton, NJ: Princeton University Press, 2012), 84.

38. The GOP hit their House maximum in the elections of 1968 and 1972. The Senate figure, for the election of 1970, includes James Buckley of New York, who won on the Conservative Party line but immediately joined the Senate GOP.

39. Nicol Rae, *Southern Democrats* (Oxford: Oxford University Press, 1994), 73–79.

40. "Words of the Week," *Jet*, October 7, 1976.

41. Earl Black and Merle Black, *The Rise of Southern Republicans* (Cambridge, MA: Harvard Belknap, 2002), 175.

42. Dennis D. Loo and Ruth-Ellen M. Grimes, "Polls, Politics, and Crime: The 'Law and Order' Issue of the 1960s," *Western Criminology Review* 5 (2004): 53.

43. Hazel Erskine, "The Polls: Fear of Violence and Crime," *Public Opinion Quarterly* 38 (1974): 131–145.

44. Donald J. Mulvahill, Lemvin M. Tumin, and Lynn A. Curtis, *Crimes of Violence*, staff report from the Task Force on Individual Acts of Violence to National Commission on the Causes and Prevention of Violence (Washington, DC: Government Printing Office, 1968), https://archive.org/stream/crimesofviolence 12mulvrich/crimesofviolence12mulvrich_djvu.txt.

45. Steven Pinker, "Decivilization in the 1960s," *Human Figurations* 2 (2013), https://quod.lib.umich.edu/h/humfig/11217607.0002.206/--deciviliza tion-in-the-1960s?rgn=main;view=fulltext.

46. Richard M. Scammon and Ben J. Wattenberg, *The Real Majority* (New York: Coward, McCann, and Geoghegan, 1970), 71.

47. Hindelang Criminal Justice Research Center, University at Albany, Sourcebook of Criminal Justice Statistics Online, https://www.albany.edu/sourcebook/pdf /t31062012.pdf.

48. Barry Latzer, *The Rise and Fall of Violent Crime in America* (New York: Encounter, 2016), 114.

49. Richard Nixon, "Address Accepting the Presidential Nomination at the Republican National Convention in Miami Beach, Florida," August 8, 1969, American Presidency Project, University of California–Santa Barbara, https://www .presidency.ucsb.edu/.

50. Hubert H. Humphrey, "Address Accepting the Presidential Nomination at the Democratic National Convention in Chicago," August 29, 1968, American Presidency Project, University of California–Santa Barbara, https://www.pres idency.ucsb.edu/.

51. Latzer, *Rise and Fall*, 153.

52. William G. Mayer, *The Changing American Mind: How and Why American Public Opinion Changed between 1960 and 1988* (Ann Arbor: University of Michigan Press, 1992), 19–22.

53. Gallup Poll, "Death Penalty," https://www.gallup.com/.

54. Second Kennedy–Nixon presidential debate, October 7, 1960, http://debates .org/.

55. John D. Morris, "GOP Brands Tax Bill a Gamble with Economy," *New York Times*, September 21, 1963, https://www.nytimes.com/.

56. HR 8363, Passage, 88th Congress, September 25, 1963, https://www.govtrack .us/congress/votes/88-1963/h69.

57. Republican Party platform of 1964, July 13, 1964, American Presidency Project, University of California–Santa Barbara, https://www.presidency.ucsb.edu/.

58. In 1978, inflation-adjusted property taxes per person were about 50 percent higher than they had been in 1960. Jason Sisney Brian Uhler and Carolyn Chu, "Proposition 13 Report: More Data on California Property Taxes," Legislative Analyst's Office, September 22, 2016, https://lao.ca.gov/LAOEconTax/Article/Detail/209.

59. Donald T. Critchlow, *The Conservative Ascendancy: How the GOP Right Made Political History* (Cambridge, MA: Harvard University Press, 2007), 164–165.

60. Irving Kristol, *Neoconservatism: The Autobiography of an Idea* (New York: Free Press, 1995).

61. Tom W. Smith, "The Polls: American Attitudes toward the Soviet Union and Communism," *Public Opinion Quarterly* 47 (1983): 277–292.

62. Jimmy Carter, "Address at Commencement Exercises at the University of Notre Dame," May 22, 1977, American Presidency Project, University of California–Santa Barbara, https://www.presidency.ucsb.edu/; Frank Reynolds interview of Jimmy Carter, ABC World News Tonight, December 31, 1979.

63. Republican Party Platform of 1976, August 18, 1976, American Presidency Project, University of California–Santa Barbara, https://www.presidency.ucsb.edu/.

64. Smith, "Polls."

65. Louis Harris, "Democratic Voters Agree with Kennedy, Not Carter, on Platform Issues," ABC News–Harris Survey, August 11, 1980, https://theharrispoll.com/wp-content/uploads/2017/12/Harris-Interactive-Poll-Research-DEMOCRATIC-VOTERS-AGREE-WITH-KENNEDY-NOT-CARTER-ON-PLATFORM-ISSUES-1980-08.pdf.

66. Jules Witcover, *Very Strange Bedfellows: The Short and Unhappy Marriage of Richard Nixon and Spiro Agnew* (New York: Public Affairs, 2007), 74.

67. Fred Lindecke, "Agnew Attacks 'Whole Zoo' of Dissidents," *Washington Post*, February 12, 1970, https://www.washingtonpost.com/.

68. Spiro Theodore Agnew, "Television News Coverage," Des Moines, Iowa, November 13, 1969, https://www.americanrhetoric.com/speeches/spiroagnewtvnewscoverage.htm.

69. Tim Dickinson, "Ailes, Nixon and the Plan for 'Putting the GOP on TV News,'" *Rolling Stone*, July 1, 2011, https://www.rollingstone.com/.

70. Michael Nelson, "George Bush: Texan, Conservative," in Nelson and Perry, *41: Inside the Presidency of George H. W. Bush*, 38–40.

71. Republican Party platform of 1968, August 5, 1968, https://www.presidency.ucsb.edu/.

72. Richard Nixon, "Special Message to the Congress on Problems of Population Growth," July 18, 1969, https://www.presidency.ucsb.edu/.

73. Jesse Jackson, "How We Respect Life Is the Over-Riding Moral Issue," January 1977, http://groups.csail.mit.edu/mac/users/rauch/nvp/consistent/jackson.html.

74. Kevin M. Kruse and Julian E. Zelizer, *Fault Lines: A History of the United States since 1974* (New York: Norton, 2018), 89–91.

75. Mark J. Rozell, "Religious Presidents," in *Whose God Rules? Is the United States a Secular Nation or a Theolegal Democracy?*, ed. Nathan C. Walker and Edwin J. Greenlee (New York: Springer, 2011), 108.

76. William Martin, *With God on Our Side: The Rise of the Religious Right in America* (New York: Broadway Books, 1996), 173.

77. Republican Party platform of 1980, July 15, 1980, American Presidency Project, University of California–Santa Barbara, https://www.presidency.ucsb.edu/.

CHAPTER 2. REAGAN, BUSH, AND THE REPUBLICANS

1. William Strauss and Neil Howe, *Generations: The History of America's Future, 1584 to 2069* (New York: Morrow, 1991), 463.

2. Author's calculation from US Census, "Table 1: Voting and Registration, by Single Years of Age and Sex," November 1988, https://www2.census.gov/programs-surveys/cps/tables/p20/440/tab01.pdf.

3. US Census, *Statistical Abstract of the United States* (Washington, DC: Government Printing Office, 1990), 343.

4. George H. W. Bush, "Address Accepting the Presidential Nomination at the Republican National Convention in New Orleans," August 18, 1988, American Presidency Project, University of California–Santa Barbara, https://www.presidency.ucsb.edu/.

5. "George Herbert Walker Bush: 12 June 1924–30 November 2018," Naval History and Heritage Command, February 10, 2015, https://www.history.navy.mil/.

6. Rolfe L. Hillman, "Lt. J. G. George H. W. Bush and USS *Finback* (230): A Focused Narration of the Silent Services WWII Lifeguard Operations," *Undersea Warfare* 55 (2014), https://www.public.navy.mil/subfor/underseawarfaremagazine/Issues/PDF/USW_Summer_2014.pdf.

7. George H. W. Bush, *All the Best, George Bush: My Life in Letters and Other Writings* (New York: Simon & Schuster, 2014), 62.

8. Bush and Gold, *Looking Forward*, 83.

9. Bush and Gold, *Looking Forward*, 85.

10. Letter to Marjorie Arsht, July 28, 1964, in Bush, *All the Best*, 88.

11. Meacham, *Destiny and Power*, 194.

12. John J. Pitney Jr., "Republican Alternatives to the Great Society," in *Politics, Professionalism, and Power: Modern Party Organization and the Legacy of Ray C. Bliss*, (Lanham, MD: University Press of America, 1994), 205–217.

13. *Congressional Record*, July 30, 1968, 24342.

14. *Congressional Record*, July 30, 1968, 24343.

15. Simone M. Caron, "Birth Control and the Black Community in the 1960s: Genocide or Power Politics?," *Journal of Social History* 31 (1998): 545–569.

16. Robert E. Johnson, "Legal Abortion: Is It Genocide or Blessing in Disguise?," *Jet*, March 22, 1973.

17. Bush, *All the Best*, 109.

18. Herbert S. Parmet, *Richard Nixon and His America* (Boston: Little, Brown, 1990), 515.
19. Bush, *All the Best*, 128.
20. Bush and Gold, *Looking Forward*, 110.
21. Bush, *All the Best*, 142.
22. Nicholas Lemann, "Bush and Dole: The Roots of a Feud," *Washington Post*, February 28, 1988, https://www.washingtonpost.com/.
23. Taped conversation between Richard Nixon and George H. W. Bush, November 29, 1972, http://nixontapes.org/ghwb/156-016.mp3.
24. Herbert S. Parmet, *George Bush: The Life of a Lone Star Yankee* (New Brunswick, NJ: Transaction, 2001), 159.
25. Bush, *All the Best*, 190–191.
26. Karl Rove, *Courage and Consequence* (New York: Threshold, 2010), 38.
27. Ford aide Robert Hartmann wrote: "Ford thought Reagan was a phony, and Reagan thought Ford was a lightweight." Robert T. Hartmann, *Palace Politics: An Inside Account of the Ford Years* (New York: McGraw-Hill, 1980), 336.
28. Bush, *All the Best*, 233–234.
29. Gerald R. Ford, "Letter to the Chairman of the Senate Armed Services Committee Concerning the Nomination of George Bush to Be Director of Central Intelligence," December 18, 1975, https://www.presidency.ucsb.edu/.
30. A faithless Ford elector actually voted for Reagan, but in an alternative scenario, he would have provided Ford with the 270th electoral vote. Otherwise, a deadlocked Electoral College would have sent the election to the Democratic House, where Carter would have won.
31. "Double-Entendre," *Newsweek*, August 8, 1977.
32. Raymond L. Garthoff, "Estimating Soviet Military Intentions and Capabilities," Central Intelligence Agency, 2007, https://www.cia.gov/.
33. Parmet, *George Bush: The Life of a Lone Star Yankee*, 209–210.
34. Bush, *All the Best*, 279.
35. Philip Klinkner, *The Losing Parties: Out-Party National Committees, 1956–1993*, (New Haven, CT: Yale University Press, 1994), 149–150.
36. William Yale, "Jackson Urges GOP To Appeal to Blacks," *Washington Post*, January 21, 1978, https://www.washingtonpost.com/.
37. Adam Clymer, "Jesse Jackson Tells Receptive GOP It Can Pick Up Votes of Blacks," *New York Times*, January 21, 1978, https://www.nytimes.com/.
38. Morton Kondracke and Fred Barnes, *Jack Kemp: The Bleeding-Heart Conservative Who Changed America* (New York: Sentinel, 2015), 21.
39. Douglas Frantz, "Army Allowed Kemp to Skip Army Call-up for an Injury," *New York Times*, August 18, 1996, https://www.nytimes.com/.
40. Kondracke and Barnes, *Jack Kemp*, 38.
41. David S. Broder, "House GOP Sees Deep Tax Cut as Election Issue," *Washington Post*, July 23, 1979, https://www.washingtonpost.com/.
42. Richard Reeves, "Why Reagan Won't Make it," *Esquire*, May 8, 1979.
43. Andrew E. Busch, *Reagan's Victory: The Presidential Election of 1980 and the Rise of the Right* (Lawrence: University Press of Kansas, 2005).

44. Robert G. Kaiser, "Minority Leader Held the Key to Carter's Canal Victory," *Washington Post*, March 19, 1978, https://www.washingtonpost.com/.

45. "Senate Leaders and the Panama Canal Treaties," United States Senate, April 18, 1978, https://www.senate.gov/.

46. Jonathan Moore, ed., *The Campaign for President: 1980 in Retrospect* (Cambridge, MA: Ballinger, 1981), 7.

47. Moore, *Campaign for President: 1980 in Retrospect*, 2–3.

48. Richard L. Lyons, "Bush's Victory Surprises Baker in Maine Voting," *Washington Post*, November 4, 1979, https://www.washingtonpost.com/.

49. Moore, *Campaign for President: 1980 in Retrospect*, 44.

50. Hugh Winebrenner, "The Evolution of the Iowa Precinct Caucuses," *Annals of Iowa* 46 (1983): 618–635.

51. Moore, *Campaign for President: 1980 in Retrospect*, 12.

52. "Poll Shows Bush Even with Reagan after Iowa," *Washington Post*, January 24, 1980, https://www.washingtonpost.com/.

53. Anthony Lewis, "Through a Glass Darkly," *New York Times*, February 28, 1980, https://www.nytimes.com/.

54. Moore, *Campaign for President: 1980 in Retrospect*, 13.

55. Reagan was paraphrasing a line from the 1949 movie *State of the Union*, in which political hacks try to keep a heroic political figure (Spencer Tracy) off the air: "Don't cut me off, I paid for this broadcast!"

56. Jeff Greenfield, *The Real Campaign: How the Media Missed the Story of the 1980 Campaign* (New York: Summit, 1982), 47–48.

57. Nicol Rae, *The Decline and Fall of the Liberal Republicans: From 1952 to the Present* (Oxford: Oxford University Press, 1989), 128.

58. Robert Shogan, "Bush Accuses Reagan of 'Economic Madness,'" *Los Angeles Times*, April 11, 1980.

59. See, e.g., the ad by the Florida Conservative Union in the *Pensacola News-Journal*, March 9, 1980.

60. Jules Witcover, "The Dynasty that Almost Wasn't," *Politico*, September 15, 2015, https://www.politico.com/.

61. Parmet, *George Bush*, 245–246.

62. Whitney Lauraine Court, "The Risks and Rewards of Selecting Vice Presidential Nominees," PhD diss., University of Kansas, 2012, https://kuscholarworks.ku.edu/bitstream/handle/1808/10431/Court_ku_0099D_12001_DATA_1.pdf. For California data, see Mervin D. Field, "As a Vice Presidential Candidate, Bush Is More of an Asset to Reagan than Mondale Is to Carter," Field Institute, September 18, 1980, http://ucdata.berkeley.edu/pubs/CalPolls/1098.pdf.

63. Bush, *All the Best*, 303.

64. Stanley Kelley, *Interpreting Elections* (1983; reprint, Princeton, NJ: Princeton University Press, 2014), 169.

65. John T. Pother, "The Partisan Bias in Senate Elections," *American Politics Quarterly* 12 (1984): 89–100.

66. See National Election Studies data in Harold W. Stanley and Richard G. Niemi,

Vital Statistics on American Politics, 2011–2012 (Washington, DC: CQ/Sage, 2011), 107–108.

67. William F. Connelly Jr. and John J. Pitney Jr., *Congress' Permanent Minority? Republicans in the US House* (Lanham, MD: Rowman & Littlefield, 1994), 55.

68. Roderick A. DeArment, oral history interview conducted by Richard Norton Smith, Robert J. Dole Institute of Politics, April 13, 2007, http://dolearchivecollections.ku.edu/collections/oral_history/pdf/dearment_rod_2007-04-13.pdf.

69. *Congressional Record,* August 17, 1982, 21416.

70. Timothy B. Clark, "The Clout of the 'New' Bob Dole," *New York Times Magazine,* December 12, 1982, https://www.nytimes.com/.

71. Tim Sabik, "Recession of 1981–82," Federal Reserve History, July 1981–November 1982, https://www.federalreservehistory.org/essays/recession_of_1981_82. During the Great Recession, unemployment peaked at 10.0 percent. See Bureau of Labor Statistics, "Databases, Tables and Calculators by Subject," https://data.bls.gov/timeseries/LNS14000000.

72. Dale Russakoff, "The Making of Bruzzy Wilders," *Washington Post,* September 10, 1980, https://www.washingtonpost.com/.

73. Ben A. Franklin, "Reagan 'Hard Hat' Back on TV, but for Democrats," *New York Times,* September 18, 1982, https://www.nytimes.com/. The worker was angry that Republicans had not helped him get a job with the postal service. National Republican Congressional Committee spokesman Rich Galen explained, "You can't promise a job. It's against the law." See "Star of 1980 Reagan Ad Changes His Tune," United Press International, May 24, 1982, https://www.upi.com/.

74. "The Failing Presidency," *New York Times,* January 9, 1983, https://www.nytimes.com/.

75. "O'Neill Says Reagan Can't Win Reelection," United Press International, May 22, 1983.

76. Sean Trende, *The Lost Majority* (New York: Palgrave Macmillan, 2012), 174–175.

77. Barry Sussman, "Plenty of Blame to Go Around on Economy," *Washington Post,* October 26, 1982, https://www.washingtonpost.com/.

78. Douglas A. Jeffrey and Dennis Teti, "A Political Party in Search of Itself: Republican Realignment and the Dallas Platform of 1984," in *The 1984 Election and the Future of American Politics,* ed. Peter W. Schramm and Dennis J. Mahoney (Durham, NC: Carolina Academic Press, 1987), 59.

79. William Safire, "The Wicked Which and the Comma," *New York Times,* September 2, 1984, https://www.nytimes.com/.

80. Safire, "Wicked Which."

81. Ronald Reagan, "Remarks at the Annual Convention of the National Association of Evangelicals in Orlando, Florida," March 8, 1983, https://www.presidency.ucsb.edu/.

82. Public support for the freeze was actually shallower and more ambivalent than top-line poll results suggested—a feature of the debate that news coverage frequently obscured. J. Michael Hogan and Ted J. Smith III, "Polling on the Issues: Public Opinion and the Nuclear Freeze," *Public Opinion Quarterly* 55 (1991): 534–569.

83. Jeane J. Kirkpatrick, "Blame America First," keynote address, Republican National Convention, Dallas, TX, August 20, 1984, https://speakola.com/political/jeane-kirkpatrick-blame-america-first-gop-1984.

84. Peter W. Kaplan, "Convention in Dallas: The Republicans; Introducing Reagan: Images and a Theme Song," *New York Times*, August 21, 1994, https://www.nytimes.com/.

85. Dwight D. Eisenhower, "The President's News Conference," August 24, 1960. https://www.presidency.ucsb.edu/.

86. Dale Russakoff, "Bush Boasts of Kicking 'A Little Ass' at Debate," *Washington Post*, October 13, 1984, https://www.washingtonpost.com/.

87. Gerald M. Boyd, "Aide to Ferraro Demands Bush Make Apology," *New York Times*, October 14, 1984, https://www.nytimes.com/.

88. Ellis Sandoz and Cecil V. Crabb Jr., eds., *Election '84: Landslide without a Mandate?* (New York: New American Library, 1985).

89. Museum of the Moving Image, The Living Room Candidate: Presidential Campaign Commercials, 1952–2016, "Prouder, Stronger, Better," http://www.livingroomcandidate.org/.

90. In response to the derisive laughter, Reagan said, "I said something funny? [Laughter]." Ronald Reagan, "Address Before a Joint Session of the Congress on the State of the Union," January 25, 1984, https://www.presidency.ucsb.edu/.

91. William F. Buckley Jr., *Four Reforms: A Program for the Seventies* (New York: Putnam, 1972); Bill Bradley, *The Fair Tax* (New York: Pocket, 1984).

92. Bernard Weinraub, "Buchanan Sees Political Gain for GOP in Reagan Tax Plan," *New York Times*, May 17, 1985, https://www.nytimes.com/.

93. Jack Nelson, "'A Political Wash': Neither Party Seen Gaining from Tax Bill," *Los Angeles Times*, August 24, 1986.

94. David E. Rosenbaum, "Tax Revision Bill Wins Passage in the House on Shift in GOP Votes," *New York Times*, December 18, 1985, https://www.nytimes.com/.

95. Karlyn Bowman, Heather Sims, and Eleanor O'Neil, "Public Opinion on Taxes: 1937 to Today," AEI Public Opinion Study, April 2016, http://www.aei.org/wp-content/uploads/2016/04/Bowman_Taxes_April-2016-2.pdf.

96. Adam Clymer, "Poll Finds Approval Rating for Reagan Is High as Ever," *New York Times*, May 4, 1986, https://www.nytimes.com/.

97. Associated Press, "Oil and Farm States Hard Hit: 138 Banks Failed in US Last Year, Regulators Say," *Los Angeles Times*, January 5, 1987.

98. *Congressional Record*, September 12, 1985, 23540.

99. *Congressional Record*, March 21, 1986, 5887.

100. Doyle McManus, "Reagan Impeachment Held Possible: It's Likely if He Knew of Profits Diversion, Hamilton Says," *Los Angeles Times*, June 15, 1987.

101. Fred Barnes, "A Donkey's Year," *New Republic*, February 29, 1988, 16–18.

CHAPTER 3. THE DEMOCRATS IN THE 1980S

1. Lou Harris, "Poll: Hart, Kennedy Top Voters' List," *Florida Today*, April 29, 1985.

2. Chris Matthews, "How Kennedy Brought Down Nixon," Daily Beast, September 13, 2009, https://www.thedailybeast.com/.

3. Matthew L. Wald, "Kennedy, Citing Senate Goals, Rules Out '88 Presidential Bid," *New York Times,* December 20, 1985, https://www.nytimes.com/.

4. Andrew Rosenthal, "Dukakis, Angered, Defends War Role," *New York Times,* August 23, 1988, https://www.nytimes.com/.

5. Richard Gaines and Michael Segal, *Dukakis and the Reform Impulse* (Boston: Quinlan Press, 1987), 21.

6. Michael Dukakis, "Making a Difference," Swarthmore College, 2004, https://www.swarthmore.edu/.

7. Robin Toner, "Dukakis Likens GOP Attacks to McCarthy's," *New York Times,* September 10, 1988, https://www.nytimes.com/.

8. Dukakis, "Making a Difference."

9. James Brooke, "A Friend Finds Dukakis a Cut Above," *New York Times,* August 25, 1988, https://www.nytimes.com/.

10. Alan Riding, "Lima Journal: Miguel Dukakis for President! 'Mom' Is So Proud," *New York Times,* October 20, 1988, https://www.nytimes.com/.

11. Kenney and Turner, *Dukakis,* 38.

12. Andrew Rosenthal, "A Foreign Policy View that Goes beyond East vs. West," *New York Times,* September 2, 1988, https://www.nytimes.com/.

13. Dukakis oral history interview.

14. Paul R. Henggeler, *The Kennedy Persuasion: The Politics of Style Since JFK* (Chicago: Ivan R. Dee, 1995), 225.

15. Dukakis oral history interview.

16. Dukakis oral history interview.

17. Gaines and Segal, *Dukakis and the Reform Impulse,* 42.

18. "Michael Dukakis, Former Massachusetts Governor," video, Harvard T. H. Chan School of Public Health, November 16, 2011, https://www.hsph.harvard.edu/voices/events/dukakis/.

19. Kenney and Turner, *Dukakis,* 61.

20. Kenney and Turner, *Dukakis,* 62.

21. Gaines and Segal, *Dukakis and the Reform Impulse,* 54.

22. Gaines and Segal, *Dukakis and the Reform Impulse,* 60.

23. *Massachusetts v. Laird,* 400 US 886 (1970), https://caselaw.findlaw.com/us-supreme-court/400/886.html.

24. J. Anthony Lukas, "As Massachusetts Went," *New York Times,* January 14, 1973, https://www.nytimes.com/.

25. Richard A. Hogarty, "The Sargent Governorship: Leader and Legacy," *New England Journal of Public Policy* 15 (1999): 113–139.

26. Kenney and Turner, *Dukakis,* 82.

27. David M. Rosen, "Dukakis: 'Lead Pipe' Tax Promise a 'Beaut' of a Mistake," United Press International, November 7, 1975.

28. James R. Dorsey, "Dukakis Quickly Vetoes Death Penalty," United Press International, April 30, 1975.

29. "Dukakis Says Furlough Bill Would Have Hurt Rehabilitation," Associated Press, October 20, 1976.

30. Geismer, *Don't Blame Us*, 258.

31. Gaines and Segal, *Dukakis and the Reform Impulse*, 177.

32. Kenney and Turner, *Dukakis*, 170.

33. Geismer, *Don't Blame Us*, 269–270.

34. David Farrell, "Dukakis Shows Flair for Leadership Lacking in His First Term," *Boston Globe*, July 9, 1984.

35. Jonathan Moore, ed., *Campaign for President: The Managers Look at '84* (Dover, MA: Auburn House, 1986), 21.

36. Moore, *Campaign for President: The Managers Look at '84*, 18.

37. Peter Goldman and Tony Fuller, *The Quest for the Presidency, 1984* (New York: Bantam, 1985), 56.

38. Henggeler, *Kennedy Persuasion*, 186.

39. Haynes Johnson, "Ill at Ease, with Questions on the Future of the Party: Troubled Democrats Are Questioning Their Party's Role and Future," *Washington Post*, May 17, 1981, https://www.washingtonpost.com/.

40. Charles Peters, "A Neo-Liberal's Manifesto," *Washington Post*, September 5, 1982, https://www.washingtonpost.com/.

41. Matt Stoller, "How Democrats Killed Their Populist Soul," *Atlantic*, October 24, 2016, https://www.theatlantic.com/.

42. Lyndon B. Johnson, "Annual Message to the Congress: The Economic Report of the President," January 28, 1965, https://www.presidency.ucsb.edu/.

43. Gary Hart, *A New Democracy* (New York: Quill, 1983), 23.

44. Hart, *New Democracy*, 32.

45. "On the Record: The Democratic Debate; Transcript of Democratic Candidates' Debate in New York," *New York Times*, March 29, 1984, https://www.nytimes.com/.

46. Moore, *Campaign for President: The Managers Look at '84*, 12.

47. United States Bureau of the Census, "Percent of People 25 Years and Over Who Have Completed High School or College."

48. John B. Judis and Ruy Teixeira, *The Emerging Democratic Majority* (New York: Scribner, 2002), 39–49.

49. Elizabeth Bumiller, "The Change of Hart: Looking to Win," *Washington Post*, February 27, 1984, https://www.washingtonpost.com/.

50. James Ceaser and Andrew Busch, *Upside Down and Inside Out: The 1992 Elections and American Politics* (Lanham, MD: Rowman & Littlefield, 1993), 2–3.

51. Roger Bruns, *Jesse Jackson: A Biography* (Westport, CT: Greenwood Press, 2005), 15–16.

52. Jesse Jackson, "1984 Democratic National Convention Address, Delivered 18 July 1984, San Francisco," https://www.americanrhetoric.com/speeches/jessejackson1984dnc.htm.

53. Senator Jesse Helms (R-NC) had accused King of communist ties. When a reporter asked if he agreed, Reagan said, "We'll know in about 35 years, won't

we?" He was referring to the year that the FBI would unseal the King files. Ronald Reagan, "The President's News Conference," October 19, 1983, https://www.presidency.ucsb.edu/.

54. Lee Roderick, "Jackson Proves Dream Still Lives," Scripps-Howard, November 14, 1983.

55. Goldman and Fuller, *Quest for the Presidency, 1984*, 114.

56. Mary McGrory, "Jackson Broke Presidential Campaign out of Cycle of Boredom," *Washington Post*, January 5, 1984, https://www.washingtonpost.com/.

57. "Key Sections from Transcripts of Democrats' Debate in Iowa," *New York Times*, February 13, 1984, https://www.nytimes.com/.

58. Rick Atkinson, "Peace with American Jews Eludes Jackson," *Washington Post*, February 13, 1984, https://www.washingtonpost.com/.

59. Rick Atkinson, "Jackson Denounces 'Hounding' from Jewish Community," *Washington Post*, February 22, 1984, https://www.washingtonpost.com/.

60. "Jackson Admits Making Ethnic Slur," Jewish Telegraphic Agency, February 28, 1984, https://www.jta.org/1984/02/28/archive/jackson-admits-making-ethnic-slur.

61. Ronald Smothers, "Jackson Scouring New England in Drive to Show Appeal to White Voters," *New York Times*, February 7, 1984, https://www.nytimes.com/.

62. Moore, *Campaign for President: The Managers Look at '84*, 67.

63. Samuel L. Popkin, *The Reasoning Voter: Communication and Persuasion in Presidential Campaigns*, 2nd ed. (Chicago: University of Chicago Press, 1994), 193–194.

64. Hedrick Smith, "Polls Outline Bases of Hart's Victory," *New York Times*, March 1, 1984, https://www.nytimes.com/.

65. Alec M. Gallup and Frank Newport, eds., *The Gallup Poll: Public Opinion, 2004* (Lanham, MD: Rowman & Littlefield, 2006), 42.

66. Marty Cohen, David Karol, Hans Noel, and John Zaller, *The Party Decides: Presidential Nominations Before and After Reform* (Chicago: University of Chicago Press, 2008), 198–203.

67. Patricia L. Southwell, "The 1984 Democratic Nomination Process: The Significance of Unpledged Superdelegates," *American Politics Quarterly* 14 (1986): 75–88.

68. James W. Ceaser, Andrew E. Busch, and John J. Pitney Jr., *Defying the Odds: The 2016 Elections and American Politics* (Lanham, MD: Rowman & Littlefield, 2017), 3–4.

69. Fay S. Joyce, "Jackson Criticizes Remarks Made by Farrakhan as 'Reprehensible,'" *New York Times*, June 29, 1984, https://www.nytimes.com/. Some reports said that he had used the term "gutter religion." He insisted that he had said "dirty religion"—a distinction without a difference.

70. In summer 1984, a CBS/New York Times survey found that 53 percent of African American registered Democrats were for Mondale, 31 percent for Jackson, and 7 percent for Hart. "Black Democrats in a Poll Prefer Mondale to Jackson as Nominee," *New York Times*, July 10, 1984, https://www.nytimes.com/.

71. Chris Matthews, *Hardball*, rev. ed. (New York: Touchstone, 1999), 170–171.

72. Tom Shales, "What Mudd Slung," *Washington Post*, March 15, 1984, https://www.washingtonpost.com/.

73. Moore, *Campaign for President: The Managers Look at '84*, 86.

74. Popkin, *Reasoning Voter*, 206–207.

75. Bernard Weinraub, "From Gloom to Exultation: Mondale's Long Campaign," *New York Times*, June 8, 1984, https://www.nytimes.com/.

76. Popkin, *Reasoning Voter*, 201–202.

77. Don Phillips, "O'Neill: Mondale Must Attack 'Cold, Mean' Reagan," United Press International, July 19, 1984, https://www.upi.com/.

78. Walter F. Mondale, "Address Accepting the Presidential Nomination at the Democratic National Convention in San Francisco," July 19, 1984, https://www.presidency.ucsb.edu/.

79. John Dillin, "Pollster: Beware the Political Poll Taken Too Early in Race," *Christian Science Monitor*, July 25, 1984, https://www.csmonitor.com/.

80. William Schneider, "The Democrats in '88," *Atlantic*, April 1987, https://www.theatlantic.com/.

81. John Marcus, "Mass. Governor Eyes Run for Presidency," *Fort Lauderdale News*, December 16, 1986.

82. David Osborne, *Economic Competitiveness: The States Take the Lead* (Washington, DC: Economic Policy Institute, 1987), https://archive.org/stream/ERIC_ED291307/ERIC_ED291307_djvu.txt.

83. Al From, oral history interview conducted by Russell Riley, Darby Morrisroe, and Jessica Steiner, Miller Center, April 27, 2006, https://millercenter.org/.

84. Al From, *The New Democrats and the Return to Power* (New York: Palgrave Macmillan, 2011), 50.

85. Phil Gailey, "Dissidents Defy Top Democrats; Council Formed," *New York Times*, March 1, 1985, https://www.nytimes.com/.

86. Charles S. Bullock III, "The Nomination Process and Super Tuesday," in *The 1988 Presidential Election in the South: Continuity Amidst Change in Southern Party Politics*, ed. Laurence W. Moreland, Robert P. Steed, and Tod A. Baker (Westport, CT: Greenwood Press, 1991), 4.

87. William G. Mayer and Andrew E. Busch, *The Front-Loading Problem in Presidential Nominations* (Washington, DC: Brookings Institution, 2004), 13–14.

CHAPTER 4. THE REPUBLICAN NOMINATION CONTEST

1. Joel K. Goldstein, *The White House Vice Presidency: The Path to Significance, Mondale to Biden* (Lawrence: University Press of Kansas, 2016), 107.

2. James A. Baker III, oral history interview conducted by Morton Kondracke, March 13, 2013, https://www.jackkempfoundation.org/.

3. Richard Ben Cramer, *What It Takes* (New York: Vintage, 1993), 10.

4. Cramer, *What It Takes*, 577.

5. Margaret Garrard Warner, "Bush Battles the 'Wimp Factor,'" *Newsweek*, October 19, 1987.

6. E. J. Dionne Jr., "Poll Shows Reagan Approval Rating at 4-Year Low," *New York Times*, March 3, 1987, https://www.nytimes.com/.

7. Federal Election Commission, Advisory Opinion 1986-06, March 14, 1986, https://www.fec.gov/files/legal/aos/66847.pdf.

8. Paul S. Ryan, "'Testing the Waters' and the Big Lie: How Prospective Presidential Candidates Evade Candidate Contribution Limits While the FEC Looks the Other Way," Campaign Legal Center, February 2015, http://www.campaign legalcenter.org/sites/default/files/Testing%20the%20Waters-Full%20Paper .pdf.

9. James P. Pinkerton, oral history interview conducted by James McCall, Beatriz Lee, Russell Riley, and Sidney Milkis, Miller Center, February 6, 2001, https://millercenter.org/.

10. Chris Weston, "Bush Names South Carolinian Chairman of 'Action' Committee," *Greenville News,* January 11, 1986.

11. Stefan Forbes and Noland Walker, transcript of "Boogie Man: The Lee Atwater Story," *PBS Frontline,* November 11, 2008, https://www.pbs.org/.

12. Ed Rollins with Tom DeFrank, *Bare Knuckles and Back Rooms* (New York: Broadway Books, 1996), 143.

13. Eric Pooley with S. C. Gwynne, "How George Got His Groove," *Time,* June 14, 1999, http://www.cnn.com/ALLPOLITICS/time/1999/06/14/bush.groove .html.

14. E. J. Dionne Jr., "Bush vs. Dole: Behind the Turnaround," *New York Times,* March 17, 1988, https://www.nytimes.com/.

15. Runkel, *Campaign for President,* 104–105.

16. Interview with Doug Wead, "The Jesus Factor," *PBS Frontline,* November 18, 2003, https://www.pbs.org/.

17. Patricia Montemmuri and William J. Mitchell, "12 Ex-Backers of Robertson Switch to Bush," *Detroit News,* December 4, 1987.

18. Henry Olsen, *The Working Class Republican: Ronald Reagan and the Return of Blue-Collar Conservatism* (New York: Broadside Books, 2017).

19. Runkel, *Campaign for President,* 33.

20. George F. Will, "George Bush: The Sound of a Lapdog," *Washington Post,* January 30, 1986, https://www.washingtonpost.com/.

21. Runkel, *Campaign for President,* 34.

22. Pinkerton oral history interview.

23. Steven V. Roberts, "Jack Kemp's Year of Decision," *New York Times,* February 3, 1985, https://www.nytimes.com/.

24. Roberts, "Jack Kemp's Year of Decision."

25. Bill Peterson, "Conservatives Split Sharply on Next Leader: Kemp Beats Bush in Poll as Conference Ends," *Washington Post,* March 5, 1985, https://www .washingtonpost.com/.

26. James F. Clarity and Warren Weaver Jr., "Briefing: A Grand Ol' Surprise?," *New York Times,* September 4, 1985, https://www.nytimes.com/.

27. Timothy E. Cook, *Making Laws and Making News: Media Strategies in the US House of Representatives* (Washington, DC: Brookings Institution, 1989), 59.

28. Mary Battiata, "Jack Kemp, Out Front," *Washington Post,* October 16, 1986, https://www.washingtonpost.com/.

29. Battiata, "Jack Kemp, Out Front."

30. Jack Nelson, "Kemp Revamps Campaign amid Staff Woes, Debt," *Los Angeles Times,* May 14, 1987.

31. Richard L. Berke, "Washington Lobbyists Find Skies over Iowa Are Friendly," *New York Times,* February 5, 1988, https://www.nytimes.com/.

32. Morton Kondracke, "Symposium: Jack Kemp and the 1988 Republican Presidential Primary," Jack Kemp Foundation, April 14, 2012, https://www.jackkempfoundation.org/.

33. Morton Kondracke, "Symposium: Kemp Congressional Staff," Jack Kemp Foundation, September 19, 2011, https://www.jackkempfoundation.org/.

34. Herbert E. Alexander and Monica Bauer, *Financing the 1988 Election* (Boulder, CO: Westview Press, 1991), 24.

35. Kondracke and Barnes, *Jack Kemp,* 203.

36. "I have a plaque on my desk in the office that says what I firmly believe, and that is there is no limit to what a man can accomplish if he doesn't—what he can do and where he can go if he doesn't care who gets the credit." Ronald Reagan, "Remarks at the Inaugural Luncheon at the Capitol," January 21, 1985, https://www.presidency.ucsb.edu/.

37. Jack Kemp, "GOP Victory in 1988," *Policy Review* 45 (1988): 4.

38. Kondracke, "Symposium: Jack Kemp and the 1988 Republican Presidential Primary."

39. Jack Kemp, "Announcement for the Presidency of the United States by Congressman Jack Kemp, April 6, 1987," 4President.org, http://www.4president.org/speeches/1988/jackkemp1988announcement.htm.

40. R. W. Apple, "Politics; Kemp, Swiveling Right and Left in Speeches, Aims for Ultimate Goal," *New York Times,* March 10, 1986, https://www.nytimes.com/.

41. Sidney Blumenthal, "Jack Kemp at the Vanishing Point," *Washington Post,* March 5, 1988, https://www.washingtonpost.com/.

42. Martin, *With God on Our Side,* 172.

43. Pat Scales, "The Path to Growth for the Christian Broadcasting Network," United Press International, September 3, 1984, https://www.upi.com/.

44. Robert Pear, "Falwell Denounces Tutu as a 'Phony,'" *New York Times,* August 21, 1985, https://www.nytimes.com/.

45. Gary Langer, "Measuring Falwell's Popularity over His Lifetime," ABC News, February 9, 2009, https://abcnews.go.com/.

46. Moore, *Campaign for President: The Managers Look at '84,* 185.

47. Garrett Epps, "Pat Robertson's a Pastor, but His Father Was a Pol," *Washington Post,* October 19, 1986, https://www.washingtonpost.com/.

48. Hedrick Smith, "Those Fractious Republicans," *New York Times,* October 25, 1987, https://www.nytimes.com/.

49. David John Marley, *Pat Robertson: An American Life* (Lanham, MD: Rowman & Littlefield, 2007), 81.

50. Charles Krauthammer, "Politics of Resentment," *Washington Post,* February 12, 1988, https://www.washingtonpost.com/.

51. Runkel, *Campaign for President,* 28.

52. Robin Toner, "Robertson Hints a Bush Link to Disclosures on Swaggart," *New York Times*, February 24, 1988, https://www.nytimes.com/.

53. T. R. Reid, "Painfully, Robertson Corrects Record; Marriage Date, 10 Weeks before Birth of Son, Is Acknowledged," *Washington Post*, October 8, 1987, https://www.washingtonpost.com/.

54. Runkel, *Campaign for President*, 30.

55. The original log cabin candidate, William Henry Harrison, grew up rich on a lavish plantation. Edward Pessen, *The Log Cabin Myth: The Social Backgrounds of the Presidents* (New Haven, CT: Yale University Press, 1984), 19–21.

56. "Bob Dole's Odyssey: Democracy in America '96," CNN, October 20, 1996, http://www.cnn.com/ALLPOLITICS/1996/resources/democracy/dole/troops.shtml.

57. Bernard Weinraub, "Dole Makes His Presidential Bid Official," *New York Times*, November 10, 1987, https://www.nytimes.com/.

58. Bernard Weinraub, "The Anger in Bob Dole Is One Key to His Power," *New York Times*, February 8, 1988, https://www.nytimes.com/.

59. William Saletan, "The Dark Side: What You Need to Know about Bob Dole," *Mother Jones*, January/February 1996, https://www.motherjones.com/.

60. John J. Pitney Jr., *The Art of Political Warfare* (Norman: University of Oklahoma Press, 2000), 13–14.

61. Martin Tolchin and Jeff Gerth, "The Contradictions of Bob Dole," *New York Times*, November 8, 1987, https://www.nytimes.com/.

62. "Bush, Dole Wind Down War of Words," *Detroit Free Press*, January 14, 1988.

63. Maureen Dowd, "One Incumbent Too Many," *New York Times*, May 12, 1996, https://www.nytimes.com/.

64. William B. Lacy, oral history interview conducted by Brien R. Williams, Robert J. Dole Oral History Project, June 18, 2008, http://dolearchivecollections.ku.edu/collections/oral_history/pdf/lacy_bill_2008-06-18.pdf.

65. Senator William E. "Bill" Brock, oral history interview conducted by Richard Richard Norton Smith, Robert J. Dole Oral History Project, June 26, 2007, http://dolearchivecollections.ku.edu/collections/oral_history/pdf/brock_william_2007-06-26.pdf.

66. Lacy oral history interview.

67. Thomas B. Edsall, "Du Pont Tells Liberal Republicans How Conservative He Is," *Washington Post*, April 27, 1986, https://www.washingtonpost.com/.

68. Associated Press, "New GOP Group Criticizes Right and Is Assailed in Turn," *New York Times*, April 28, 1986, https://www.nytimes.com/.

69. Runkel, *Campaign for President*, 1–2.

70. Marjorie Williams, "Pete du Pont and the Search for a Spark," *Washington Post*, February 2, 1988, https://www.washingtonpost.com/.

71. Michael D'Antonio, *Never Enough: Donald Trump and the Pursuit of Success* (New York: Thomas Dunne, 2015), 181.

72. Ilan Ben-Meir, "That Time Trump Spent Nearly $100,000 on an Ad Criticizing US Foreign Policy," *BuzzFeed*, July 10, 2015, https://www.buzzfeednews.com/.

73. Fox Butterfield, "New Hampshire Speech Earns Praise for Trump," *New York Times*, October 23, 1987, https://www.nytimes.com/.

74. D'Antonio, *Never Enough*, 185.

75. "Donald Trump Teases a Presidential Bid during a 1988 Oprah Show Appearance," video, Oprah Winfrey, April 25, 1988, http://www.oprah.com/.

76. Sidney Blumenthal, "Election and the Wall Street Bypass: In Anxious Times, Taking Stock of the Presidential Candidates," *Washington Post*, April 21, 1988, https://www.washingtonpost.com/.

77. "Individual Contributions," Federal Election Commission, https://www.fec.gov/data/receipts/individual-contributions/?two_year_transaction_period=1988&contributor_name=trump%2C+donald+j.&min_date=01%2F01%2F1987&max_date=12%2F31%2F1988.

78. Simply America, "Donald Trump Interview 1988 Republican Convention," Vimeo, originally aired on *Larry King Live*, August 17, 1988, https://vimeo.com/137083308.

79. Phil Gailey, "GOP Taking First Step toward '88 in Michigan," *New York Times*, August 3, 1986, https://www.nytimes.com/.

80. Phil Gailey, "Bush's Hopes in Michigan Races Are Supported by a Poll of Voters," *New York Times*, August 6, 1986, https://www.nytimes.com/.

81. Paul Taylor, "Unofficial Results Show Bush Wins Plurality in Michigan," *Washington Post*, August 7, 1986, https://www.washingtonpost.com/.

82. Remer Tyson, "Bush, Robertson Both Claim Precinct Election Victory," *Detroit Free Press*, August 15, 1986, http://www.newspapers.com/image/99344329/.

83. "Symposium: Jack Kemp and the 1988 Republican Presidential Primary, April 14, 2012," Jack Kemp Oral History Project, http://www.jackkempfoundation.org/wp-content/uploads/2015/10/JKF-88-Campaign-Panel-2__oht.pdf.

84. Transcript of Republican presidential debate, *Firing Line*, October 28, 1987, https://digitalcollections.hoover.org/images/Collections/80040/80040_fls101_trans.pdf.

85. Republican presidential debate, *Firing Line*, October 28, 1987.

86. David S. Broder, "Round 1 Goes to George Bush," *Washington Post*, October 30, 1987, https://www.washingtonpost.com/.

87. Pinkerton oral history interview.

88. David Lightman, "Jackson, Bush Frontrunners in Poll, but Leads Shaky," *Hartford Courant*, October 1, 1987.

89. Runkel, *Campaign for President*, 34.

90. E. J. Dionne Jr., "Robertson's Victory in Ballot Shakes Rivals in GOP Race," *New York Times*, September 14, 1987, https://www.nytimes.com/.

91. Mark Matthews, "Son's 'Cockroach' Crack Causes Trouble for Bush," *Baltimore Sun*, November 25, 1987, http://www.newspapers.com/image/226707936/.

92. Martin, *With God on Our Side*, 290.

93. United States Congress, House Select Committee to Investigate Covert Arms Transactions with Iran, 1987, *Report of the Congressional Committees Investigating the Iran-Contra Affair: With Supplemental, Minority, and Additional Views*, H.

Rept./100th Congress, 1st Session, No. 100-433 (Washington, DC: US House of Representatives Select Committee to Investigate Covert Arms Transactions with Iran, 1987), 21, https://ia802205.us.archive.org/16/items/reportofcongress87unit/reportofcongress87unit.pdf.

94. Stephen Engelberg, "Panel Says Memo Calls Bush 'Solid' for Iran Arms Sale," *New York Times*, December 18, 1987, https://www.nytimes.com/.

95. Michael Oreskes, "Bush Is Target of Foes at Iowa Debate," *New York Times*, January 9, 1988, https://www.nytimes.com/.

96. Runkel, *Campaign for President*, 67.

97. "Text of Dan Rather's Interview with George Bush," *Washington Post*, January 27, 1988, https://www.washingtonpost.com/.

98. E. J. Dionne Jr., "Bush Camp Feels Galvanized after Showdown with Rather," *New York Times*, January 27, 1988, https://www.nytimes.com/.

99. Runkel, *Campaign for President*, 68.

100. Robin Toner, "Poll Finds Rather Clash Is Failing to Ease Bush's Iran–Contra Woes," *New York Times*, February 2, 1988, https://www.nytimes.com/.

101. Thomas B. Edsall, "Bush Victory in Michigan Strains Coalition of Kemp, Robertson Forces," *Washington Post*, January 16, 1988, https://www.washingtonpost.com/.

102. Kondracke, "Symposium: Jack Kemp and the 1988 Republican Presidential Primary."

103. E. J. Dionne Jr., "Poll Shows Discontent on Reagan Helps Dole Outpace Bush in Iowa," *New York Times*, January 8, 1988, https://www.nytimes.com/.

104. Gerald M. Boyd, "Bush, in Iowa, Speaks Softly on Farming," *New York Times*, August 2, 1987, https://www.nytimes.com/.

105. E. J. Dionne Jr., "Dole Wins in Iowa, With Robertson Next," *New York Times*, February 9, 1988, https://www.nytimes.com/.

106. Bush, *All the Best*, 378.

107. William Schneider, "When Citizens Choose Change," *Los Angeles Times*, February 14, 1988.

108. Edward Walsh and James R. Dickenson, "Dole Support Surges in New Hampshire," *Washington Post*, February 11, 1988, https://www.washingtonpost.com/.

109. "Poll Shows Dole, Bush about Even in New Hampshire," United Press International, February 11, 1988, https://www.upi.com/.

110. E. J. Dionne Jr., "In Debate, Bush Issues a Plea for Help," *New York Times*, February 15, 1988, https://www.nytimes.com/.

111. Bush, *All the Best*, 378.

112. Gary Maloney, ed., *The Almanac of 1988 Presidential Politics* (Falls Church, VA: American Political Network, 1989), 40.

113. John Sununu, oral history interview conducted by James Young, Erwin Hargrove, and Sidney Milkis, Miller Center, June 9, 2000, https://millercenter.org/.

114. Runkel, *Campaign for President*, 37–38.

115. Frank Clifford, "Dole, Bush Spar with Conservatives: Neither Dominates Crucial GOP Debate in New Hampshire," *Los Angeles Times*, February 15, 1988.

116. Smith, *'88 Vote*, 345–346.

117. "Bob Dole's Temper May Get Him into Trouble with Voters," transcript, *NBC Nightly News,* February 17, 1988, https://archives.nbclearn.com/portal/site/k-12/flatview?cuecard=33616.

118. Judy Woodruff, interview with Lee Atwater, *MacNeil/Lehrer NewsHour,* February 17, 1988.

119. Peter Goldman and Tom Mathews, *The Quest for the Presidency: The 1988 Campaign* (New York: Simon & Schuster/Touchstone, 1989), 281.

120. Smith, *'88 Vote,* 351–354.

121. Edward Walsh, "Two Top Consultants Fired from Dole's Campaign," *Washington Post,* February 26, 1988, https://www.washingtonpost.com/.

122. Bill Peterson, "Illinois Is Must-Win State For Dole, but May Not Sift Out Democrats," *Washington Post,* March 9, 1988, https://www.washingtonpost.com/.

123. Bernard Weinraub, "Dole Makes Plea in Half-Hour TV Ad," *New York Times,* March 13, 1988, https://www.nytimes.com/.

124. Pinkerton oral history interview.

125. Pinkerton oral history interview.

126. J. Danforth Quayle, oral history interview conducted by James Young and colleagues, Miller Center, March 12, 2002, https://millercenter.org/.

127. Quayle oral history interview.

128. Ronald Brownstein, "Playing Politics for Baby Boomers," *Los Angeles Times,* January 4, 1987.

129. Richard F. Fenno Jr., *The Making of a Senator: Dan Quayle* (Washington, DC: CQ Press, 1989).

130. Jack W. Germond and Jules Witcover, *Whose Broad Stripes and Bright Stars? The Trivial Pursuit of the Presidency, 1988* (New York: Warner Books, 1989), 386.

131. George Bush, "News Conference by Vice President Bush and Senator Dan Quayle," August 17, 1988, American Presidency Project, University of California–Santa Barbara, https://www.presidency.ucsb.edu/.

132. Lawrence M. Baskir and William A. Strauss, *Chance and Circumstance: The Draft, the War, and the Vietnam Generation* (New York: Vintage Books, 1978), 48–51.

133. Goldman and Mathews, *Quest for the Presidency: The 1988 Campaign,* 324–325.

134. Helen Dewar, "Quayle's Kin Helped Him Join Guard, Campaign Says," *Washington Post,* August 19, 1988, https://www.washingtonpost.com/.

135. "Deer in the Headlights," Word Detective, April 24, 2009, http://word-detective.com/.

136. Gerald M. Boyd, "Question of Selection; Bush Took Secrecy over Consensus in Choosing Quayle as Running Mate," *New York Times,* August 29, 1988, https://www.nytimes.com/.

137. David S. Broder and Bob Woodward, "In 1988, 'Control Freak Loses Control,'" *Washington Post,* January 7, 1992, https://www.washingtonpost.com/.

138. George H. W. Bush, "Address Accepting the Presidential Nomination."

139. Peggy Noonan, *What I Saw at the Revolution: A Political Life in the Reagan Era* (New York: Random House, 1990), 310–311.

140. Noonan, *What I Saw at the Revolution,* 307.

CHAPTER 5. THE DEMOCRATIC NOMINATION CONTEST

1. Rowland Evans and Robert Novak, "Joseph Biden: Kennedy's Exit Gives Him Running Room," *Asheville Citizen-Times*, December 26, 1985.

2. Henggeler, *Kennedy Persuasion*, 198.

3. "Excerpts from Transcript of 5 Candidates Debate in Atlanta," *New York Times*, March 12, 1984, https://www.nytimes.com/.

4. Runkel, *Campaign for President*, 18.

5. Gary Lee, "Hart, Gorbachev Discuss Arms, Human Rights," *Washington Post*, December 16, 1986, https://www.washingtonpost.com/.

6. Robin Toner, "Hart, Stressing Ideals, Formally Enters the 1988 Race," *New York Times*, April 14, 1987, https://www.nytimes.com/.

7. E. J. Dionne Jr. "Gary Hart: The Elusive Front-Runner," *New York Times Magazine*, May 3, 1987, https://www.nytimes.com/.

8. James G. Driscoll, "The Buck Had More to Do with Hart Exit than Donna Rice," *Sun-Sentinel*, May 24, 1987, https://www.sun-sentinel.com/.

9. Matt Bai, *All the Truth Is Out: The Week Politics Went Tabloid* (New York: Vintage, 2015), 121.

10. Bai, *All the Truth Is Out*, 38.

11. Bai, *All the Truth Is Out*, 95.

12. Dan Thomasson and Tim Wyngaard, "Kennedy, Giancana, and John Roselli Had One Thing in Common," *El Paso Herald Post*, December 18, 1975.

13. David Maraniss, "On Brink of Running, Clinton Called It Off," *Washington Post*, February 7, 1995, https://www.washingtonpost.com/.

14. George Gallup Jr., "Sympathy for Hart, Barbs for Media," (Santa Rosa, CA) *Press-Democrat*, May 12, 1987.

15. Phil Gailey, "Politics; Biden: Something About '88 Keeps Beckoning," *New York Times*, December 19, 1985, https://www.nytimes.com/.

16. Runkel, *Campaign for President*, 20.

17. Don Campbell, "New Directions Plotted for Dem Party," *Lansing State Journal*, October 27, 1985.

18. Howard Kurtz, "Choosing His Battles, Working by Consensus," *Washington Post*, December 9, 1986, https://www.washingtonpost.com/.

19. Maureen Dowd, "Biden's Debate Finale: An Echo from Abroad," *New York Times*, September 12, 1987, https://www.nytimes.com/.

20. John Corrigan, in Runkel, *Campaign for President*, 77.

21. Maureen Dowd, "Biden Is Facing Growing Debate on His Speeches," *New York Times*, September 16, 1987, https://www.nytimes.com/.

22. E. J. Dionne Jr., "Biden Admits Plagiarism in School but Says It Was Not 'Malevolent,'" *New York Times*, September 18, 1987, https://www.nytimes.com/.

23. E. J. Dionne Jr., "Biden Admits Errors and Criticizes Latest Report," *New York Times*, September 22, 1987, https://www.nytimes.com/.

24. Goldman and Mathews, *Quest for the Presidency: The 1988 Campaign*, 110.

25. United States Bureau of the Census, Statistical Abstract of the United States, 2010, Table 1095, "Utilization of Selected Media," http://www2.census.gov/library/publications/2010/compendia/statab/129ed/tables/10s1095.xls.

26. Stephen E. Frantzich, *Founding Father: How C-SPAN's Brian Lamb Changed Politics in America* (Lanham, MD: Rowman & Littlefield, 2008), 38–40.

27. Alert readers will note that I just swiped a line from Rutger Hauer's speech in *Blade Runner* (https://www.youtube.com/watch?v=NoAzpaix7jU).

28. "History of Women in the US Congress," Center for American Women in Politics, Rutgers Eagleton Institute of Politics, https://cawp.rutgers.edu/history-women-us-congress.

29. Maureen Dowd, "Schroeder: At Ease with Femininity and Issues," *New York Times*, August 23, 1987, https://www.nytimes.com/.

30. "FEC Releases Information on 1987 Presidential Spending," United States Federal Election Commission, February 11, 1988, https://transition.fec.gov/press/archive/1988/19880211_PresSpend1987.pdf.

31. Alexander and Bauer, *Financing the 1988 Election*, 21–22.

32. Richard L. Berke, "For Dukakis Campaign, the Money Keeps Rolling In," *New York Times*, April 24, 1988, https://www.nytimes.com/.

33. Richard L. Berke, "Heeding Plato, Greek-Americans Aid in Effort to Raise Money for Dukakis," *New York Times*, December 27, 1987, https://www.nytimes.com/.

34. Richard L. Berke, "Campaign Finance; Mastermind of the Dukakis Success," *New York Times*, March 21, 1988, https://www.nytimes.com/.

35. Bob Drogin, "Dukakis on Tightrope: He Can't Just Win in NH, He Needs to Win Big," *Los Angeles Times*, September 26, 1987.

36. Runkel, *Campaign for President*, 3.

37. Kenneth S. Baer, *Reinventing Democrats: The Politics of Liberalism from Reagan to Clinton* (Lawrence: University Press of Kansas, 2000), 107.

38. Randall Rothenberg, *The Neoliberals* (New York: Simon & Schuster, 1984), 126.

39. Edmund Burke, *Reflections on the French Revolution* (1790), https://www.bartleby.com/.

40. Hendrik Hertzberg, "First Returns," *New Republic*, February 28, 1988.

41. Marvin Kalb and Hendrick Hertzberg, *Candidates '88* (Dover, MA: Auburn House, 1988), 238–239.

42. "Presidential Candidates Debate," video, C-SPAN, December 1, 1987, https://www.c-span.org/.

43. Runkel, *Campaign for President*, 6.

44. "Democratic Debate '88," video, *Saturday Night Live*, January 30, 1988, https://www.nbc.com/saturday-night-live/video/democratic-debate/2859797.

45. Terry Michael in Runkel, *Campaign for President*, 16.

46. E. J. Dionne Jr., "The Dozen's Debate: Splits Both Deep and Shallow," *New York Times*, December 3, 1987, https://www.nytimes.com/.

47. Runkel, *Campaign for President*, 15.

48. Runkel, *Campaign for President*, 21.

49. Bill Turque, *Inventing Al Gore: A Biography* (New York: Houghton Mifflin Harcourt, 2014), 161.

50. "Perry Lauds Democrats," *Hood County News*, January 23, 1988.

51. "Gore Announcement," video, C-SPAN, June 29, 1987, https://www.c-span.org/.

52. David Mikkelson, "Did Al Gore Say 'I Invented the Internet'? ," Snopes.com, May 5, 2005, https://www.snopes.com/.

53. Sandra Roberts, "Al Gore: A Better Public Official Than He Is a Candidate," (Rochester, NY) *Democrat and Chronicle,* April 13, 1988.

54. Myra McPherson, "Leading Jackson's Charge on the Apple," *Washington Post,* April 11, 1988, https://www.washingtonpost.com/.

55. Evans Witt, "Jackson Launches Second Bid for the Presidency," Associated Press, October 10, 1987.

56. Sidney Blumenthal, "Jackson and the Brain Trust," *Washington Post,* April 5, 1988, https://www.washingtonpost.com/.

57. Jesse Jackson, "A Chance to Serve" (announcement in Raleigh, NC, October 10, 1987), in *Keep Hope Alive: Jesse Jackson's 1988 Presidential Campaign,* ed. Frank Clemente and Frank Watkins (Boston: South End Press, 1989), 27.

58. Robert J. Samuelson, "Jackson Program Gives Budget Debate a Shove," *Washington Post,* June 1, 1988, https://www.washingtonpost.com/.

59. Michael Knight, "Vermont Socialist Plans Mayoralty with Bias toward Poor," *New York Times,* March 8, 1981, https://www.nytimes.com/.

60. Mark Johnson, "Rainbow Coalition Seeing Plus Signs in Sanders' Bid," *Burlington Free Press,* February 18, 1986.

61. Bernie Sanders, *Outsider in the White House* (New York: Verso Books, 2015).

62. Steve Cobble, "Watch: When Bernie Sanders Endorsed Jesse Jackson for President," video, *Nation,* February 17, 2016, https://www.thenation.com/.

63. Bernie Sanders, *Our Revolution* (New York: Macmillan, 2016), 93.

64. Runkel, *Campaign for President,* 24.

65. Jackson, "Chance to Serve," 31.

66. Frank Newport and Joseph Carroll, "History Shows January Frontrunner Often Does Not Win Democratic Nomination," Gallup, January 6, 2004, https://www.gallup.com/.

67. "Hart Leaps Ahead in Iowa Poll," *New York Times,* December 21, 1987, https://www.nytimes.com/.

68. David Handelman, "Gary Hart: Campaignus Interruptus," *Rolling Stone,* March 24, 1988, https://www.rollingstone.com/.

69. t4change, "US Democrats—Richard Gephardt 1988 Video 2," Hyundai ad, posted March 5, 2007, https://www.youtube.com/watch?v=L1df9V40RDQ.

70. Runkel, *Campaign for President,* 140.

71. Runkel, *Campaign for President,* 141.

72. E. J. Dionne Jr., "Gephardt's Iowa Campaign Resurges," *New York Times,* January 19, 1988, https://www.nytimes.com/.

73. Iowa State University Center for Industrial Research and Service, "Manufacturing in Iowa," January 2018, https://www.ciras.iastate.edu/files/publications/Manufacturing_In_Iowa_2018.pdf.

74. "Babbitt Hits Simon's Deficit Plan as 'Laughable,'" Associated Press, January 6, 1988.

75. Runkel, *Campaign for President,* 16.

76. Hugh Winebrenner and Dennis J. Goldford, *The Iowa Precinct Caucuses: The Making of a Media Event* (Iowa City: University of Iowa Press, 2010), 169.

77. R. W. Apple, "Stunning Result Carries a Grim Message for Bush," *New York Times*, February 9, 1988, https://www.nytimes.com/.

78. Winebrenner and Goldford, *Iowa Precinct Caucuses*, 171.

79. Michael Oreskes, "Gephardt and Simon Fight for 2d Place," *New York Times*, February 14, 1988, https://www.nytimes.com/.

80. Germond and Witcover, *Whose Broad Stripes and Bright Stars?*, 224.

81. Robert Shrum, *No Excuses: Confessions of a Serial Campaigner* (New York: Simon & Schuster, 2007).

82. Maura Dolan, "Fuming Dukakis Warns Gephardt of 'Scrappy' Race," *Los Angeles Times*, February 26, 1988.

83. Mickey Kaus and Eleanor Clift, "The Many Faces of Dick Gephardt," *Newsweek*, March 7, 1988, 46.

84. Runkel, *Campaign for President*, 170.

85. Runkel, *Campaign for President*, 182.

86. Maloney, *Almanac of 1988 Presidential Politics*, 44.

87. Michael Oreskes, "Gore, in Texas Debate, Spars with Dukakis and Gephardt," *New York Times*, February 19, https://www.nytimes.com/.

88. Roy M. Neel, oral history interview conducted by Russell Riley and Stephen F. Knott, Miller Center, November 14, 2002, https://millercenter.org/.

89. Sidney Blumenthal, *Pledging Allegiance: The Last Campaign of the Cold War* (New York: HarperCollins, 1990), 221.

90. Smith, *'88 Vote*, 232–303.

91. Charles D. Hadley and Harold W. Stanley, "Super Tuesday 1988: Regional Results and National Implications," *Publius* 19 (1989): 28, https://faculty.smu.edu/hstanley/Publications/ST%201988.Publius%201989.pdf.

92. Elaine Kamarck, *Primary Politics*, 2nd ed. (Washington, DC: Brookings Institution, 2016), 38.

93. Smith, *'88 Vote*, 242, 292.

94. Paul M. Green, "Illinois' 1988 Presidential Primaries: Voter Turnout, Margins, Percentages," June 1988, https://www.lib.niu.edu/1988/ii880621.html.

95. Runkel, *Campaign for President*, 25.

96. Walter Shapiro, "Win, Jesse, Win," *Time*, April 4, 1988, 21.

97. Maloney, *Almanac of 1988 Presidential Politics*, 124.

98. Michael Oreskes, "Dukakis Rebounds, Defeating Jackson in Connecticut Bid," *New York Times*, March 30, 1988, https://www.nytimes.com/.

99. Orlando Bagwell and Jeanne Jordan, "Running with Jesse," *PBS Frontline*, February 7, 1989, VHS recording, transcription by author.

100. Goldman and Mathews, *Quest for the Presidency: The 1988 Campaign*, 159.

101. Joyce Purnick and Michael Oreskes, "Jesse Jackson Aims for the Mainstream," *New York Times*, November 29, 1987, https://www.nytimes.com/.

102. E. J. Dionne Jr., "Democrats Close in on Bush Nationally, Latest Survey Shows," *New York Times*, March 25, 1988, https://www.nytimes.com/.

103. Richard L. Berke, "Rural Wisconsin Town Turns Out for Jackson," *New York Times,* April 2, 1988, https://www.nytimes.com/.

104. Garth Johnson, "Remembering Ed Koch's Scandalous Third Term," *Gothamist,* February 1, 2013, http://gothamist.com/2013/02/01/ed_koch_and_the _curse_of_the_third.php.

105. Richard J. Meislin, "New Yorkers Say Race Relations Have Worsened in the Last Year," *New York Times,* January 10, 1988, https://www.nytimes.com/.

106. Joyce Purnick, "Koch Says Jackson Lied about Actions after Dr. King Was Slain," *New York Times,* April 18, 1988, https://www.nytimes.com/.

107. Ralph Blumenthal, "Homicides Hit a Record in New York," *New York Times,* December 26, 1988, https://www.nytimes.com/.

108. Robert Shogan, "Gore, Dukakis Tangle during NY Debate," *Los Angeles Times,* April 13, 1988.

109. Christopher Graff, "Jackson Win Official in Vermont," Associated Press, April 28, 1988, https://apnews.com/b1fdd8a9afe37741682107d0326ecd41.

110. E. J. Dionne Jr., "Jackson Share of Votes by Whites Triples in '88," *New York Times,* June 13, 1988, https://www.nytimes.com/.

111. Gerald M. Pomper, "The Presidential Nominations," in *The Election of 1988: Reports and Interpretations,* ed. Gerald M. Pomper (Chatham, NJ: Chatham House, 1989), 46–47.

112. Michael Oreskes, "Jackson Says He Is Best Choice for Vice President," *New York Times,* June 11, 1988, https://www.nytimes.com/.

113. Andrew Rosenthal, "Jackson Runs 1st For the No. 2 Spot," *New York Times,* July 6, 1988, https://www.nytimes.com/.

114. Runkel, *Campaign for President,* 108.

115. William Greider, "Is the Democrats' New Harmony for Real?," *Rolling Stone,* September 8, 1988, https://www.rollingstone.com/.

116. Democratic Party Platform of 1988, July 18, 1988, https://www.presidency.ucsb .edu/. See John J. Pitney Jr., "Comparing the National Party Platforms of 1960 and 1988," paper presented at the 1989 annual meeting of the Western Political Science Association, Salt Lake City, UT, March 30–April 1, 1989.

117. Kamarck, *Primary Politics,* 120.

118. David E. Rosenbaum, "Man in the News; A Candidate Who Is More Like Bush: Lloyd Millard Bentsen Jr.," *New York Times,* July 13, 1988, https://www.ny times.com/.

119. Rae, *Southern Democrats,* 105.

120. David E. Rosenbaum, "Bentsen, Longtime Foe of Busing, Supported Most Other Rights Bills," *New York Times,* July 14, 1988, https://www.nytimes.com/.

121. Democratic National Committee, *Official Proceedings of the 1988 Democratic National Convention* (Washington, DC: Democratic National Committee, 1988), 222.

122. Democratic National Committee, *Official Proceedings,* 321.

123. Democratic National Committee, *Official Proceedings,* 302.

124. Democratic National Committee, *Official Proceedings,* 336.

125. Democratic National Committee, *Official Proceedings,* 474.

126. "Dukakis Lead Widens, According to New Poll," *New York Times*, July 26, 1988, https://www.nytimes.com/.

CHAPTER 6. THE GENERAL ELECTION: THE TRIUMPH OF THE FUNDAMENTALS

1. Michael Oreskes, "Bush Overtakes Dukakis in a Poll," *New York Times*, August 23, 1988, https://www.nytimes.com/.
2. Lawrence J. DeMaria, "Stocks Plunge 508 Points, a Drop of 22.6%; 604 Million Volume Nearly Doubles Record," *New York Times*, October 20, 1987, https://www.nytimes.com/.
3. Everett Carll Ladd, "The 1988 Elections: Continuation of the Post–New Deal System," *Political Science Quarterly* 104 (1989): 1–18.
4. Gregory B. Markus, "The Impact of Personal and National Economic Conditions on Presidential Voting, 1956–1988," *American Journal of Political Science* 36 (1992): 829–834.
5. "Bentsen Text: We Agree a Good Job Is Passport to Opportunity," *Los Angeles Times*, July 22, 1988, https://www.latimes.com/.
6. Kenneth J. Robinson, "Savings and Loan Crisis, 1980–1989," Federal Reserve History, November 22, 2013, https://www.federalreservehistory.org/essays /savings_and_loan_crisis.
7. William Greider, *Who Will Tell the People? The Betrayal of American Democracy* (New York: Simon & Schuster, 1992), 75.
8. Greider, *Who Will Tell the People,* 75.
9. Ronald Reagan, "The President's News Conference Following the Soviet–United States Summit Meeting in Moscow," June 1, 1988, American Presidency Project, University of California–Santa Barbara, https://www.presidency.ucsb .edu/.
10. Bill Keller, "US Military Is Termed Prepared for Any Move against Nicaragua," *New York Times*, June 4, 1985, https://www.nytimes.com/.
11. Alan I. Abramowitz, "An Improved Model for Predicting Presidential Election Outcomes," *Political Science and Politics* 21 (1988): 843–847.
12. "Presidential Job Approval," https://www.presidency.ucsb.edu/.
13. "Still, strategists say the surest bet is that Dukakis will win because Bush is vulnerable on two fronts: His limited ability to harangue Dukakis as weak on defense and his stance as the status quo candidate." Gloria Borger, "Potential for Problems All Around," *US News and World Report*, July 4, 1988.
14. Alexander and Bauer, *Financing the 1988 Election,* 41.
15. Goldman and Mathews, *Quest for the Presidency: The 1988 Campaign,* 308–313.
16. Blumenthal, *Pledging Allegiance,* 146.
17. Goldman and Mathews, *Quest for the Presidency: The 1988 Campaign,* 346.
18. E. J. Dionne Jr., "Political Memo; Dukakis Remains on Course, Dismissing Polls and Advice," *New York Times*, July 11, 1988, https://www.nytimes.com/.
19. *Saturday Night Live*, October 8, 1988, quotes at http://www.imdb.com/title /tt0694525/trivia?tab=qt&ref_=tt_trv_qu.
20. Runkel, *Campaign for President,* 136.

21. Runkel, *Campaign for President,* 110.

22. Pinkerton oral history interview.

23. Data from "Crime—National or State Level: State-by-State and National Crime Estimates by Year(s)," US Department of Justice, Federal Bureau of Investigation, Uniform Crime Reports, Uniform Crime Reporting Statistics, https://www.ucrdatatool.gov/Search/Crime/State/StatebyState.cfm.

24. Compilation of survey data at Gallup News, "Death Penalty," https://www.gallup.com/.

25. Roger Simon, *Road Show* (New York: Farrar, Straus & Giroux, 1990), 207–209.

26. "Winners of Pulitzer Prizes in Journalism, Letters and the Arts," *New York Times,* April 1, 1988, https://www.nytimes.com/.

27. Robin Toner, "Prison Furloughs in Massachusetts Threaten Dukakis Record on Crime," *New York Times,* July 5, 1988, https://www.nytimes.com/.

28. Robert James Bidinotto, "Getting Away with Murder," *Reader's Digest,* July 1988.

29. Maureen Dowd, "Bush Portrays His Opponent as Sympathetic to Criminals," *New York Times,* October 8, 1988, https://www.nytimes.com/.

30. Pinkerton oral history interview.

31. Tom Raum, "Bush: Dukakis' Furlough Program Coddled Criminal," Associated Press, June 19, 1988.

32. Robin Toner, "Prison Furloughs in Massachusetts Threaten Dukakis Record on Crime," *New York Times,* July 5, 1988, https://www.nytimes.com/.

33. Tali Mendelberg, *The Race Card: Campaign Strategy, Implicit Messages, and the Norm of Equality* (Princeton, NJ: Princeton University Press, 2001), 145–147.

34. Maralee Schwartz and Lloyd Grove, "Bush Rejects Assistance of 'Security' PAC," *Washington Post,* June 25, 1988, https://www.washingtonpost.com/.

35. Federal Election Commission, MUR 2638, June 28, 1988, https://www.fec.gov/files/legal/murs/2638.pdf.

36. Video and transcript of the ad are available at Museum of the Moving Image, The Living Room Candidate: Presidential Campaign Commercials, 1952–2016, "Willie Horton," http://www.livingroomcandidate.org/.

37. Morgan Whitaker, "The Legacy of The Willie Horton Ad Lives On, 25 Years Later," MSNBC, October 21, 2013, http://www.msnbc.com/.

38. Letters of Lee Atwater (September 12, 1988) and James A. Baker III (September 27, 1988) to Elizabeth Fedlay, Federal Election Commission, MUR 3069, January 16, 1992, https://www.fec.gov/files/legal/murs/3069.pdf.

39. Jan Baran, quoted in John Brady, *Bad Boy: The Life and Politics of Lee Atwater* (Reading, MA: Addison-Wesley, 1997), 208.

40. Jeffrey Toobin, "The Dirty Trickster," *New Yorker,* June 2, 2008, https://www.newyorker.com/.

41. Ben Smith, "Trump's Birther Play," *Politico,* March 28, 2011, https://www.politico.com/.

42. Garance Franke-Ruta, "Karl Rove: Here Are the 2 Tactical Fails that Cost Romney the Election," *Atlantic,* June 27, 2013, https://www.theatlantic.com/.

43. Saul Friedman, "GOP Charts Southern Strategy," *Newsday,* July 10, 1988, 15.

44. Runkel, *Campaign for President*, 119.

45. Stephen Engelberg, "Bush, His Disavowed Backers and a Very Potent Attack Ad," *New York Times*, November 3, 1988, https://www.nytimes.com/.

46. Eric Levenson, "'Willie Horton' and the Rise (and Fall?) of Mass Incarceration," *Boston Globe*, May 14, 2015.

47. Kerwin Swint, *Dark Genius: The Influential Career of Legendary Political Operative and Fox News Founder Roger Ailes* (New York: Union Square Press, 2008), 95.

48. Richard Stengel, "The Man Behind the Message," *Time*, August 22, 1988, http://www.cnn.com/ALLPOLITICS/1997/08/25/back.time/.

49. Federal Election Commission, MUR 3069, January 16, 1992, https://www.fec.gov/files/legal/murs/3069.pdf.

50. Federal Election Commission, MUR 3069, January 16, 1992, https://www.fec.gov/files/legal/murs/3069.pdf.

51. Museum of the Moving Image, The Living Room Candidate: Presidential Campaign Commercials, 1952–2016, "Revolving Door," http://www.livingroomcandidate.org/.

52. Lloyd Grove, "Campaign Ads Play Fast and Loose with The Truth," *Washington Post*, October 21, 1988, https://www.washingtonpost.com/.

53. Andrew Rosenthal, "Foes Accuse Bush Campaign of Inflaming Racial Tension," New York Times, October 24, 1988, https://www.nytimes.com/.

54. Mendelberg, *Race Card*, 173–178; John Sides, "It's Time to Stop the Endless Hype of the 'Willie Horton' Ad," *Washington Post*, January 6, 2016, https://www.washingtonpost.com/.

55. Robert Scheer, "Nuclear Deterrence: Dukakis Not Ruling Out First Use," *Los Angeles Times*, May 26, 1988.

56. Richard Cohen, "Why Is Bush Saying Those Things about Dukakis?," *Washington Post*, September 1, 1988, https://www.washingtonpost.com/.

57. Barbara G. Farah and Ethel Klein, "Public Opinion Trends," in Pomper, *Election of 1988*, 116.

58. *West Virginia State Board of Education v. Barnette*, 319 US 624 (1943).

59. Supreme Judicial Court of Massachusetts, Opinions of Justices to Governor, 372 Mass. 874, at 875, May 16, 1977, http://masscases.com/.

60. "Veto of Flag Salute Overriden by House," United Press International, June 15, 1977. Citing the legal issues that had led Dukakis to veto the bill, the state's education department never enforced the law.

61. Paul Taylor, "Dukakis Returns Fire on Pledge of Allegiance," *Washington Post*, August 24, 1988, https://www.washingtonpost.com/.

62. Goldman and Mathews, *Quest for the Presidency: The 1988 Campaign*, 339.

63. James Gerstenzang, "'Capture the Flag' a Vital Game in '88 Campaign," *Los Angeles Times*, September 21, 1988.

64. The ad showed a sign reading "Danger Radiation Hazard No Swimming." It was located near a navy yard where nuclear submarines had repairs had long ago taken place. Lloyd Grove, "Campaign Ads Play Fast and Loose with the Truth," *Washington Post*, October 21, 1988, https://www.washingtonpost.com/.

65. Owen Thomas, "Dukakis, Bush, EPA to Blame for Boston Harbor. Cleanup of the Nation's Dirtiest Harbor Was Task No Politician Wanted," *Christian Science Monitor,* September 15, 1988, https://www.csmonitor.com/.

66. George H. W. Bush, "Address Accepting the Presidential Nomination."

67. National data on defense employment appear in United States General Accounting Office, "Defense Sector: Trends in Employment and Spending," GAO/NSIAD-95-105BR, April 1995, https://www.gao.gov/assets/80/78984.pdf.

68. Josh King, "Dukakis and the Tank," *Politico,* November 17, 2013, https://www.politico.com/.

69. Museum of the Moving Image, The Living Room Candidate: Presidential Campaign Commercials, 1952–2016, "Tank Ride," http://www.livingroomcandidate.org/.

70. Andrew Rosenthal, "Dukakis Questions Bush's Leadership," *New York Times,* August 6, 1988, https://www.nytimes.com/.

71. "Historical Tables: Budget of the United States Government, Fiscal Year 2018," United States Office of Management and Budget, Bureau of the Budget, https://www.whitehouse.gov/sites/whitehouse.gov/files/omb/budget/fy2018/hist03z1.xls.

72. Farah and Klein, "Public Opinion Trends," 114.

73. John Geer charted the negativity of presidential campaign spots in *In Defense of Negativity: Attack Ads in Presidential Campaigns* (Chicago: University of Chicago Press, 2008), 119.

74. Museum of the Moving Image, The Living Room Candidate: Presidential Campaign Commercials, 1952–2016, "Hey Pal," http://www.livingroomcandidate.org/.

75. "Carl Cannon, "4 Bush Aides Are Linked to Lobbyists for the Bahamas," *Philadelphia Inquirer,* September 8, 1988.

76. David Lightman, "Lobbyists Defend Work for Bahamas," *Hartford Courant,* September 9, 1988.

77. David Hoffman and Ann Devroy, "The Complex Machine behind Bush," *Washington Post,* November 13, 1988, https://www.washingtonpost.com/.

78. Bob Drogin, "Dukakis Steps Up Attack on Bush Camp–Bahamas Ties," *Los Angeles Times,* September 11, 1988.

79. Museum of the Moving Image, The Living Room Candidate: Presidential Campaign Commercials, 1952–2016, "Counterpunch," http://www.livingroomcandidate.org/.

80. Goldman and Mathews, *Quest for the Presidency: The 1988 Campaign,* 339.

81. Museum of the Moving Image, The Living Room Candidate: Presidential Campaign Commercials, 1952–2016, "Furlough from the Truth," http://www.livingroomcandidate.org/.

82. "Kitty Dukakis, Wife of Democratic Presidential Nominee Michael Dukakis," United Press International, August 25, 1988, https://www.upi.com/.

83. Robin Toner, "Kitty Dukakis Stings GOP With Her Attack," *New York Times,* September 25, 1988, https://www.nytimes.com/.

84. Ronald Reagan, "Remarks on the Veto of the National Defense Authorization Act, Fiscal Year 1989, and a Question-and-Answer Session with Reporters," August 3, 1988, American Presidency Project, University of California–Santa Barbara, https://www.presidency.ucsb.edu/.
85. Runkel, *Campaign for President*, 159.
86. Bob Drogin, "Aide's Remarks Prompt Dukakis Apology to Bush," *Los Angeles Times*, October 21, 1988.
87. Presidential Candidates Debates, "Presidential Debate in Winston-Salem, North Carolina," September 25, 1988, American Presidency Project, University of California–Santa Barbara, https://www.presidency.ucsb.edu/.
88. Gerald M. Boyd, "Bush Camp Offers a Clarified Stand about Abortions," *New York Times*, September 27, 1988, https://www.nytimes.com/.
89. Natcher motion on HR 4783, September 9, 1988, *1988 CQ Almanac* (Washington, DC: Congressional Quarterly Press, 1989), 96-H.
90. Noah Bierman, "'Senator, You're No Jack Kennedy' Almost Didn't Happen. How It Became the Biggest VP Debate Moment in History," *Los Angeles Times*, October 4, 2016.
91. Quayle–Bentsen vice presidential debate, October 5, 1988, http://debates.org/.
92. Museum of the Moving Image, The Living Room Candidate: Presidential Campaign Commercials, 1952–2016, "Crazy," http://www.livingroomcandidate.org/.
93. Presidential Candidate Debates, "Presidential Debate at the University of California in Los Angeles," October 13, 1988, American Presidency Project, University of California–Santa Barbara, https://www.presidency.ucsb.edu/.
94. Maloney, *Almanac of 1988 Presidential Politics*, 72.
95. Abramowitz, "Improved Model."
96. Robin Toner, "In Blur of Rallies, Dukakis Steps up Attacks on Rival," *New York Times*, November 7, 1988, https://www.nytimes.com/.
97. Thomas B. Edsall and Richard Morin, "Reagan's 1984 Voter Coalition Is Weakened in Bush Victory," *Washington Post*, November 9, 1988, https://www.washingtonpost.com/.
98. Gerald M. Pomper, "The Presidential Election," in Pomper, *Election of 1988*, 133–134.
99. Smith, *'88 Vote*, 18.
100. Judis and Teixeira, *Emerging Democratic Majority*, 48.
101. Author's calculations from US Census Bureau, "Voting and Registration Tables," https://www.census.gov/topics/public-sector/voting/data/tables.html.
102. E. J. Dionne Jr., "The 1988 Elections; Bush Is Elected by a 6–5 Margin with Solid GOP Base in South," *New York Times*, November 9, 1988, https://www.nytimes.com/.
103. Smith, *'88 Vote*, 22.
104. Smith, *'88 Vote*, 22.
105. Smith, *'88 Vote*, 21.
106. Steven J. Rosenstone, Roy L. Behr, and Edward H. Lazarus, *Third Parties in America*, 2nd ed. (Princeton, NJ: Princeton University Press, 1996), ch. 9.

107. Richard E. Cohen and James E. Barnes, *The Almanac of American Politics, 2018* (Washington, DC: National Journal, 2017), 2035.

108. Rove, *Courage and Consequence*, 71.

109. Kenneth Pins, "With Spring to Election Day On, Dukakis Leads Iowa, Bush US," *Des Moines Register*, November 6, 1988.

110. Michael Tackett, "Iowa's Swing to Republicans Is a Matter of (Lacking a) Degree," *New York Times*, October 14, 2017, https://www.nytimes.com/.

111. Howard L. Reiter and Jeffrey M. Stonecash, *Counter Realignment: Political Change in the Northeastern United States* (Cambridge: Cambridge University Press, 2011), 138–139.

112. "Population Distribution by Race/Ethnicity, Timeframe: 2016," Henry J. Kaiser Family Foundation, State Health Facts, https://www.kff.org/other/state-indicator/distribution-by-raceethnicity/?currentTimeframe=1&sortModel=%7B%22colId%22:%22Location%22,%22sort%22:%22asc%22%7D.

113. Jack Segal, "Illinois's Shift to the Left: How a Bellwether State Diverged from National Trends," undergraduate thesis, Claremont McKenna College, 2017, https://scholarship.claremont.edu/.

114. Nixon was the GOP's vice presidential nominee in 1952 and 1956, and its presidential nominee in 1960, 1968, and 1972. In 1968, Nixon's official residence was in New York, but few people thought of him as a New Yorker because his political career had played out in California. After his election, he reestablished California residency by buying a home in San Clemente.

115. David Lauter and Bob Drogin, "Will Slam-Dunk Foe, Dukakis Tells UCLA Rally," *Los Angeles Times*, November 8, 1988.

116. Ross K. Baker, "The Congressional Elections," in Pomper, *Election of 1988*, 153–155.

117. Michael Nelson, "Constitutional Aspects of the Elections," in Nelson, *Elections of 1988*, 195.

118. Baker, "Congressional Elections," 160–162.

119. Gary Jacobson, "Congress: A Singular Continuity," in Nelson, *Elections of 1988*, 140.

120. Thomas E. Mann, "Is the House Unresponsive to Political Change?," in *Elections American Style*, ed. A. James Reichley (Washington, DC: Brookings Institution, 1987), 277.

121. George Bush, "Inaugural Address," January 20, 1989, American Presidency Project, University of California–Santa Barbara, https://www.presidency.ucsb.edu/.

122. Bush, *All the Best*, 408.

123. Ronald Reagan, "The President's News Conference," December 8, 1988, American Presidency Project, University of California–Santa Barbara, https://www.presidency.ucsb.edu/.

124. David S. Broder, "When Wars End, Voters Want New Governments," *Washington Post*, November 22, 1989, https://www.washingtonpost.com/.

CHAPTER 7. CAMPAIGNS HAVE CONSEQUENCES

1.   Paul Taylor and David S. Broder, "Evolution of The TV Era's Nastiest Presidential Race," *Washington Post*, October 28, 1988, https://www.washingtonpost.com/.

2.   *George Bush: Leadership on the Issues* (Washington, DC: Republican National Committee, 1988), 210.

3.   Michel McQueen and John Harwood, "Bush's Schedule Shows He Spends Little Time on Domestic Concerns," *Wall Street Journal*, October 28, 1991.

4.   Maureen Dowd, "Political Memo: Weary and Feeling the Presidency's Weight," *New York Times*, August 16, 1992, https://www.nytimes.com/.

5.   Charles Kolb, *White House Daze: The Unmaking of Domestic Policy in the Bush Years* (New York: Free Press, 1994, 11.

6.   John Samples, *The Fallacy of Campaign Finance Reform* (Chicago: University of Chicago Press, 2008), 236.

7.   Kolb, *White House Daze*, 9.

8.   James P. Pinkerton, *What Comes Next: The End of Big Government—And the New Paradigm Ahead* (New York: Hyperion, 1995, 4).

9.   Robert Schlesinger, *White House Ghosts: Presidents and Their Speechwriters* (New York: Simon & Schuster, 2008), 398.

10. Lyndon B. Johnson, "Remarks in Memorial Hall, Akron University," October 21, 1964, American Presidency Project, University of California–Santa Barbara, https://www.presidency.ucsb.edu/.

11. Pinkerton oral history interview.

12. George Bush, "Statement on the Federal Budget Negotiations," June 26, 1990, American Presidency Project, University of California–Santa Barbara, https://www.presidency.ucsb.edu/.

13. Bud Newman, "Bush Says Tax Revenue Increases Needed," United Press International, June 26, 1990, https://www.upi.com/.

14. Gallup job approval numbers for George H. W. Bush, American Presidency Project, University of California–Santa Barbara, https://www.presidency.ucsb.edu/.

15. "Labor Force Statistics from the Current Population Survey," US Department of Labor, Bureau of Labor Statistics, https://www.bls.gov/cps/.

16. Mel Steely, *The Gentleman from Georgia: The Biography of Newt Gingrich* (Macon, GA: Mercer University Press, 2000), 226–227.

17. Rollins with DeFrank, *Bare Knuckles*, 206–207.

18. Michael R. Kagay, "History Suggests Bush's Popularity Will Ebb," *New York Times*, May 22, 1991, https://www.nytimes.com/.

19. Peter Goldman, Thomas M. DeFrank, Mark Miller, Andrew Murr, and Tom Matthews, *Quest for the Presidency, 1992* (College Station: Texas A&M University Press, 1994), 621.

20. Museum of the Moving Image, The Living Room Candidate: Presidential Campaign Commercials, 1952–2016, "Second," http://www.livingroomcandidate.org/.

21. Museum of the Moving Image, The Living Room Candidate: Presidential Cam-

paign Commercials, 1952–2016, "Trickle Down," http://www.livingroomcan didate.org/.

22. Second half debate transcript, Commission on Presidential Debates, October 15, 1992, http://debates.org/.

23. Gerald M. Pomper, "The Presidential Election," in *The Election of 1992: Reports and Interpretations,* ed. Gerald M. Pomper (Chatham, NJ: Chatham House, 1993), 146; Glenn Kessler, "Grover Norquist's History Lesson: George H. W. Bush, 'No New Taxes,' and the 1992 Election," *Washington Post,* November 27, 2012, https://www.washingtonpost.com/.

24. George W. Bush, *41: A Portrait of My Father* (New York: Crown, 2014), 218.

25. Dave Skidmore, "Gingrich Reminds Republicans of Bush Defeat in Pressing for Tax Cut," Associated Press, March 22, 1995.

26. "Republican Presidential Candidate Debate in Ames, Iowa," August 11, 2011, American Presidency Project, University of California–Santa Barbara, https://www.presidency.ucsb.edu/.27. Presidential Candidate Debates, "Presidential Debate in Winston-Salem, North Carolina," September 25, 1988, American Presidency Project, University of California–Santa Barbara, https://www.presidency.ucsb.edu/.

28. Meacham, *Destiny and Power,* 502.

29. Jon A. Shields, *The Democratic Virtues of the Christian Right* (Princeton, NJ: Princeton University Press, 2009), 129.

30. Brooks Jackson, "The Christian Coalition and George Bush," CNN, August 19, 1992, http://www.cnn.com/ALLPOLITICS/1997/08/19/christian.coalition/.

31. Republican National Convention, August 19, 1992, video and transcript, https://www.c-span.org/.

32. George Bush, "Remarks to the Christian Coalition Road to Victory Conference in Virginia Beach, Virginia," September 11, 1992, American Presidency Project, University of California–Santa Barbara, https://www.presidency.ucsb. edu/.

33. Presidential Candidates Debates: "Republican Presidential Candidates Debate in Des Moines, Iowa," December 13, 1999, American Presidency Project, University of California–Santa Barbara, https://www.presidency.ucsb.edu/.

34. Jon Ward, "Transcript: Donald Trump's Closed-Door Meeting with Evangelical Leaders," Yahoo!, June 22, 2016, https://www.yahoo.com/news/transcript -donald-trumps-closed-door-meeting-with-evangelical-leaders-195810824.html.

35. Sarah Pulliam Bailey, "White Evangelicals Voted Overwhelmingly for Donald Trump, Exit Polls Show," *Washington Post,* November 9, 2016, https://www .washingtonpost.com/.

36. Eric M. Uslaner and Marc Lichbach, "Identity versus Identity: Israel and Evangelicals and the Two-Front War for Jewish Votes," *Religion and Politics* 2 (2009): 395–415, http://www.gvptsites.umd.edu/uslaner/uslanerlichbachpoliticsand religion.pdf.

37. Ira M. Sheskin, "Geography, Demography, and the Jewish Vote," in *American Politics and the Jewish Community,* ed. Bruce Zuckerman, Dan Schnur, and Lisa Ansell (West Lafayette, IN: Purdue University Press, 2013), 51.

38. "US Presidential Elections: Jewish Voting Record (1916–Present)," Jewish Virtual Library, https://www.jewishvirtuallibrary.org/jewish-voting-record-in-u-s-presidential-elections.

39. Lee Atwater, "Toward a GOP Rainbow," *New York Times,* February 26, 1989, https://www.nytimes.com/.

40. Louis Bolce, Gerald De Maio, and Douglas Muzzio, "Blacks and the Republican Party: The 20 Percent Solution," *Political Science Quarterly* 107 (1992): 63–79.

41. Eric Alterman, "GOP Chairman Lee Atwater: Playing Hardball," *New York Times Magazine,* April 30, 1989.

42. Walter Mears, "David Duke: Win or Lose, He's Trouble for the GOP," Associated Press, November 10, 1991.

43. "Howard Students Continue Atwater Protest," Associated Press, May 7, 1989, https://apnews.com/61457cf0f1c1404086dc8f24b260dfeb.

44. Memorandum for Lee Atwater, March 27, 1989 (photocopy).

45. *Congressional Record,* October 24, 1990, S16562.

46. Matthew Rees, "Black and Right," *New Republic,* September 29, 1991.

47. Memorandum for Lee Atwater, March 27, 1989 (photocopy).

48. Michael Catalini, "Biden Calls Republican Candidate's Ad the 'Return of Willie Horton,'" Associated Press, October 12, 2017, https://www.bloomberg.com/news/articles/2017-10-12/biden-calls-new-republican-ad-return-of-willie-horton.

49. Associated Press, "Gravely Ill, Atwater Offers Apology," *New York Times,* January 13, 1991, https://www.nytimes.com/.

50. Brady, *Bad Boy,* 316.

51. John Geer, "The News Media and the Rise of Negativity in Presidential Campaigns," Center for the Study of Democratic Institutions, Vanderbilt University, Working Paper 2-2012, https://www.vanderbilt.edu/csdi/research/CSDI_WP_2-2012.pdf.

52. Rick Perlstein, "Exclusive: Lee Atwater's Infamous 1981 Interview on the Southern Strategy," *Nation,* November 13, 2012y.

53. Forbes and Walker, "Boogie Man."

54. David Mikkelson, "Dan Quayle Quotes: Did Dan Quayle Say He Wished He'd Brushed Up on Latin before His Trip to Latin America?," Snopes.com, updated December 18, 2014, https://www.snopes.com/.

55. Isabell Sawhill, "20 Years Later, It Turns Out Dan Quayle Was Right about Murphy Brown and Unmarried Moms," *Washington Post,* May 25, 2012, https://www.washingtonpost.com/.

56. John Broder, "Clinton Assails Out-of-Wedlock Births," *Los Angeles Times,* September 10, 1994.

57. Frank Newport, "Quayle Never Caught On with Republican Voters," Gallup, September 28, 1999, https://www.gallup.com/.

58. Bush, *All the Best,* 574.

59. "New World Coming: American Security in the 21st Century—Major Themes and Implications," United States Commission on National Security/21st Cen-

tury, September 15, 1999, http://govinfo.library.unt.edu/nssg/Reports/NWC .pdf.

60. Andrew Sarris, "*Naked Gun* Takes Aim at Politics," *Washington Post*, January 5, 1992, https://www.washingtonpost.com/.

61. "The American President, 1995," American Rhetoric Movie Speeches, https://www.americanrhetoric.com/MovieSpeeches/moviespeechtheamericanpresident.html.

62. George Stephanopoulos, *All Too Human: Political Education* (Boston: Little, Brown, 1999), 47.

63. Museum of the Moving Image, The Living Room Candidate: Presidential Campaign Commercials, 1952–2016, "Leaders 2," http://www.livingroomcandidate.org/.

64. Charles T. Royer, ed., *Campaign for President: The Managers Look at '92* (Hollis, NH: Hollis, 1994), 42.

65. "In Her Own Disputed Words," *Washington Post*, June 16, 1992, https://www.washingtonpost.com/.

66. Sheila Rule, "Racial Issues: Rapper, Chided by Clinton, Calls Him a Hypocrite," *New York Times*, June 17, 1992, https://www.nytimes.com/.

67. David S. Broder and Thomas B. Edsall, "Clinton Finds Biracial Support for Criticism of Rap Singer," *Washington Post*, June 16, 1992, https://www.washingtonpost.com/.

68. Mary Matalin and James Carville with Peter Knobler, *All's Fair: Love, War, and Running for President* (New York: Random House, 1994, 357).

69. George Bush, "Letter to George W. Bush on Advice Regarding 'New Friends,'" May 9, 1988, American Presidency Project, University of California–Santa Barbara, https://www.presidency.ucsb.edu/.

70. Philip Shenon, "Bush Consultant Peddled Influence at HUD, He Says," *New York Times*, June 21, 1989, https://www.nytimes.com/.

71. R. W. Apple, "Bush's Court Choice; Sununu Tells How and Why He Pushed Souter for Court," *New York Times*, July 25, 1990, https://www.nytimes.com/.

72. Bill Turque and John Barry, "Was Bush Really 'Out of the Loop,'" *Newsweek*, October 5, 1992, 43.

73. David Johnston, "Weinberger Faces 5 Counts in Iran–Contra Indictment," *New York Times*, June 17, 1992, https://www.nytimes.com/.

74. "Transcript of Eisenhower's Speech to the GOP Convention," *New York Times*, July 15, 1964, https://www.nytimes.com/.

75. George Bush, "The President's News Conference with Prime Minister Brian Mulroney of Canada at Camp David, Maryland," January 16, 1993, American Presidency Project, University of California–Santa Barbara, https://www.presidency.ucsb.edu/.

76. Tim Dickinson, "How Roger Ailes Built the Fox News Fear Factory," *Rolling Stone*, June 9, 2011, https://www.rollingstone.com/.

77. George H. W. Bush (@GeorgeHWBush), "He wasn't perfect, but Roger Ailes was my friend & I loved him. Not sure I would have been President w/o his

great talent, loyal help. RIP," Twitter, May 18, 2017, 8:36 a.m., https://twitter
.com/GeorgeHWBush/status/865229585415274496.

78. Peter Baker, "Both Bush Presidents Worry Trump Is Blowing Up the GOP,"
    New York Times, November 4, 2017, https://www.nytimes.com/.

79. Mark Davis, "Writing for a President Indifferent to Speeches," *Los Angeles
    Times,* January 17, 1993.

80. Bush, "Inaugural Address."

81. Davis, "Writing for a President Indifferent to Speeches."

82. Heclo, "George Bush and American Conservatism," 77.

83. Connelly and Pitney, *Congress' Permanent Minority?,* 80.

84. *Congressional Record,* January 12, 1991, 1124.

BIBLIOGRAPHIC ESSAY

The World Wide Web did not exist until 1989, so it is a bit harder to find certain kinds of information for the 1988 race than for later elections. Accordingly, researchers have to do much of their work the old-fashioned way, with print documents. For information on campaign finance, television advertising, and public opinion, a good reference is Gary Maloney, ed., *The Almanac of 1988 Presidential Politics* (Falls Church, VA: American Political Network, 1989). A rich source of state-level survey data is Carolyn Smith, ed., *The '88 Vote* (New York: Capital Cities/ABC, 1989). Both are out of print and hard to get, but well worth the effort. On public opinion data more generally, one book I constantly return to is William G. Mayer, *The Changing American Mind: How and Why American Public Opinion Changed between 1960 and 1988* (Ann Arbor: University of Michigan Press, 1992).

Excellent journalistic and academic works exist on the 1988 election over the several years that followed. For revelations about the lives and characters of presidential candidates, a landmark work is Richard Ben Cramer, *What It Takes* (New York: Vintage, 1993). Jack W. Germond and Jules Witcover present a cynical take in *Whose Broad Stripes and Bright Stars? The Trivial Pursuit of the Presidency, 1988* (New York: Warner Books, 1989). Sidney Blumenthal, *Pledging Allegiance: The Last Campaign of the Cold War* (New York: HarperCollins, 1990) contains a critical insight in the form of its subtitle. Other journalistic accounts include Elizabeth Drew, *Election Journal: Political Events of 1987–1988* (New York: William Morrow, 1988); and Roger Simon, *Road Show* (New York: Farrar, Straus & Giroux, 1990). Especially useful for its documentary appendices is Peter Goldman and Tom Mathews, *The Quest for the Presidency: The 1988 Campaign* (New York: Simon & Schuster/Touchstone, 1989). Peggy Noonan has a beautifully written firsthand account of the Reagan and Bush in *What I Saw at the Revolution: A Political Life in the Reagan Era* (New York: Random House, 1990). James P. Pinkerton gives a brief but essential account of the Bush administration in *What Comes Next: The End of Big Government—And the New Paradigm Ahead* (New York: Hyperion, 1995).

Two indispensable collections of scholarly analysis are Michael Nelson, ed., *The Elections of 1988* (Washington, DC: CQ Press, 1989), and Gerald M. Pomper, ed., *The Election of 1988: Reports and Interpretations* (Chatham, NJ: Chatham House, 1989). The practice of campaign finance was very different in those days, and one may find a sharp snapshot of the subject in Herbert E. Alexander and Monica Bauer, *Financing the 1988 Election* (Boulder, CO: Westview Press, 1991).

For decades, the Institute of Politics at the Harvard Kennedy School has held quadrennial conferences where presidential campaign staffs have provided insights on the electoral battles they have just fought. For 1988, the resulting volume is David R. Runkel, *Campaign for President: The Managers Look at '88* (Dover, MA: Auburn House, 1989). Before the election, the Kennedy School hosted held a series of forums with the major candidates. For the transcripts, see Marvin Kalb and Hendrick Hertzberg, *Candidates '88* (Dover, MA: Auburn House, 1988).

George H. W. Bush never wrote a complete set of memoirs, but the closest thing is his authorized biography: Jon Meacham, *Destiny and Power: The American Odyssey of George Herbert Walker Bush* (New York: Random House, 2015). Another thorough treatment is Herbert S. Parmet, *George Bush: The Life of a Lone Star Yankee* (New Brunswick, NJ: Transaction, 2001). Bush was a prodigious letter writer who collected some remarkably revealing examples in *All the Best, George Bush: My Life in Letters and Other Writings* (New York: Simon & Schuster, 2014). Bush's 1988 campaign biography is George H. W. Bush and Victor Gold, *Looking Forward* (New York: Doubleday, 1987). It contains some useful bits of information, though the genre does not lend itself to deep candor. For the 41st president's place in the conservative firmament, see Hugh Heclo, "George Bush and American Conservatism, " in *41: Inside the Presidency of George H. W. Bush*, ed. Michael Nelson and Barbara A. Perry (Ithaca, NY: Cornell University Press, 2014). In the same volume, Michael Nelson has a valuable essay: "George Bush: Texan, Conservative." Bush's tenure in the vice presidency was the prelude to his years in the White House, and a valuable work on the development of the office is Joel K. Goldstein, *The White House Vice Presidency: The Path to Significance, Mondale to Biden* (Lawrence: University Press of Kansas, 2016).

John Brady deserves a special mention for *Bad Boy: The Life and Politics of Lee Atwater* (Reading, MA: Addison-Wesley, 1997). Having worked in the Bush campaign and the Republican National Committee, I knew Atwater (though he never quite remembered my name). My former coworkers and I learned many things from this book that we had not known.

For biographical information on Michael Dukakis, see Charles Kenney and Robert L. Turner, *Dukakis: An American Odyssey* (Boston: Houghton Mifflin, 1988); Richard Gaines and Michael Segal, *Dukakis and the Reform Impulse* (Boston: Quinlan Press, 1987); and David Nyhan, *The Duke: The Inside Story of a Political Phenomenon* (New York: Warner Books, 1988). My Claremont McKenna College friend and colleague Lily Geismer offers a rich historical analysis of Dukakis's home territory in *Don't Blame Us: Suburban Liberals and the Transformation of the Democratic Party* (Princeton, NJ: Princeton University Press, 2015).

Gary Hart's 1984 campaign manifesto, *A New Democracy* (New York: Quill, 1983), is worth reading for a glimpse of neoliberal thinking in the early 1980s. A more recent work on the collapse of the Hart campaign is Matt Bai, *All the Truth Is Out: The Week Politics Went Tabloid* (New York: Vintage, 2015). For Jesse Jackson, see Roger Bruns, *Jesse Jackson: A Biography* (Westport, CT: Greenwood Press, 2005), 15–16. Frank Clemente and Frank Watkins collected Jackson's campaign speeches and issue papers in *Keep Hope Alive: Jesse Jackson's 1988 Presidential Campaign* (Boston: South End Press, 1989). In *The New Democrats and the Return to Power* (New

York: Palgrave Macmillan, 2011), Al From chronicles the political movement that advanced Al Gore, Richard Gephardt, and Lloyd Bentsen. For a look at how 1988 propelled Gore into national politics, there is Bill Turque, *Inventing Al Gore: A Biography* (New York: Houghton Mifflin Harcourt, 2014). On the world of Democratic activists and intellectuals during the decade, see Kenneth S. Baer, *Reinventing Democrats: The Politics of Liberalism from Reagan to Clinton* (Lawrence: University Press of Kansas, 2000), and Randall Rothenberg, *The Neoliberals* (New York: Simon & Schuster, 1984), 126

For the other 1988 Republican contenders, see Morton Kondracke and Fred Barnes, *Jack Kemp: The Bleeding-Heart Conservative Who Changed America* (New York: Sentinel, 2015), and David John Marley, *Pat Robertson: An American Life* (Lanham, MD: Rowman & Littlefield, 2007),

Bush may have grown up in the Northeast, but he made his career in the South. The foundational text is V. O. Key, *Southern Politics in State and Nation* (New York: Vintage, 1949). Other works on the politics of this region are Earl Black and Merle Black, *The Rise of Southern Republicans* (Cambridge, MA: Harvard Belknap, 2002), and Nicol Rae, *Southern Democrats* (Oxford: Oxford University Press, 1994).

Opposition research is as old as electoral politics itself, and a good contrarian argument for its value is in Kyle Mattes and David P. Redlawsk, *The Positive Case for Negative Campaigning* (Chicago: University of Chicago Press, 2014). On racial messages in campaigns, see Tali Mendelberg, *The Race Card: Campaign Strategy, Implicit Messages, and the Norm of Equality* (Princeton, NJ: Princeton University Press, 2001).

For congressional elections, the ur-source is Norman J. Ornstein, Thomas E. Mann, and Michael J. Malbin, *Vital Statistics on Congress* (Washington, DC: Brookings Institution, 2017). Gary C. Jacobson sums up the state of knowledge in the late 1980s in *The Electoral Origins of Divided Government* (Boulder, CO: Westview Press, 1990).

A work such as this relies heavily on books that supply panoramic views of political history and presidential elections in general. In *The Gamble: Choice and Chance in the 2012 Presidential Election* (Princeton, NJ: Princeton University Press, 2013), John Sides and Lynn Vavreck explain the fundamentals that have long presidential voting. The analysis in this book owes much to them. For its sweep and political savvy, I have enormous admiration for Michael Barone, *Our Country: The Shaping of America from Roosevelt to Reagan* (New York: Free Press, 1990). A classic work on the interplay of demographics and generational change is James L. Sundquist, *Dynamics of the Party System*, rev. ed. (Washington, DC: Brookings Institution, 1983). A. James Reichley provides an essential narrative on American political parties in *The Life of the Parties: A History of American Political Parties* (Lanham, MD: Rowman & Littlefield, 2000). For a prescient discussion of the political impact of educated professionals, see John B. Judis and Ruy Teixeira, *The Emerging Democratic Majority* (New York: Scribner, 2002). Two valuable recent works are Sam Rosenfeld, *The Polarizers: Postwar Architects of Our Partisan Era* (Chicago: University of Chicago Press, 2018), and Kevin M. Kruse and Julian E. Zelizer, *Fault Lines: A History of the United States since 1974* (New York: Norton, 2018). And although not primarily a study of politics, one particular book informs just about any discussion of political generations: William Strauss and Neil Howe, *Generations: The History of America's Future, 1584 to 2069* (New York: Morrow, 1991).

Previous elections set the table for the 1988 race. The 1968 race was especially important, and the state-of-the-art work of political science on the subject is Michael Nelson, *Resilient America: Electing Nixon in 1968, Channeling Dissent, and Dividing Government* (Lawrence: University Press of Kansas, 2014). During the first Nixon term, a highly influential analysis of social trends was Richard M. Scammon and Ben J. Wattenberg, *The Real Majority* (New York: Coward, McCann, and Geoghegan, 1970). Reagan molded the politics of the 1980s, and a splendid study of his 1980 election is Andrew E. Busch, *Reagan's Victory: The Presidential Election of 1980 and the Rise of the Right* (Lawrence: University Press of Kansas, 2005).

INDEX

Atkinson, Rick, 73
Atwater, Lee
    and Black, Manafort, Stone, and
        Atwater firm, 83, 157
    as H. W. Bush's campaign manager,
        9, 82–85, 93, 98, 99–100, 101,
        102, 103–106, 107, 144–145, 146,
        163
    and personal attacks on Dukakis in
        1988 campaign, 158–159, 183
    RNC and, 9–10, 39, 179–180
    and Willie Horton ads in 1988
        campaign, 150–151, 179–180
Austin, Gerald, 125, 135
Aykroyd, Dan, 122

Babbitt, Bruce, 78–79, 95, 97, 120,
    122–123, 129, 130, 131
Baer, Kenneth, 122
Bai, Matt, 115
Baier, Bret, 176
Bailey, Douglas, 43, 44
Baker, Howard, 43, 44, 54, 96
Baker, James, 41, 52, 80, 82, 144–145,
    146–147, 150, 157, 160
Bakker, Jim, 91
Barnes, Cliff, 147, 148
Barnes, Fred, 57
Barone, Michael, 17
Beckel, Robert, 75
Bentsen, Lloyd, 36, 78, 138–139, 142,
    143, 160–161, 168, 181–182
Berke, Richard, 121
Berlin Wall, 3, 156, 200n17
Biden, Joseph, 53, 113, 116–120, 133, 145,
    180, 182–183
Big Sleep, The (film), 173
birth control and reproductive rights,
    14, 28, 34–35, 176–177. See also
    abortion
Black, Charles, 83, 87, 88, 102
Black, Manafort, Stone, and Atwater
    (consulting firm), 83, 157
Bliss, Ray C., 34
Blum, Liz, 137

Blumenthal, Sidney, 145
Bond, Richard, 93–94, 97
Bonfire of the Vanities, The (Wolfe),
    136
Bork, Robert, 117–118
Borosage, Robert, 126, 138
Bradley, Bill, 54
Bradley, Tom, 72
Brazile, Donna, 159
Brezhnev, Leonid, 25
Brock, Bill, 41, 94, 107
Broder, David, 99, 170
Brokaw, Tom, 31, 105–106
Brooke, Edward, 72
Brountas, Paul, 62
Brown, George, 33
Brown, Pat, 17, 19
Brown, Willie, 125
Brownstein, Ron, 108
Brown v. Board of Education, 18, 60
Bryan, William Jennings, 72
Brzezinski, Zbigniew, 26
Buchanan, Pat, 19, 27, 54, 96, 187
Buckley, James, 203n38
Buckley, John, 87
Buckley, William F., Jr., 18, 54, 98
Burns, James MacGregor, 13
Bush, Barbara (Pierce), 32, 159
Bush, George H. W.
    and abortion, 29, 47, 159–160, 176–
        177
    and African American voters, 10, 34,
        35, 163, 179–180
    background of, 31–36, 41
    Bob Dole as rival of and ally to,
        37–38, 54, 81–82, 190
    as CIA director, 39–41, 85
    Congress and, 170, 172–173
    and crime issue in 1988 campaign,
        9, 111, 147–152, 153, 164, 179–180
    and Dan Quayle as 1988 vice
        president pick, 108–110, 141,
        181–182
    death of, 1, 190
    on Donald Trump, 188–189

African Americans and, 6, 12, 16, 19, 20, 21–22, 71–72, 184–185, 212n70
crime and, 78
cultural issues and, 27–29
demographic and ideological shifts affecting, 2–6, 11–13, 15–16, 20–22
DLC and, 78–79, 117, 122, 127, 168
foreign policy and, 25–27
George McGovern and, 21, 177, 184
Hispanic voters and, 6, 163–164, 166–167
John Kennedy and, 59, 64
and neoliberalism, 69–70, 77, 78, 79, 122
in 1988 congressional elections, 2–3, 167–169
and 1988 electoral vote, 2, 164–167
and 1988 popular vote, 2, 162–164
and Southern Democrats, 5, 15–16, 19–20, 22, 79, 124–125, 139, 172
Walter Mondale's 1984 defeat and, 77–78
See also Democratic Party candidates and leaders individually by name
demographics, politics and, 11–13, 133, 165, 166–167
Dewey, Thomas, 13, 14
Dillon, Douglas, 13
Dionne, E. J., Jr., 114
DLC, 78–79, 117, 122, 127, 168
Doak, David, 131
Dole, Bob
as Ford's 1976 running mate, 40, 44, 53, 92
H. W. Bush as rival of and ally to, 37–38, 54, 81–82, 190
in 1974 midterm elections, 38
and 1980 Republican nomination campaign, 44, 92, 94
and 1988 presidential campaign, 81–82, 88, 92–95, 96–97, 98, 99, 100, 102, 103, 105–107, 111, 148
and 1996 presidential campaign, 4, 182, 190

as Republican Senate leader, 54, 92, 94, 182
and tax increases, 48–49, 51, 55, 189
as World War II veteran, 37, 40, 93, 189–190
Dole, Elizabeth, 92, 93, 105
Donahue, Phil, 97
Dornan, Bob, 85
Dowd, Maureen, 94, 118
Drudge, Matt, 188
Dukakis, Kitty, 3, 65, 158, 161
Dukakis, Michael S.
and African American voters, 6, 60–61
background of, 59–64
crime and, 3, 65, 111, 136–137, 147–152, 153, 154, 158, 161, 164
and Hispanic voters, 6, 133, 139, 158, 163–164
H. W. Bush's 1988 campaign attack strategy on, 147–152, 155, 156, 157–159, 179–180, 181, 183, 185
H. W. Bush's 1988 defeat of, 2, 162–163, 164–167
on JFK, 61–62
as Massachusetts governor, 64–67, 77
military service of, 61
and 1988 campaign attack strategy on H. W. Bush, 156–157, 158, 159
and 1988 Democratic National Convention, 139–140
in 1988 Democratic nomination campaign, 113, 118, 119, 120, 121–122, 127–129, 130–137
and 1988 Democratic platform, 138
and 1988 election debates, 159–162
and 1988 election issues, 152–156, 157–158, 159–160, 164, 172, 174, 227n60
and 1988 vice president pick, 138–139
and 1992 presidential election, 184
and suburban Democratic voters, 5–6, 13, 70
and Vietnam War opposition, 63

Johnson, Lyndon, *continued*
    as JFK's vice president, 12, 33–34
    military service of, 4, 200n19
    and neoliberalism, 69–70
    1964 landslide election of, 18, 36, 167
    and televised debates, 30
    and Vietnam War, 20, 173

Kamarck, Elaine, 133
Kefauver, Estes, 58
Kelly, Megyn, 188
Kemp, Jack
    and antitax Republicans, 51, 182
    as Bob Dole's 1996 running mate, 182
    and Kemp–Roth legislation, 41–42, 46–47, 48
    and 1988 presidential campaign, 83, 86–89, 96–98, 102, 106–107, 108
    and Reagan tax cuts, 24–25, 41–42, 48
    social conservatism and, 88
Kennedy, Edward "Ted," 58–59, 62, 112, 113, 116, 117–118, 120, 180
Kennedy, John F.
    Al Gore compared to, 124
    anticommunism of, 20
    assassination of, 33–34, 58
    Democratic Party and, 59, 64
    Dukakis on, 61–62
    evangelicals and, 29
    Gary Hart influenced by, 68, 113
    Joe Biden comparisons to, 116
    military service of, 4, 11, 200n19
    in 1960 presidential election, 12, 24, 30, 52, 68, 79, 116, 124
    in Quayle–Bentsen vice presidential debate, 160–161
    Soviet Union and, 199–200n15
    and tax cuts, 24, 41–42
Kennedy, Robert F., 20, 21, 58, 68, 117, 118, 119–120
Kenney, Charles, 63
Kerrey, Bob, 168
Kerry, John, 66, 162

Kimmitt, Robert, 108, 110
King, Ed, 65–66, 145
King, Larry, 97
King, Martin Luther, Jr., 23, 36, 41, 71, 72, 136, 211–212n53
Kinnock, Neil, 118, 119–120
Kirk, Russell, 84
Kirkpatrick, Jeane, 26, 52, 96
Kissinger, Henry, 37
Klein, Joe, 93
Koch, Ed, 136
Kolb, Charles, 172–173
Korean War, 59, 106, 144
Krauthammer, Charles, 91
Kristol, Irving, 25
Kunin, Madeleine, 126
Kuwait, Iraq invasion of, 4, 172, 175

Lacy, William, 94, 105
Laffer, Arthur, 42
La Guardia, Fiorello, 19
Lamb, Brian, 30, 119
LaRouche, Lyndon, 158
Latzer, Barry, 23
Lawrence Eagle-Tribune, 147, 148
Laxalt, Paul, 96
League of Women Voters, 159
Levenson, Russell, 1
Levin, Carl, 60
Lewis, Anthony, 45
liberalism, 29, 49, 69–70, 78, 113, 140, 145, 184. *See also* neoliberalism
liberal media bias, 27–28, 102, 157
Libya, 155
Limbaugh, Rush, 188
Lincoln Day dinners, GOP, 40, 89
Lincoln-Douglas debates, 119
Lindsay, John, 19
Lodge, Henry Cabot, 15
Loeb, William, 84–85
Long, Gillis, 77–78
Long, Huey, 72
Lord, Jeffrey, 118
Los Angeles Times, 103, 152–153, 154
Lott, Trent, 94

Nixon, Richard, *continued*
    and 1960 presidential election, 11,
        12, 15, 22, 24, 30, 92
    and 1966 midterms, 41
    and 1968 presidential election, 3, 11,
        17–18, 23, 35–36, 92, 102, 108
    and 1972 reelection campaign, 4, 11,
        58, 169
    Republican Party and, 13, 15, 19, 28,
        167, 230n114
    and Southern Democrats, 172
    and televised debates in 1960
        campaign, 11, 24, 30
    and US–Soviet relations, 25, 26
    as vice president to Dwight
        Eisenhower, 13, 52, 81, 230n114
    and Watergate, 38, 39, 58
Noonan, Peggy, 110–111
Novak, Robert, 47, 113
NSPAC (National Security Political
    Action Committee), 149–152

Obama, Barack, 2, 4, 7, 76, 135, 138,
    162, 167
O'Connor, Sandra Day, 50
O'Neill, Tip, 50, 76
Orlando Sentinel, 159
Other America, The (Harrington),
    22

patriotism, 27, 52, 60, 67, 140, 154
Paul, Ron, 164
Pearson, Drew, 14
Percy, Charles, 53–54
Perry, Rick, 45, 124
Peters, Charles, 69
Pinkerton, James P., 82, 85–86, 99,
    107–108, 146–147, 148, 154,
    173–174
Planned Parenthood, 14
*Pledging Allegiance: The Last Campaign
    of the Cold War* (Blumenthal),
    153–154
Powell, Adam Clayton, 18
Powell, Lewis, 117

Proposition 13, California, 24, 41, 66,
    204n58
PTL (Praise the Lord) Club, 91

Quayle, Dan, 97, 108–110, 141, 158,
    160–161, 181–182

Rae, Nicol, 139
Rainbow Coalition, 126, 185
Rather, Dan, 100–102, 135, 146, 157,
    187, 188
Reader's Digest, 148, 149
Reagan, Nancy, 47, 96
Reagan, Ronald, 215n36
    abortion issue and, 28, 47, 50
    African American voters and, 72,
        180, 211–212n53
    and approval ratings, 144, 162, 165
    assassination attempt on, 96
    and Bork Supreme Court
        nomination, 117
    as California governor, 19, 24, 28
    Cold War and, 8, 51, 56, 143, 164, 170
    Gerald Ford's relationship with, 39,
        47, 108, 206n27
    H. W. Bush as vice president to, 47,
        49, 52, 55, 80–81, 88, 108
    and immigration reform, 7
    Iran–Contra and, 8, 56, 81, 100, 143,
        144, 156–157, 186, 187
    on Michael Dukakis in 1988
        campaign, 158–159
    military service of, 200n19
    and 1968 presidential election, 19,
        35
    and 1980 presidential election,
        42–43, 45–47, 50–51, 52, 53, 55–56,
        67, 83, 141, 159, 206n30
    and 1984 presidential election, 4, 59,
        72, 76, 86, 112, 162, 163, 169
    and Republican Party conservatism,
        84
    Soviet Union and, 4, 8, 51–52, 56,
        114, 143, 170, 201n82
    and Syria, 72–73

H. W. Bush and, 189, 190
and 1988 presidential election, 92,
96–97, 162, 165, 166
and Obama birther myth, 7
and tax cuts, 176
television and rise of, 89, 90, 97
and 2016 presidential election, 7, 71,
96, 112, 178, 188–189
Tsongas, Paul, 72, 121, 179, 184
Turner, Robert L., 63

Updegrove, Mark, 189
U.S. News & World Report, 1
USSR. *See* Soviet Union

Van Buren, Martin, 143, 168
Vance, Cyrus, 26
Vavreck, Lynn, 9
Vietnam War, 20, 21, 27, 35, 63, 109–
110, 124–125, 173, 185
Volcker, Paul, 49
Voting Rights Act (1965), 20, 71–72

Wallace, George, 19, 35
Walsh, Edward, 107
Wanniski, Jude, 42
Warner, Margaret, 81
Washington, Harold, 134
Washington Post, 73, 87, 103, 107, 116,
125, 163, 185
Watergate, 21, 38, 39, 43, 58, 64, 115,
141, 144
Wattenberg, Ben J., 22–23
Wead, Doug, 84, 100, 106
Weinberger, Casper, 187
West Virginia v. Barnette, 154

Weyrich, Paul, 29, 169
*What It Takes: The Way to the White
House* (Cramer), 2, 80
White, Kevin, 63, 64
White, Theodore H., 11, 12–13, 20–21
*Whose Broad Stripes and Bright Stars?
The Trivial Pursuit of the Presidency,
1988* (Germond, Witcover),
153–154
Wilder, Douglas, 72, 185
Will, George, 85
Willkie, Wendell, 13
Wilson, Pete, 55
Wilson, Woodrow, 15, 69
Winfrey, Oprah, 97
Witcover, Jules, 47, 109
World War I, 14, 32
World War II
Bob Dole and, 37, 40, 93, 189–190
Greatest Generation as veterans of,
31
H. W. Bush and, 11, 31, 32, 37, 83,
189–190
JFK and, 11, 59
and "new generation" of American
presidents, 4, 200n19
Richard Nixon and, 11
and veterans in Congress, 169, 189–
190
Wright, Betsey, 116
Wright, Jim, 143

Yarborough, Ralph, 33, 34, 36
Young, Andrew, 21–22

Zorinsky, Edward, 167–168